THE
EXPERT
GUIDE

TO YOUR LIFE IN SWITZERLAND

Selected chapters were originally written in German and translated into English by Ashley Curtis.

English Edition: ISBN 978-3-03869-076-4 (Printed in Czech Republic)
German Edition: ISBN 978-3-03869-077-1 (Printed in Czech Republic)

Also available as an ebook, and, outside of Europe, in a print-on-demand edition wherever books are sold.

Bergli Books received a structural grant from the Swiss Ministry of Culture 2016–2020

THE
EXPERT
GUIDE
TO YOUR LIFE IN SWITZERLAND

EDITED BY DICCON BEWES

Dimitri Burkhard, Angelica Cipullo, Daniel Dreier, Christina Fryer,
Clive Greaves, Rebekka Hänggi, Caroline Kaufmann,
Christian Langenegger, Isobel Leybold-Johnson, Cornelia Lüthy,
Nicolas Mossaz, Margaret Oertig, Andie Pilot, Felix Schneuwly,
Greg Zwygart

CONTENTS

NTRODUCTION

One in four. It might be hard to believe but out of every four people in Switzerland, one of them isn't Swiss. That means that as a foreigner living here, you're not on your own. But being one of thousands doesn't always make it easier to fit in or understand the rules. Sometimes you need a helping hand from someone in the know. That's where this book comes in.

Each chapter is written by an expert living in Switzerland, giving you the benefit of their experience and knowledge. Crucial subjects such as housing or tax are covered in detail so you can navigate the red tape. The same goes for everyday matters like recycling or health insurance, or even how to greet the locals.

But there's more to life in Switzerland than that. This book is bursting with inspiration for making the most of this beautiful country. From train trips and wild swims to finding friends and eating fondue, we've plenty of ideas for enjoying a Swiss life to the full.

To make things easier for you, we've highlighted essential words and phrases that are trickier to translate. They are underlined the first time they appear in any chapter, and you can find them in the glossary at the back along with German and French translations. Plus there's an appendix with useful extras, such as details of all the cantons and important facts about Switzerland.

I hope you love living in Switzerland as much as we all do.

Diccon Bewes
February 2020
Bern, Switzerland

MEET YOUR EXPERT

Cornelia Lüthi has been vice-director and a member of the Board of Management at the State Secretariat for Migration (SEM) since 2016. Her areas of responsibility include entry requirements, naturalisation, residence and work permits, the free movement of persons between Switzerland and the EU, and measures to promote integration. She is a lawyer and holds a doctorate in law, and has completed an Executive Master of Public Administration at the London School of Economics. Before joining the SEM she worked at the Federal Office of Justice, as an attorney in a number of law offices, and in the Department of Education of Canton Zurich.

ARRIVAL

Would you like to move to Switzerland? Perhaps you are wondering what requirements you have to fulfil in order to enter the country. Or maybe you are trying to make sense out of the jungle of work and residence permits, deadlines and documents. Perhaps you are already here and want to register properly or renew your residence permit. This chapter will help you to find some order in the bureaucratic thicket.

We won't be able to go into every last detail or consider every possible exception. Instead we will lay out generally valid points, explaining complicated processes in a simple and easily understandable way and pointing out important connections. Depending on whether you are entering the country, already working in Switzerland, or wish to renew a permit, the following questions may be relevant:

- Under what conditions can I enter Switzerland?
- What types of permit exist?
- How and where do I apply for or extend my permit?

THE LOWDOWN
- The rules of entry and immigration
- Residency permits and which one's right for you
- The essential requirements for living here long term

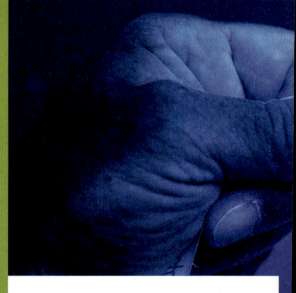

THREE CRUCIAL FACTORS

1. Switzerland is not a member of the European Union, but has signed a treaty with the EU governing the <u>free movement of persons</u>. Free movement of persons means that, under certain circumstances, people in Europe can freely choose their place of work and residence. EU and EFTA (European Free Trade Association) citizens receive preferential treatment compared to citizens of other countries.
2. A central question is the reason for your move to Switzerland: are you coming primarily for reasons of work, education or training, or purely for private reasons? A further reason to come to Switzerland might be forced migration, but this will not be addressed in this chapter.
3. Finally, the length of the planned stay plays a role. As in many other countries, there is a threshold at three months. Stays longer than 90 days require a <u>permit</u>.

THREE QUESTIONS

For entry and residence the following three questions are decisive:
*   Do I come from an EU/EFTA country?
*   What is the reason for my stay in Switzerland?
*   How long do I wish to remain?

MIGRATION

The Swiss migration system is complex. The admission of foreigners generally falls under the competence of the 26 cantons. The legal demands and requirements are the same in all cantons, but in practice differences can arise between one canton and another. This means that a person who would like to live and work in Switzerland has no choice but to make contact with the authorities in their future work or residence canton. This is also the case for people who are already in Switzerland.

Entry and visa requirements are determined at national level (via the Schengen laws). The points of contact here are the Swiss embassies in the future resident's country of origin. There you will find all the information you need about visas and the requirements that need to be fulfilled before crossing the border into Switzerland.

If the free movement of persons has recently been extended to a country, for example as a result of joining the EU, there may still be temporary restrictions on free movement. Currently such restrictions apply to Croatia, for whose citizens there are still time-limited quotas and other requirements that apply to residence in Switzerland. These restrictions will expire at the latest in 2023.

ENTRY

Anyone who wants to enter Switzerland needs to have a valid and officially recognised travel document and, unless they are exempt from the visa requirement, a visa. EU/EFTA citizens do not need a visa. A few other countries also benefit from a partial or total visa exemption.

WITHOUT A VISA

Citizens of the following countries do not need a visa to enter Switzerland: EU countries (including the United Kingdom), EFTA countries, Andorra, Brunei, Japan, Malaysia, Monaco, New Zealand, San Marino, Singapore and Vatican City.

VISA OR PERMIT?

The terms visa and permit are sometimes used as synonyms in English. This can lead to misunderstandings in Switzerland. Switzerland distinguishes between a visa (entry visa) and a residence or work permit.

A visa is issued after a preliminary check of whether a person fulfils the requirements for entry into Switzerland. The embassy examines the travel documents to see if they are officially recognised and valid, and considers the purpose and length of stay. It further insists on accountability for sufficient financial means of support and for the credibility of a timely departure from the country.

A work or residence permit grants the right to remain in Switzerland to live and/or work. These permits are issued by the cantonal employment and migration authorities.

The visa must be requested and issued before you cross the border into Switzerland. The visa application can be submitted to the Swiss embassy in the applicant's country of origin. Visa application forms can be downloaded from the website of the relevant embassy. In larger countries, such as the USA and Canada, Swiss consulates in various cities can provide many of the same services as the embassy (for purposes of brevity, we refer only to embassies below).

For most third-country nationals, a visa is mandatory for entering Switzerland. At the Swiss border the requirements are checked once again: purpose of the stay, valid travel document, financial means of support, and no indication of danger to public order and security. Third-country nationals who intend to live and work in Switzerland need residence and work permits in addition to a visa in order to enter the country.

EFTA/EEA

The European Free Trade Association (EFTA) was founded to promote the growth and prosperity of its member countries and to intensify economic cooperation. Switzerland, Iceland, Norway and Liechtenstein are not part of the EU, but are members of EFTA. As regards entry requirements, EFTA citizens are treated in the same manner as persons from the EU. The European Economic Area (EEA) comprises the EU countries and the other EFTA countries, but not Switzerland.

RESIDENCY

EU/EFTA citizens need to know the following.

With employment: anyone who comes to Switzerland via the free movement of persons and wants to work here needs a residence permit, which serves simultaneously as a work permit. The requirement for this is a written declaration of employment or an employment contract. The residence permit should be requested in the municipality of residence, in general no later than 14 days after entry. People planning only a short stay in Switzerland (up to and including 90 days) do not need a residence permit. Only written notice is required, which can be provided online.

Without employment: for a stay of up to 90 days without employment neither a permit nor written notice to the migration authorities is required. For a longer stay (more than 90 days) written notice to the relevant cantonal authorities is required, along with a confirmation of sufficient financial means of support and possession of the obligatory health insurance. The same requirements are valid for people who come to study or to join their families in Switzerland.

EXTENSION

For the extension of a permit the application must generally be submitted no later than two weeks before the expiry date. Time-limited permits can be extended if the conditions continue to be fulfilled. A person with a B residence permit can request a C settlement permit after five years' residency at the earliest.

In the case of the time-unlimited C permit, the permit itself (not the permission, but the actual ID card) expires after five years. The card must be presented to the authorities for renewal before it has expired.

CROSS-BORDER WORKERS

People who wish to work in a Swiss border canton while residing in a neighbouring foreign country can request a G permit. Standard requirements for salary and working conditions must be fulfilled, and priority is given to Swiss residents. The G permit is closely coordinated with the border regions and is thus subject to certain restrictions (eg in the case of a change of employment).

PERMITS FOR EMPLOYEES

Requirements	Validity	Renewable
L permit = short residence permit		
EU/EFTA: • Employed or seeking employment *Third-country nationals:* • Time-limited work contract for a maximum of 12 or 24 months • No comparable workers available in Switzerland • Strong qualifications • Quota not yet filled • Standard salary and working conditions	*EU/EFTA:* Time-limited. Duration depends on employment situation (can be prolonged/renewed). *Third-country nationals:* Up to 12 months, subsequently renewable for up to a total of 24 months	*EU/EFTA* Yes, extendable for up to a maximum of 12 months total, and then renewable. *Third-country nationals:* Up to a maximum of 12 months, then renewable for up to a total of 24 months.
B permit = residence permit		
EU/EFTA: • Employment for at least one year or sufficient financial means of support • Mandatory insurance *Third-country nationals:* • Employment for at least one year or important public interest (eg taxes) • Employment contract • Swiss residents have priority • Strong qualifications • Quota not yet filled • Standard salary and working conditions • Knowledge of the national language spoken at the place of residence	*EU/EFTA:* 5 years *Third-country nationals:* 1 year	*EU/EFTA:* Yes, for 5 years at a time. For 1 year, if the person has been involuntarily unemployed for 12 months. *Third-country nationals:* Yes, by 1 to 2 years at a time.
C permit = settlement permit		
EU/EFTA/Third-country nationals: • At least 5 years' residence in Switzerland • Integrated in the community (including language abilities)	Unlimited. ID valid for 5 years	Renewal of ID every 5 years

THIRD COUNTRIES

Third-country nationals who would like to work in Switzerland have a harder time of it. The number of work permits is limited. Once the national quota has been filled, no more permits can be issued. In addition, a 'domestic preference' applies. This means that Swiss or EU/EFTA citizens with the same qualifications have priority. Employers have to prove that salary and working conditions meet the standards of the relevant sector. The procedure for acquiring a permit for third-country nationals is thus significantly more involved than that for citizens of EU/EFTA countries. In the following we have ordered the process chronologically (i.e. in the same order in which the documents must be submitted or requested):

A third-country national would like to come to Switzerland for purposes of employment.

1. The employer submits a request for a work permit to the relevant authorities in the canton of employment. The canton checks whether:
    *   The employment is in the overall economic interest of Switzerland
    *   No equally qualified person from Switzerland or an EU/EFTA country can be found, nor could another person currently resident in Switzerland do the job
    *   The canton still has not reached its quota
    *   The person has strong professional qualifications
    *   The salary and working conditions meet the standards of the relevant sector.

2. If all of these requirements are fulfilled, the application is sent on to the State Secretariat for Migration (SEM), which checks that laws are applied in a similar manner across Switzerland.
3. If the SEM approves the application of the canton, it informs the cantonal authorities and the employer of the positive decision. At the same time a message is sent to the relevant embassy in the employee's country of origin with the authorisation to issue an entry visa.
4. After arriving in Switzerland the person registers with the cantonal authorities within two weeks and receives a residence permit.

If only a short stay in Switzerland (less than four months) is foreseen, some of the requirements are not applicable: the quota regulation is not relevant, and registration with the cantonal migration authorities is not necessary.

Third-country nationals without employment: for residence without employment, the length of the stay again becomes significant. For a residence of over three months a permit must be obtained prior to entry. In contrast to residency related to employment, where the employer submits the application, here the foreigners must themselves contact the migration authorities of the future canton of residence. A residence of longer than three months may be permitted for education or training, for retired people, for medical treatment or in specific exceptional cases. The same procedure applies to family reunification.

For a stay of up to 90 days no residence permit is necessary. In the course of the visa application procedure, however, assurance of a timely departure is required, as well as proof of sufficient financial means of support. A residence permit is not required.

LANGUAGE SKILLS

For issuing or extending a residence permit (B) or a settlement permit (C), knowledge of the national language spoken at the place of residence is required. Permits that grant more extensive rights also demand stronger language skills (residence permit: oral and written A1, settlement permit: oral A2 and written A1). For those coming to join their families, a confirmation of registration for a language course is generally sufficient. For caregivers and teachers the bar is set higher (oral B1, written A1).

MEET YOUR EXPERT

Caroline Kaufmann is the founder and director of Silver Nest Relocation based in Zurich. Born and raised in both the French- and German-speaking parts of Switzerland, she studied International Hospitality Management, then travelled the world for 10 years before settling back in Switzerland with her husband and their three small children. Her dedication to her clients as well as her local knowledge and relationships make Silver Nest Relocation the perfect provider of relocation solutions: housing, tours, schooling, or simply answering all the questions newcomers have when settling in Switzerland.

HOUSING

It doesn't take long after arriving to Switzerland to discover that nearly everyone has a story to tell about their first apartment-hunting adventure. These can be funny but also frustrating experiences at times.

The housing market in the larger cities such as Zurich or Geneva can be very challenging because demand for most types of housing far exceeds the supply. This can make it difficult if you have to make compromises such as down-sizing or paying higher rents than expected – unless you are moving to Switzerland from an area which is even tougher.

It is easier to move to Switzerland if you already have an employment contract with a company, as this will facilitate home search. If you don't have a job yet, I suggest that you stay in temporary accommodation for a couple of months, look for a job and then focus on permanent housing.

Housing in Switzerland has many positive facets such as high-quality buildings, fair rules for tenants, safe neighbourhoods, great city infrastructure, access to public transport and reliable electricity and drinking water.

THE LOWDOWN
- How to successfully find a place to rent or buy
- The Do's and Don'ts, and the written and unwritten Swiss rules in the Swiss housing market
- Know your rights during an apartment handover

A NEW HOME

The process of finding permanent housing can be complex and time-consuming. First, you will need to understand the local rental market in the area you are planning to live, and be ready to deal with estate agencies. It's worth noting that the entire housing and rental process normally takes place in the local language (French, German or Italian). Therefore, it is highly recommended that you obtain the assistance of a relocation specialist in order to avoid pitfalls and potentially costly mistakes.

You will need to be physically present in Switzerland to view permanent housing options, so it's good to decide whether you prefer to travel to Switzerland to apartment hunt or whether you'd be fine with temporary accommodation for a few weeks after arrival.

Temporary accommodation: unlike in other countries, finding temporary accommodation in Switzerland can be difficult. In the larger cities, some furnished 1–2-bedroom apartments are available on 1–6 months rental agreements, but if you plan to move with children that may not be enough space. The best places to look are Vision apartments, PABS, UMS as well as Airbnb.

Permanent accommodation: if you're looking for housing, here's where to look:
- internet: comparis.ch, homegate.ch, immostreet.ch, immobilier.ch
- property section in your local newspaper
- property management companies: Livit, Wincasa or Privera and others have their own websites
- relocation specialists
- tell everyone you know! You should not underestimate the impact and power of networking in Switzerland.

It is very important to properly target potential apartments. Prepare a list of properties you would like to see. I suggest creating an Excel file with the following columns: address, postal code, city/village, rooms, sq. meters, price, available date, contact name, contact phone, website. Then colour code for where you are in the process.

Then, visit as many properties as you can, especially in the larger cities. The viewing schedule should be like a pipeline: load it as much as possible first, then add more visits to maintain the flow.

SWISS SPECIALTIES

- 'Number of rooms' refers to the total number of rooms, not bedrooms. As an example, a 4.5-room apartment has three separate bedrooms, one living/dining area (counted as one room) and a kitchen (counted as half a room). Bathrooms and corridors usually don't count towards the number of rooms. Reality however shows that this rule doesn't always work and there may be some variance. Best to review the square meters indicated in the advertisement.
- Likewise, the total square meters listed refers to usable space inside the apartment. Communal areas, stairways, laundry room in the basement and cellars are not included.
- Apartments in Switzerland are usually rented unfurnished, often even without light fittings. When you view a property, check whether the fridge, freezer and oven will be included (they usually are in the German and Italian parts but not always in the French part of Switzerland).
- Many flats, especially older and smaller ones (1.5-room–3.5-room apartments) tend to have communal laundry rooms, usually in the cellar, with time slots for each party. However, provided space allows, you may be able to buy your own.
- In cities with lakes, such as Zurich or Geneva, the closer to water, the higher the rent.
- Estate agencies don't charge any fees for showing apartments nor do they take commissions. They are usually paid by the property owners.
- It's quite normal to have a balcony, unless you live in a historic building or up under the roof.
- You can expect your flat to come with separate and lockable storage space in the cellar and/or attic where you can store things like suitcases, wine and sports equipment.
- Don't expect to walk along the street and see For Sale or To Let signs as is common in other countries. You have to research vacancies yourself (see opposite).

SIGNING THE DEAL

In the main cities, the rental market is very competitive. It is very important to visit each place in person. Pictures can be deceiving. Make an appointment with the agency or landlord, or by joining an official viewing with pre-set date and time. Keep in mind:

- for official viewings expect a queue.
- obviously, be on time; dress smart casual; always remain polite, patient and respectful.
- if you are viewing an occupied property, ask if you should take off your shoes before entering.
- make sure you have the correct contact details for the application.

Once you're ready to apply, in addition to the completed application form signed by potential new tenants (maximum two adults, both should sign even if only one is currently employed), you'll need to include copies of these documents in your application:

- passport or ID for all adults
- references from employer and previous landlord including name, phone number and email
- for those who have lived in Switzerland for more than six months, an extract from the debt collection register proving you are not being pursued by debt collection authorities
- employment contract, ideally showing your salary
- work permit and/or residence permit

When applying to agencies, there is no need to include a motivational latter or a picture of your family, or to send flowers or other gifts. If you are dealing with a private landlord, a picture or short description of yourself or your family can add a nice touch, as they tend to be more emotional towards people living in their apartment.

It is recommended that you only apply to one apartment per agency. Once you have signed a rental contract, withdraw any other pending applications to avoid being charged a penalty (100–250Fr depending on the canton).

EXPECTED TIMEFRAME

- Lease contracts typically begin on the 1st or 15th of every month.
- Follow up a couple of days after sending the application to ensure that your form has been received and is being processed. Ask if additional documents are required to facilitate the decision-making process.
- Answers from the agency can usually be expected within one week.

CRUCIAL FACTORS

Things to bear in mind when making important decisions:

- first come is not first served.
- your income, employer, and family situation, the first impression you leave, and the quality of your references are the most important factors.
- agencies prefer quiet and reliable tenants who will pay their rent on time.
- as a rule of thumb, please note that the monthly rent should be no more than one quarter of your gross monthly salary (combined salary for couples or families).
- your nationality or cultural background is not a deciding factor for agencies, but if they might prefer non-smoking tenants without large pets. However, if you deal with private landlords, they might have prejudices in some cases. According to a study by swissinfo.ch 'people with a Kosovar or Turkish name have a clearly lower chance of being invited to a viewing.

GOOD TO KNOW

If you decide to apply for an apartment, do it quickly. The best is to send the application via email right after viewing a property. Don't wait! It shows the agency you are serious. You will either have received an application form during the viewing or you can download it on the agency's website. Complete the application in an official language (French/German/Italian) and not English. It may increase your chances at agencies with no English speakers.

MOVING IN

Once you have received confirmation over the phone or via email, but before you receive a rental contract, the estate agency or landlord will ask you to confirm your acceptance of the rental agreement. Any questions or uncertainties should be clarified now. A withdrawal later might be subject to a penalty (usually 100–250Fr, as indicated on the application form).

If you are new to Switzerland, it might make sense to have your rental contract reviewed by a relocation specialist, as it normally doesn't cost more than a few hundred francs. This will also give you the security that you understand the terms and conditions before signing.

If the contract looks good, correct any mistakes and have all parties initial the changes made. Sign the contract within five business days and send it back to the agency or landlord by mail (scanned copies are usually not accepted). Don't forget to withdraw any other pending applications!

THE CONTRACT

Item	Issues
Deposit	2–3 months' rent is common, but never more than 3 months.
House rules	Smoking, pets, noise, correct airing etc.
Inventory	If the apartment is furnished
Keys	Keys are not supposed to be replicated by the tenant. If you lose one, you should inform the agency right away and have the locks changed (your liability insurance may cover this).
Monthly rent	Is it what you agreed upon? What are the conditions for future rent increases?
Names	All adult occupants must sign the rental contract. This insures the lease is not terminated without common consent. Check your personal details.
Parking	This can either be included in the monthly rent or contracted separately. In large underground garages, the parking spots could even be rented out by another agency or landlord so it is worth checking if there is a second contract to sign and a different invoice to pay.
Pets	If you decide to add a pet to your family (eg dog, cat, parrot, reptile) or install a larger aquarium you need written permission.
Private appliances	If you decide to buy your own appliances that will, which use existing water connections (dishwasher, washing machine, dryer) you should first get written approval first.
Redecoration	Covers whether you expect any items to be taken care of before you move in (eg painting). Keep in mind that the apartment should be handed back in the same condition when you move out, apart from normal wear and tear.
Repairs	Generally, you are responsible for minor repairs of up to 150–200Fr (eg replacing light bulbs, mirrors, baking trays, shower hose).
Sublease	Generally permitted with the written approval of the agency or landlord, and can only be prohibited if the tenant tries to make a profit. The main tenant will always be liable for damages made by the subtenant.
Term	A 12–15-month minimum is standard.
Term of notice	Three to six months is common but some contracts allow notice to be given at the end of every month, while others allow you to quit twice a year, at the end of March and September. This means your termination notice must reach the landlord by 31 December or 30 June, respectively.
Utilities	Which utilities are included, and which ones are invoiced separately. It's common to deduct an average amount per month and then invoice/pay back the difference at the end of the fiscal year.

THE HANDOVER

If you have a particular moving date in mind, let the estate agency know before you sign the contract. Taking over a rental property is a formal process and involves certain obligations. Expect it to last one to three hours, and bring all relevant documents: proof of first month's rent and deposit payment, and a copy of your insurance policy (if available).

Handovers in Switzerland include a thorough examination of the current state of the property at the rental starting date. The assessment and handover protocol will be completed in the local language, and may include maintenance responsibilities for the new tenant. It is important to document any defects that occurred prior to yourt moving in.

You will be asked to sign the completed handover protocol, which forms part of the formal rental contract. You may want to enlist the help of a professional, who is familiar with the local language and Switzerland's property market and is willing to accompany you. Note that you will have 14 days to try everything out in the apartment (eg electrical appliances, water pressure etc). Should you discover some defects, report them to the agency or landlord via email or mail. Make sure these items are added to the handover protocol.

INSPECTION TIPS

- Bring a camera, pen and paper and a few stickers to label the doorbell and mailbox.
- Check that defects are clearly listed on the protocol.
- Check window frames, windows, walls and ceiling for holes, marks and other damage. Take pictures of damages, including any scratches or marks, and have them noted in the protocol.
- Check that all doors have a key and that they really work for the relevant door(s).
- Open and close blinds and sun shades.
- Check light fixtures; flush the toilet; test faucets in the sink, shower, kitchen; inspect fridge and freezer and any electrical appliances.
- Check the cellar, communal laundry room and garage/parking spots.
- Inquire about your responsibilities with regard to service contracts for electrical appliances, snow removal, and garden maintenance (if applicable).

SECURITY DEPOSIT

Most estate agencies will have you set up a bank account for your rental deposit. It is free of charge and you'll earn interest. Alternatively, SwissCaution can reduce the deposit to 1.5 months rent, but note that there is a charge for this service.

UTILITIES

You can expect electricity and water, while gas is less common – but all of these will be set up by your landlord. You'll have to set up TV, telephone, and internet and register for Serafe. It's best to get your apartment's previous tenant's name and ask about previous third-party providers. Make inquiries two to three weeks before your move. Ask for a contract and request that the services be operational when you move in. If you need help from an electrician, simply find one on local.ch. While expensive by international standards, you can count on them to be efficient and dependable.

Item	Issues	Who pays
Cleaning of common space	Common spaces are staircases, elevators, garbage containers, washing areas etc.	Landlord
Electricity	The Swiss energy market is regional and privatized, and you probably won't be able to choose your provider. Generally not covered in the ancillary costs listed in the contract except for the basic connection fees.	Renter
Gardening	Common green areas and playgrounds in housing estates	Landlord
	Your own private garden	Renter or dedicated gardener if stated in the rental agreement
Insurance	A private liability and household insurance is strongly recommended (see 'Money' chapter)	Renter
Landline, internet and cable TV	Connections are available in all apartments, but you will need to sign up with local providers.	Renter
Serafe	Switzerland's radio and television fee (365Fr per household) is mandatory for all households with TVs, radio or internet.	Renter
Water and sewage	The basic fee for water connection and waste water is included in the rent but not the actual water consumption.	Renter

DISPUTES

In certain cases, conflicts with your landlord can't be avoided. If trouble strikes, here's where to turn.

Tenants' association: for a 100Fr yearly fee, experts in each canton are available to answer questions, provide free legal advice, and lobby for your interests. (mieterverband.ch/asloca.ch)

The Swiss Homeowner's Association: this association supports property owners and helps with tenancy law issues as well as disputes with neighbours. (hev-schweiz.ch)

The Swiss Estate Association SVIT: this association serves as a lobby for the interests of the housing market, and represents professional property service providers. (svit.ch)

Conciliation boards: conciliation authorities help both tenants and landlords to resolve disputes. These services are free of charge. (search at mietrecht.ch)

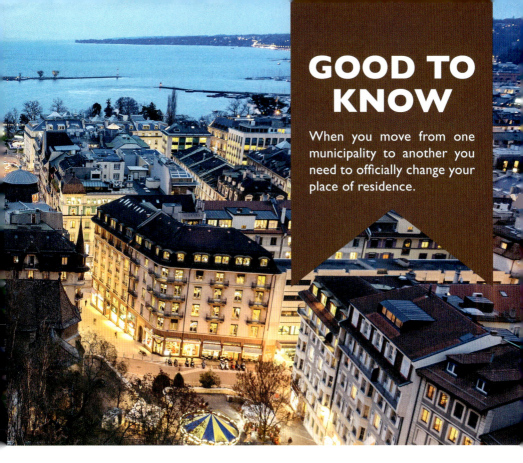

DEPARTING

If you would like to leave your apartment/house, give notice according to the terms of your contract by registered mail. If you'd like to move at a date not allowed by your contract and can't find a suitable replacement renter you may be liable for payments until the next official moving date. You must leave your home in the condition stipulated in your contract, which usually means cleaned to a pristine condition. It is highly recommended that you hire a professional cleaning company as most companies guarantee handovers. All nails should be removed, and holes repaired. You may need to paint.

You will only be liable for damages caused by you, not general wear and tear resulting from normal usage of the apartment (eg some scratches on the floor, some marks on the walls etc). Damages may result in losing some of your deposit. In case of disputes, contact the resources listed in the section opposite.

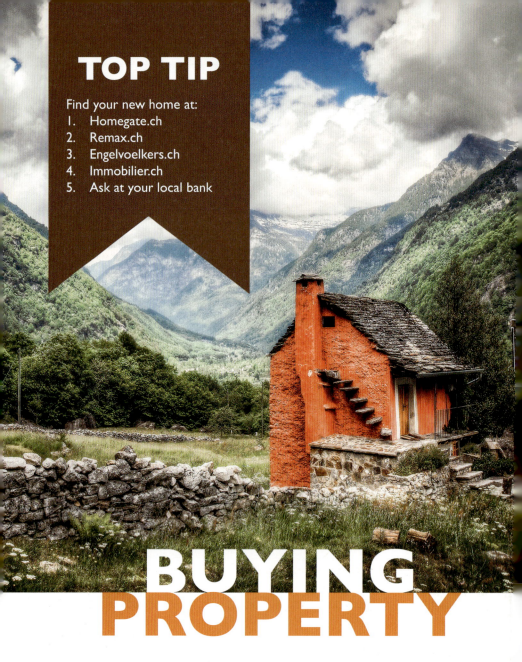

TOP TIP

Find your new home at:
1. Homegate.ch
2. Remax.ch
3. Engelvoelkers.ch
4. Immobilier.ch
5. Ask at your local bank

BUYING PROPERTY

Only 37.4% of Swiss residents owns homes. However, rents in urban areas tend to be high, so it might be the right time for you to buy. But beware, the Swiss housing market can be challenging even to experienced buyers, with house prices varying dramatically from city to city, many rules around foreign property ownership, and a unique mortgage system. See Money Matters (Chapter 7) for information on mortgages. While buying a home can be well-suited to those with stable employment and private life, it has its disadvantages. It's not ideal for short term stays, as it entails a long-term financial obligation.

FINDING A HOME

The most important sources are online portals, where estate agents list properties in their portfolio. You'll find both existing properties and future building projects planned in your search area. Another tool is to call the municipality or architects directly.

Once you have found your dream home, things can move fast and you need to be on top of them. Start by determining the highest offer you can make and deciding on a bid. Then communicate this to the seller, either through your estate representative or directly to the homeowner. Keep in mind that estate agents are typically paid by the seller.

For the buyer, it doesn't matter who is selling (estate agent or owner) as the sale itself will be handled by a notary. Once your offer has been accepted, you will be asked to pay a reservation fee (generally 20,000–50,000Fr). You will sign a written agreement, and the money will be held in an escrow account by a notary. Then, check back with your bank and advise them that your offer has been accepted. They will then liaise with the notary to finalize outstanding paperwork and move forward with the actual purchase.

In Switzerland, a notary oversees the final stages of the purchase. The notary is a neutral party. You can select a notary, or the buyer can suggest one. The notary's tasks include drafting the contract; holding the buyer's deposit or reservation fee in an escrow account; completing the official transfer of the property; registering the change of ownership; and advising both parties as to the legitimacy and legality of the transaction.

You should budget up to 5% of the purchase price for fees which include both the notary's fee (0.2–1%) and the property transfer tax (varies by canton but is usually between 1–4%). In addition, land registry fees amounting to 1–1.5% can be split between the buyer and the seller but are usually covered by the buyer.

TRANSFER TAX

Property transfer taxes vary from one canton to the next and from one village to the next, so it is difficult to provide overall percentages. To give you a simplified overview, here are the cantons with the highest and lowest property transfer taxes in alphabetical order.

The three highest:
• Bern, Lucerne, Neuchâtel

The lowest:
• Aargau, Glarus, Schaffhausen, Schwyz, Uri, Zug and Zurich

MEET YOUR EXPERT

Rebekka Hänggi has been involved with the Swiss jobs and recruiting market for many years. She is excited by economics, innovation, digitalisation, globalisation, and new models of living and working. In the end, however, it is really about one thing: people. Rebekka works at JobCloud, the leading digital enterprise dedicated to the Swiss job market. In her chapter, she hopes to help you understand how the Swiss mentality plays out in the job market, and give you insights that will help you as you work in Switzerland.

WORK

It's no wonder that Switzerland is a popular destination for foreign professionals – it has a lot to offer. A high quality of life, fair salaries, low unemployment, political stability, an international orientation, a variety of languages, a central location and a high level of innovation are just a few of its attractions. But to enjoy working and living here, you need to know a few basics.

When looking for a job you should definitely rely on your network. However, expanding this network in Switzerland might not be as easy as it was back home. At your Swiss workplace you will have new colleagues, but you won't necessarily find new friends. And with these colleagues, by the way, it's best not to speak about your salary. That simply doesn't wash in Switzerland. If you should run into a major conflict, though, Switzerland is a good place to be. The Swiss often resolve conflicts in the workplace without external assistance. That's why there are so few strikes here.

So grab a seat on the next train – it will surely be running, and on time – and read this chapter to get inspired!

THE LOWDOWN
- How to find a job
- Distinctive features of the application process
- Everything about salaries and benefits

THE SWISS JOB MARKET

One special feature of the Swiss market is that there are many linguistic regions: German, French, Italian, Romansh, and, increasingly and everywhere, English. Yet although they are taught at least one national language from an early age, most Swiss don't learn that language very well. I am a good example: I've been learning French ever since I was nine, but, hey, speak a little French with me and…It can therefore be a real advantage if you can speak two of the Swiss national languages. English is spoken mostly by city-dwellers. In Zurich people use a lot of anglicisms, and the rest of Switzerland, listening in, rolls its collective eyes. English is not as widespread in daily life among the Swiss as it is in the Netherlands or in Sweden. With the younger generation exposed to so much English on digital media, however, the level of competency should rise.

State schools in Switzerland provide a solid education. According to the State Secretariat for Education, Research and Innovation (SERI), after completing their obligatory schooling (around age 14–16), two thirds of Swiss students decide for an apprenticeship, while only a minority pursues an academic path. Apprentices attend vocational school in parallel with their hands-on work. An apprenticeship gives young people access to the working world and allows them to experience it at first hand. This kind of educational system is unfamiliar to many foreigners, and is therefore often underestimated. In Switzerland apprenticeships are highly valued, and our 'dual-track educational system' is the subject of studies all over the world.

Industry in Switzerland is multifaceted. Although the various sectors are distributed throughout the country, there are concentrations in certain cities. The pharmaceutical industry in Basel, the federal administration in Bern, the banks in Zurich, and 'Crypto Valley' in Zug all contribute many innovations to their fields. French-speaking Switzerland's watch industry is another example of a successfully ticking sector of the economy.

UNEMPLOYMENT RATE

The unemployment rate in Switzerland is low. Often the rate from the State Secretariat for Economic Affairs (SECO) is cited, but this rate is of little use for making international comparisons, as it is based on a measuring methodology that is not widespread. The ILO unemployment rate, by contrast, is internationally standardised. The ILO value always lies above the SECO value. Switzerland had an ILO unemployment rate of 4.4% in September 2018. This is quite low compared with most other countries, but not exceptional: there are eight EU nations with lower unemployment rates.

More than 84% of the Swiss population is between 15 and 64 years of age, and over a third of this age group works part-time (Labour Force Survey, 2018). Compared with other countries, this is a very high figure. In Europe only the Netherlands has a higher rate of part-time employment.

Engineers, IT developers and nurses are in short supply in Switzerland, and the unemployment rate in these professions is correspondingly low. If you are looking for a job in marketing, administration or the food service industry you'll have a harder time of it. Since July 2018, professions with an above-average unemployment rate are required to publish their vacancies with the regional employment centres (RAV), with the goal of filling them with Swiss residents. Swiss job seekers get a head start of five days, after which the vacancies can be announced publicly, and foreigners also have the opportunity to learn about them. According to SECO, this procedure is followed for one out of every ten vacancies.

THE JOB HUNT

The job hunt plays out in classical fashion in Switzerland. A 2019 study by JobCloud came to the conclusion that the vast majority of job seekers (70%) use online portals. About 50% look for a new position with help from their own contacts, only 40% use newspapers and magazines, 32% use social networks, and 13% use employment agencies. Yet in ever more areas, especially those in which there is a shortage of professionals, this classical recruiting model is no longer adequate. Employment agents now often have to actively search for suitable candidates. In addition, there are sector-specific portals that you can use if you are looking for work in a specific field.

Most job portals offer even more possibilities for simplifying the job hunt.
- **Activating a 'Job Alarm' or 'Job Subscription'** automatically sends you an email with any new vacancies that fit your search criteria.
- **Establishing a profile, filling it out as completely as possible** granting permission for it to be stored in the job portal's CV databank gives recruiters easy access to it.

WEBSITES

Businesses have realised that they not only have to market their products and services, but also need to position themselves as attractive employers in order to win over strong and suitable employees. Marketing is thus increasingly becoming an aspect of personnel departments. One consequence of this is that firms are disclosing more information than ever about what life and working conditions are like in their workplaces.

- Which businesses are active in your sector? Research!
- Study the websites of companies you are interested in. Most companies post their job openings.
- If you really like the look of a company but it has no vacancies, simply write to the recruiter. Nowadays good recruiters nurse contacts with potential employees, even when no positions are vacant at the moment.

PERSONAL CONTACTS

Networks are the key to job hunting! Use your network on the job hunt as well.
- Build up a network in Switzerland or maintain and expand your existing network.
- If you don't yet live in Switzerland, this will be more difficult. Especially since the Swiss are not known for making your first steps particularly easy. Still, it can be done.
- Visit events, workshops or specialist functions with a networking character. It is easy to start conversations at such functions, since the event itself provides a hook. Try to arrange for lunch with interesting contacts a couple of weeks after the event.
- Business networks can support you in wonderful ways. In Switzerland two portals are used the most: LinkedIn and Xing.
  LinkedIn: international but ever more prominent in Switzerland.
  Xing: only known in German-speaking areas.
  You can't go wrong if you maintain a presence on both portals, but this takes a lot of effort. If in doubt, decide for LinkedIn. Keep your profile and your contacts up to date, and make yourself visible by commenting on other members' posts and sharing interesting articles.

THE APPLICATION

Recruiters can request your application documents in various ways. Often at first you merely send an email with a CV and a motivational letter, or fill in the employer's application management tool. These tools can be frustrating to use because you have to type everything in separately. Depending on the sector, it may be common to deliver your application in person – for jobs in skilled labour or the food service industry, for example.

CV

Choose a simple design for your CV and focus on the essentials.
- Personal data: name, date of birth, marital status, residence permit
- Photograph (this is still expected in Switzerland)
- Your previous jobs, with short descriptions
- Your education
- Other skills
- Hobbies (be as concrete as possible)
- References

REFERENCES

Referees are contacted—if at all—towards the very end of the application process. In your CV it is enough to write 'References available upon request'. This has the advantage that you can notify your referees before they are contacted. Choose two or three contacts before you apply for the job and get their permission in advance. Recruiters are only allowed to contact referees after clearing it with you.

Draw on your network again during the application process. Do you know someone who works for or with the potential employer? Does your girlfriend's sister practice yoga with someone who works at the company? No joke – sometimes even remote contacts can help you get a job.

HEADHUNTER

Depending on the professional level and the sector, it can sometimes make sense for employers to work with an external headhunter, especially when seeking to fill executive positions. Find out which headhunters work with job seekers in your field. You will probably be able to find them through business networks. But be careful: if you are looking for a 'normal', less elite position, it's better to apply directly to the company. Employers generally pay headhunters a month's salary of the position to be filled. (There are no costs for the candidates.) When there are several good candidates, this mediation fee can tip the scale toward candidates who have applied directly.

AT THE INTERVIEW

Interviews can take many forms. But there are a few rules that you should always observe.

BEFORE THE INTERVIEW

You need to be well-informed about the company. As for every meeting, it is expected that you come prepared. You can expect that your interviewer will be well-informed about you as well. And he or she will have looked at your social media profile.

AT THE INTERVIEW

Show up punctually: that means three to four minutes before the appointed time. If you're half an hour early, have an espresso around the corner. If something happens that prevents you from being on time, be sure to phone while on the way!

Use the formal address ('Sie/vous'): unless you have been explicitly told otherwise, use the formal forms of address with your interviewer. More and more companies have introduced policies of informal address ('du/tu'), but if this is the case you will be informed of it at the beginning of the interview.

Handshake: in Switzerland attention is paid to a person's handshake, which should be clear, firm and friendly. A fleeting sweaty one, or a bone-crusher, is not appreciated. Your handshake should be accompanied by a clear and friendly greeting.

Eye contact: eye contact is important in Swiss culture. You don't have to continually stare the interviewer in the face, but do seek regular eye contact. If you are offered a drink—coffee, tea, orange juice—accept it! It gives the interview a more relaxed character.

Language/dialect: politely ask that the interview be carried out in Standard (High) German if you have difficulties understanding Swiss dialect.

Honesty is the best policy: okay, okay, maybe with a little fudging here and there. But stick to the truth. The Swiss like honest people. Taboo: your interviewer is not allowed to ask you anything about your plans for having a family. You don't have to answer such questions.

Money matters: at the first interview it is normal to exchange expectations regarding salary. If the interviewer doesn't bring it up, do so yourself. You need to come to the interview with an idea of the salary range you would consider. If your job is in the private sector, be prepared to negotiate the salary. And while you may be used to thinking in terms of monthly pay, in the interview you should negotiate in terms of an annual salary.

THE INTERVIEW PROCESS

The number of steps in the entire interview process depends heavily on the employer and the position. For a 'normal' position two or three interviews are usual. For a leadership position there will be more.

IN THE WORKPLACE

Working conditions in Switzerland are fair. There is no 'Hire and Fire' mentality as in the USA, but also no extreme protection for employees as in France. This explains why there are no strikes in Switzerland.

Unions: the Swiss Trade Union Federation (SGB) is the largest employee organisation in Switzerland and represents the interests of employees on the national level. Beneath this umbrella organisation there are individual unions such as Unia, which is the largest one. Unia negotiates collective labour agreements with employers and employer associations to regulate working conditions. Not all employers are party to collective labour agreements. You can find out more about unions by clicking on 'Labour' on the SECO homepage at seco.admin.ch.

HARD WORKER

Switzerland is one of the European countries with the longest working weeks. Working hours must be recorded—with a few exceptions—for the protection of employees. The lunch break does not count as work time, and overtime is generally compensated.

- **Working hours:** on average 42 hours per week
- **Lunch break:** at least a half hour is mandated by labour laws (but the lunch break doesn't count as work time)
- **Statutory minimum annual leave:** four weeks

In case of conflict: conflict situations sometimes arise in the workplace, but very rarely escalate so that the parties end up facing each other in court. The Swiss are in general very polite and usually criticise one another only indirectly. Conflicts between employees can often be patched up with the help of a supervisor or the personnel department. Some employers recommend an external, confidential counselling centre that employees can turn to. In cases of bullying or harassment the procedure is similar: first speak directly with the person concerned, and only then take further action. Unlike in ordinary conflict situations, it is best to seek out witnesses in such cases.

FLEXIBLE WORK

Time- and location-independent work is not very widespread in Switzerland. But times are changing. Swiss public transport will soon reach its limits during commuting hours, so it makes sense to support time- and location-flexible work. At the same time, employees should be encouraged to set limits so that they don't end up working day and night.

Annual working time: another model with flexible hours is that of <u>annual working time</u>. Here it doesn't matter how much an employee works each week, as long as they put in the required number of hours over the course of the year. This model is not common, but I am convinced that employers will begin to open up to it.

Part-time work: <u>part-time work</u> is very widespread in Switzerland compared with other countries: over a third of Swiss employees work 'part-time'. When referring to part-time work in Switzerland, however, you should always specify the percentage. There is a big difference between working 80% and working 30%.

All in all working in Switzerland is fair and balanced for both employees and employers. Switzerland is currently in a transition phase with respect to many aspects of working life. In the coming years there will be many changes made in the direction of models based on greater flexibility and openness.

SOCIAL MATTERS

Birthdays	The person whose birthday it is brings in a snack: homemade or bought cakes, rolls, croissants, etc. The team eats them together over a cup of coffee during a morning break. You only need to invite the immediate team, and not the entire work force.
Goodbyes	When someone leaves the company – and, less frequently, also on birthdays – money is often collected in order to buy a communal present for the departing employee. Typical contributions range from 5 to 20 francs, and contributing is voluntary.
Births, Marriages	As with goodbyes, on these pleasant occasions money is often collected within the team to buy a present for the person concerned.

Celebrating with the company: usually there is a Christmas meal or party. The form of this event varies greatly. At a party it is fine to celebrate, and alcohol is often consumed. It is a company event, however, so you should go easy on the drinking. Still, at most such gatherings there will be a few people who go overboard. This will be the subject of much whispering over coffee on the following Monday morning.

Formal or informal address: this isn't necessarily determined by the size of the company: Swisscom, the leading telecom firm in Switzerland with 20,000 employees, has an informal culture, as does Tamedia, one of the largest media concerns in the country.

To orient yourself, consider the following.
- The informal 'du' or 'tu' is becoming more and more common.
- The more hierarchical and conservative the business, the more it will lean toward the formal 'Sie' or 'vous'.
- Within teams you almost always use the informal forms.
- The more digitalised and modern the company is, the more it will lean toward a completely informal culture.

Colleagues vs. friends: colleagues from work and friends are not the same thing. With colleagues you might eat lunch sometimes and even possibly, occasionally, conceivably, drink an end-of-work beer together, but that's it. This can make it somewhat difficult to make friends.

EN GUETE

On your lunch break in German-speaking Switzerland you will hear 'En Guete' called out from every corner. You'll think you hear it a thousand times. It means something like 'Bon appetit!' For some reason it's a part of Swiss culture to say it to everyone between 11:30 and 13:00.

SALARY

You surely know already that Switzerland is an expensive place to live – a 'high-price island'. Swiss salaries are correspondingly elevated.

It's generally frowned on to speak openly about your salary in Switzerland, so be careful about this. Don't ask colleagues how much they are paid. Salaries and salary ranges are rarely mentioned even in job advertisements. There are a few employers, however, who are transparent about the salaries of their employees. And occasionally it even happens that Swiss employees break the taboo and actually do talk informally about how much they earn. In the end it is the employees who benefit from transparent salary policies, which constrain companies to operate with fair salary models.

A year has 13 months: it's normal to receive 13 monthly salaries per year in Switzerland. You get your December salary twice. The typical Swiss sets this amount to the side to pay the following year's taxes. Companies are not required to pay 13 monthly salaries, but the practice is widespread.

RULE OF THUMB

Annual taxes = One month's salary

DIFFERENCES IN SALARIES

In Switzerland there are large regional and sectoral differences in salary levels. Salaries in the pharmaceutical and banking industries, for example, are higher than in the field of health care. In Zurich both the salaries and the cost of living are higher than in Bern. According to a 2016 salary structure survey by the Federal Statistical Office (FSO), women earn on average 19.6% less than men. Only a portion of this difference is due to the position held, experience, educational level, etc. The survey did not, however, take account of the industry sector. Doing so might provide a further reason for the shortfall, given that women often work in sectors of the economy that pay lower wages. Recently a popular initiative was approved to require companies with more than 100 employees to conduct and openly publish an annual study of the salaries they pay.

How much do the various professions earn? At lohncheck.ch you can enter the relevant parameters and find out.

Median annual salaries for full-time employees according to the FSO:

Overall	81,000
Executive positions	119,000
Academic positions	100,000
Technicians	86,300
Office workers	72,500
Sales and service	62,100
Skilled labour	71,500
Unskilled labour	58,500

BENEFITS

Most companies offer their employees <u>benefits</u> in addition to their salary. The larger the company, the greater the number of 'fringe benefits'. According to the FSO these benefits make up between 2% and 10% of earnings. Some of them are taxed. You can check on the tax status of your benefits either at the cantonal tax office or with a tax advisor.

Common benefits

- Company parking
- Car for private use
- Mobile phone for private use
- Sports facilities
- Restaurant for personnel
- Increased contribution to a pension plan
- Increased contribution to social security

- Life insurance premiums
- Unpaid leave
- Stock certificates
- <u>Further education</u>
- Discounts for company products/ services

Holiday entitlement: Employers are legally required to give their employees four weeks' paid leave per year – five weeks for employees under 20 years old. Many companies offer five weeks even for those over 20. In rare cases they will offer six weeks – for example, once the employee has reached a certain age, such as 50.

And by the way: in 2012 the Swiss voted on a popular initiative proposing 'Six weeks of holiday for everyone' – and hold on tight! – we rejected it. It is often very surprising to foreigners that the Swiss vote in such a business-friendly way in referendums.

SWISS PLUS

There are a few more typical Swiss benefits that some employers offer.

Reka-Checks	Reka-Checks are a means of payment for leisure activities and holidays. You can use them in restaurants, hotels, zoos, fairs, for public transportation, etc. Some employers offer them to employees at a discount.
Train tickets	Some companies pay for their employees' annual passes for public transport. Either the employer has a business account and provides the passes directly to the employees, or the employees buy the pass themselves and are reimbursed for it.
Health insurance premiums	In Switzerland it is very rare that an employer pays for employees' health insurance.
Maternity leave	The law stipulates 14 weeks of maternity leave. Some employers offer more.
Paternity leave	Parliament has approved two weeks of paternity leave for fathers, but it is unclear when this will be implemented. In practice, many employers have begun offering at least that much.

MEET YOUR EXPERT

Diccon Bewes is a British travel writer and author of five books on Switzerland, including the number one bestseller, *Swiss Watching*. He arrived back in 2005 and fell in love with Switzerland and its people (and chocolate) so started writing about his life here. In doing so, he became an accidental expat expert and regularly speaks about the joys and trials of living in Switzerland. You can follow him via his website dicconbewes.com, on Twitter (@dicconb) or on Facebook (facebook.com/ SwissWatching).

SWISS FACTS

Do you know your Rütli from your Röstigraben? Or have some idea who Dufour and Dunant were? If not, then you'll soon stand out as a foreigner when chatting to the locals. You'll either quickly lose the plot of a conversation or constantly have to ask questions that make you look daft. Worst of all, you might even end up committing an excruciating faux-pas, such as stating that cuckoo clocks are Swiss.

What you need is a quick introduction to the facts and (historical) figures that are often self-explanatory to anyone who grew up here. A shared knowledge of basic history, politics and culture is part of the national subconscious in every country, but it's unlikely you've had much exposure to the Swiss version. This chapter will help fill in some of the most important gaps, so that you won't embarrass yourself by asking what the Federal Council is or where the Fifth Switzerland can be found. It's a chance to get to know your new home better, and to whet your appetite for finding out even more about this unique country.

For more facts and stats about Switzerland, have a look at the Appendix, which lists all the cantons plus useful trivia you never thought you needed to know.

THE LOWDOWN
- The high points of Swiss history
- Swiss politics explained
- The low-down on Swiss celebrities and clichés

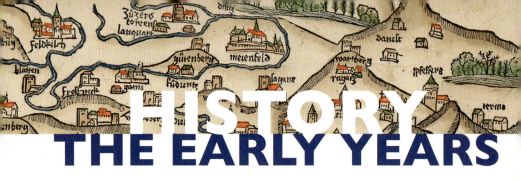

HISTORY
THE EARLY YEARS

It all began with three men who met in a lakeside meadow on 1 August 1291 and swore an oath of allegiance. Switzerland was born.

Not much of that founding story has ever been proved, least of all the date, but around that time the first three cantons did get together to resist Habsburg rule and Switzerland grew out of the initial pact. However, Rütli meadow beside Lake Lucerne is still celebrated as the nation's birthplace, with that initial vow known as the Rütli oath. .

After that, Swiss history becomes much clearer as it usually involved fighting for survival, primarily against the Habsburgs. Battles like Morgarten, Murten and Marignano are etched into the Swiss subconscious, even if few people remember who was fighting. Suffice to say, that up until the mid-1500s the Swiss were as pugnacious as any other European nation. Even after they stopped fighting their neighbours, the Swiss hired out their men as mercenaries to the monarchs of Europe; the last remnant of this is the Pope's Swiss Guard.

The Confederation grew as cities like Bern and Basel joined but there was little central control and no real structure, with each canton effectively a mini-state. All that came to an abrupt end with the French invasion of 1798 and the creation of the Helvetic Republic, the first real incarnation of a modern Swiss state. While the French occupation lasted 17 long years, the Republic was abolished after only five, replaced by a revised form of centralised control, but with six new cantons. This arrangement was swept away with Napoleon's defeat in 1815, when Swiss independence was restored, and three more cantons added.

THE NATION'S NAME

Switzerland has four national languages so uses a fifth, Latin, for its official name: Confœderatio Helvetica, which is abbreviated to CH, the initials you see on the back of cars and at the end of internet addresses. The Latin translates as Swiss Confederation, even though the country has been a federation since 1848. As for the Helvetica part, that refers to the Helvetii, a Celtic tribe that lived in these parts during the Roman era. They are long gone but they live on in name only.

TIMELINE 1291–1815

The first few centuries of Swiss history were marked by battles between the cantons and with their neighbours. Here are the most important dates:

1291 Traditional date for the foundation of Switzerland by the first three cantons, Schwyz, Uri and Unterwalden (now known separately as Nidwalden and Obwalden).

1315 Battle of Morgarten, a vital victory over the Habsburgs that ensured the new Confederation survived despite being outnumbered.

1386 Battle of Sempach, the against-the-odds victory over the Austrians, helped by the sacrifice of legendary hero Arnold von Winkelried.

1476 Battles of Grandson and Murten, with two crucial Swiss victories over the Burgundians in three months; in 1477 they won again, killing the Duke of Burgundy.

1515 Battle of Marignano, Italy, where the French inflicted a heavy defeat on the Swiss, thereby reconquering nearby Milan and ending Swiss military dominance.

1519 Ulrich Zwingli became priest at the Grossmünster in Zurich, kickstarting the Swiss Reformation with his views on eating sausages during Lent.

1541 Jean Calvin, a French Reformer, returned to Geneva and quickly transformed it into the Protestant Rome, so helping to start the Swiss watch industry.

1648 Switzerland stayed out of the Thirty Years' War and the resulting Treaty of Westphalia finally recognised Swiss independence.

1798 French invasion ended with the surrender of the Confederation and the creation of the Helvetic Republic, a centralised Swiss state under French control.

1803 The Act of Mediation abolished the Helvetic Republic and created six new cantons: Aargau, Graubünden, St Gallen, Thurgau, Ticino and Vaud.

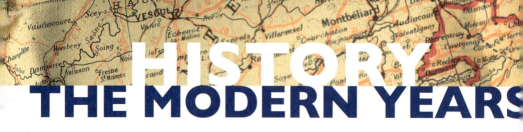

HISTORY
THE MODERN YEARS

After the French left, the old Confederation was resurrected in 1815. It didn't survive once civil war erupted in 1847 following the formation of a special alliance by seven Catholic cantons. The war was over in a month and the resulting peace turned Switzerland into a modern federation with a central government, parliament, flag and currency, building on the changes Napoleon had made 50 years earlier.

Industrialisation and innovation helped transform the Swiss economy. High-value products such as chemicals, textiles, watches and chocolate led the way, while trainlines, built initially for British tourists, became the backbone of the country. The boom ended with the First World War, which Switzerland managed to avoid but couldn't escape from the consequences: the General Strike in 1918 led to proportional representation and better working conditions.

The Swiss resisted the constant threat of invasion during World War Two and survived the war largely unscathed compared to the rest of Europe. That helped the post-war economy thrive, ushering in the 'economic miracle' and modern prosperity, built on the back of industries like pharmaceuticals and tourism. Political reforms followed slowly but surely, with consensual government and (finally) women's votes engendering stability and security.

Modern Switzerland has managed to negotiate the minefield of relations with the European Union, which completely surrounds the Alpine republic. Instead of membership, the two sides have negotiated a series of bilateral treaties covering everything from free movement of people to trade. The Swiss populist right, with its anti-EU and anti-immigration agenda, has called those treaties into question but as yet, no one has decided what the answer is. One thing is certain the Swiss themselves will make the decision, using their system of direct democracy (see page 60).

THE NATION'S FLAG

A white cross on a red background is as much a symbol of Switzerland as the Matterhorn or Heidi, but the national flag itself is actually a fairly recent creation. It dates back to the early 19th century and was only officially defined by the Federal Council in 1889. Most importantly the flag is square.

TIMELINE
1815–TODAY

The 19th and 20th centuries changed Europe completely and Switzerland was not immune. Here are the most important dates:

1815   Swiss independence and neutrality were restored at the Congress of Vienna, while three new cantons were added: Geneva, Neuchâtel and Valais.

1847   The Sonderbund War, the last conflict on Swiss soil, saw the defeat of the Catholic separatist cantons during a short civil war.

1848   A new Federal Constitution created the modern Swiss state with a federal government and parliament set up in Bern.

1918   Social unrest led to a General Strike and Swiss troops on the streets; the end result was proportional representation and a 48-hour working week.

1940   Operation Tannenbaum was the Nazi plan to conquer Switzerland, while the Swiss response was the National Redoubt of mountain fortresses.

1959   Power-sharing in the Federal Council was set in the unofficial 'magic formula', by which the seven seats are divided between the four largest parties.

1971   Women finally got the right to vote at federal level, although the last canton (Appenzell Innerrhoden) didn't relent for another twenty years.

1979   Jura became the newest canton after a separatist campaign against Canton Bern was finally decided at the ballot box and approved by referendum in 1978.

1992   Swiss voters rejected the government's proposal to join the European Economic Area (EEA), but by a narrow majority of 50.3%.

2005   After the EEA defeat, Switzerland negotiated bilateral treaties with the EU, including joining the Schengen area, which voters approved in a referendum.

LONG DIVISIONS

Today Switzerland is a unified, peaceful country but it wasn't always like that. The Swiss have been divided for centuries but, while those divisions do still exist, these days they are overcome by talking instead of fighting. Two of the deepest splits are still evident today: language and religion.

Language: Switzerland has four national languages, three of which are also official languages of state: German (63% of the population), French (23%) and Italian (8%). The fourth, Romansh (0.5%) is only an official language in its home canton of Graubünden. To further complicate things, the German used in Switzerland is split between the written version, High German (which is also the official language of state), and the various spoken dialects that are collectively known as Swiss German. Government data show that 42% of the population regularly speaks more than one language, while 23% have a mother tongue that is not a national language: English and Portuguese are the most common foreign languages.

Religion: less obvious is the religious divide. The split between Catholics and Protestants thankfully no longer precipitates armed conflict, and freedom of religion is written into the constitution. Today, 37% of the population is Catholic, 25% Protestant, with another 24% officially having no religion. The main difference you may notice is that Catholic cantons, such as Ticino or Schwyz, generally have more public holidays than Protestant ones like Bern or Vaud. For example, ten Catholic cantons recognise the Feast of the Assumption on 15 August as a holiday but no Protestant ones do.

DID YOU KNOW?

Muslims make up 5.1% of the population in Switzerland, a slightly higher percentage than in the UK.

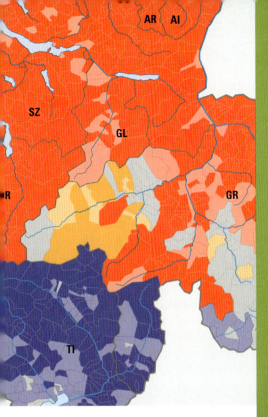

AR AI

SZ

GL

R

GR

TI

THE DITCH

The imaginary line dividing the German- and French-speaking areas is known colloquially as the *Röstigraben*, or fried-potato ditch (reflecting the fact that German-speakers typically eat lots of Rösti). This linguistic division runs through three bilingual cantons – Bern, Fribourg and Valais – but also is often used to describe the political split between the more liberal, pro-European French speakers and the rest of the country.

GRÜEZI

German and French may be the two main official languages but that doesn't mean the Swiss versions of those languages are the same as in the mother country. Both have notable 'helveticisms' that exist only in Switzerland. Here are seven to look out for:

German	Swiss-German	French	Swiss-French
Hallo (hello)	Grüezi	Salut (hello/goodbye)	Adieu
Frühstück (breakfast)	Z'morge	petit-déjeuner (breakfast)	déjeuner
Speiseeis/Eis (ice cream)	Glacé	déjeuner (lunch)	dîner
Personalausweis (ID card)	Identitätskarte	dîner (dinner)	souper
Strassenbahn (street car)	Tram	quatre-vingts (eighty)	huitante
Bürgersteig (sidewalk/pavement)	Trottoir	quatre-vingts-dix (ninety)	nonante
Tschüss (goodbye)	Adé	je t'en/vous en prie (you're welcome)	service

FEDERAL POLITICS

Modern Switzerland was created with the Federal Constitution of 1848, which replaced the old confederation with a new federation – although it kept the country's old name (Swiss Confederation) and the existing cantons. With federation came a new parliament and government in Bern, making it the de facto Swiss capital, although officially Switzerland has no capital city, with Bern simply being called the Federal City.

Federal parliament consists of two equal houses elected every four years by a popular vote. The two houses together then elect the federal government and the supreme court (although the latter is largely unpolitical).

National Council: 200 seats representing the people, with seats allocated by population. The smallest cantons, such as Uri, have one seat each while the largest, Zurich, has 35. Most members are elected by proportional representation resulting in multiple parties (currently eleven).

Council of States: 46 seats representing the cantons, with each canton having two seats regardless of size, except for the six half-cantons (see box).

It is normal for no single party to have control of either house, let alone both, so that there is no system of government and opposition. Legislation must be passed by both houses, which requires a consensus among a majority of the elected members.

Under the constitution, the federal state is responsible for national affairs, such as defence or the railways, but anything that is not specifically a federal matter is the responsibility of the cantons. Most cantons have a political structure similar to the federal one, with elected parliaments and multi-member executives.

VOTES FOR WOMEN

Swiss women won the right to vote at federal level in 1971, after (male) voters finally said yes in a referendum. At cantonal level, women could vote since 1959 in Vaud and Neuchâtel, with other cantons soon following suit until the last– Appenzell Innerrhoden – was forced to comply by a court ruling in 1990.

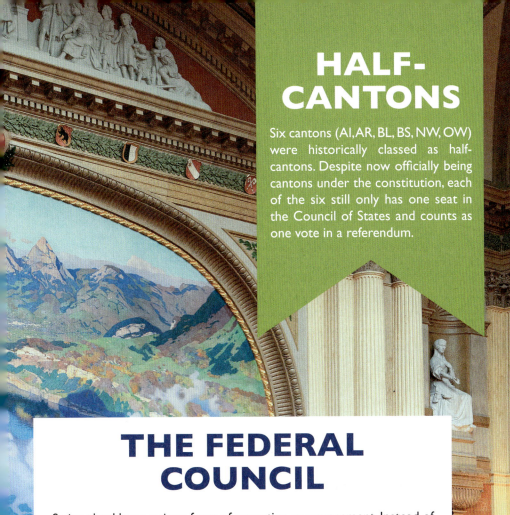

HALF-CANTONS

Six cantons (AI, AR, BL, BS, NW, OW) were historically classed as half-cantons. Despite now officially being cantons under the constitution, each of the six still only has one seat in the Council of States and counts as one vote in a referendum.

THE FEDERAL COUNCIL

Switzerland has a unique form of executive, or government. Instead of one person in charge, there are seven, known together as the Federal Council. It is elected every four years by parliament, with most members serving until they resign, retire or die. It's very rare for sitting Federal Councillors not to be re-elected; in fact, it has happened only four times in history.

To be elected, a candidate must merely be a Swiss citizen, though typically they already sit in federal parliament. There are no fixed quotas but instead an unofficial 'magic formula' is used to ensure that the Council represents not only the four largest parties in parliament but also the main regions and languages of the country. Plus, since the 1984 election of Elisabeth Kopp, the first female Councillor, the gender balance has also been a factor.

Each of the seven heads a federal department, such as Foreign Affairs, but no one has more power than any of the others. Every December parliament elects one of them to be president for a year, although he or she has no extra authority but is there simply to make speeches and shake hands.

DIRECT DEMOCRACY

Let the people decide. That fundamental principle of democracy is taken to its logical conclusion in Switzerland, where the people can decide on anything and everything. Under the Swiss system of <u>direct democracy</u>, referendums give voters the final say on legislation at every level (municipal, cantonal and national). Or citizens can trigger a vote on any issue by collecting signatures. The result is that the Swiss vote three or four times a year on a variety of topics, from opening hours and animal rights to pensions and immigration.

Amazingly, it's a system that works, partly because most Swiss voters take their responsibility seriously but also because not everything goes to a vote. About 80% of legislation is passed without the public being directly involved, but the potential for a referendum is always there, acting as a counterweight to the politicians.

The main drawback is that direct democracy is slow. It takes time to collect signatures, campaign, vote, legislate and then maybe vote again. That's one reason why women couldn't vote until 1971 and Switzerland didn't join the UN until 2002. On the plus side, contentious issues, such as abortion or gay rights, are usually decided by the people rather than parliament or the courts, and so can be less polarising than elsewhere. That doesn't mean one vote settles the issue – it can sometimes take two or three – but once a consensus is found, the topic becomes less of an issue.

Two cantons – Appenzell Innerrhoden and Glarus – still hold a *Lands-gemeinde*, or annual open-air assembly, where voters decide in person on the issues at hand.

VOTING RIGHTS

To be able to vote, you must be Swiss and over 18. Swiss nationals living abroad retain these rights, whereas foreigners living here cannot vote in federal elections or referendums. Note that the allocation of seats in federal parliament is based on the population in each canton – including any resident foreigners.

Two cantons – Jura and Neuchâtel – allow foreigners to vote at the cantonal level as long as they've been resident for long enough. At municipal level, foreigners living in five cantons (FR, GE, JU, NE, VD) have the right to vote, if they meet the relevant criteria, eg having a C permit. In three other cantons (AR, BS, GR), municipalities can extend voting rights to foreigners if they wish, though few have done so.

A PEOPLE'S VOTE

Given the central role the referendum plays in the Swiss political system, it's perhaps no surprise to learn that there is more than one type. Here's a quick guide to the three ways Swiss direct democracy works in practice at federal level.

Mandatory referendum: a compulsory vote is required for any amendment to the constitution or for accession to a supranational organisation (eg the EU). It needs a double majority to pass: that of the popular vote and also of the cantons.

Optional referendum: once parliament has passed any legislation, voters have 100 days to collect 50,000 signatures and force a referendum. It only needs a simple majority of the popular vote to either accept or reject the legislation in question.

Popular initiative: most frequent is when citizens demand a change to the constitution. To do that they must collect 100,000 signatures within 18 months and then win the subsequent vote with a double majority. Only about 10% of initiatives are passed. Those that do win normally need legislation to enact the changes.

DID YOU KNOW?

Voting is not compulsory and turnout is usually around 50%; the highest ever was 78.7% in the 1992 vote on joining the European Economic Area – and the answer was no.

MIGRATION

Historically Switzerland was a land that people left, a classic emigration country. Most went to seek a better life, keen to escape the rural poverty of 19th century Switzerland and find their fortune in places like the USA, Canada, Argentina or Australia. Some were even paid to leave so that the authorities here no longer had to look after them. This Swiss diaspora became known as the Fifth Switzerland, and today the Swiss abroad account for almost 10% of all Swiss citizens.

That all changed after the Second World War. Switzerland needed workers and Europeans needed jobs, so the country became an attractive proposition for migrants. Over the past few decades more people have moved to Switzerland than have left, so that there are now over two million foreigners living here. These non-Swiss make up 25% of the population. Although Switzerland is not a member of the European Union, bilateral treaties mean that EU citizens can live here, so that two-thirds of the resident foreigners are from the EU, principally Italy, Germany and Portugal. But many others came as refugees – the collapse of Yugoslavia in the 1990s precipitated an influx of Serbians, Kosovans and Macedonians who still live here today. Not forgetting the Sri Lankans, Eritreans, Kurds and more recently Syrians.

Switzerland still needs its foreign workers, as many do the jobs that the Swiss can't, or won't, do. Whether as doctors and teachers or waiters and farmhands, foreigners are an essential part of the Swiss economy. In sectors such as hospitality and construction, foreign workers constitute over a third of the workforce. And while some are seasonal or cross-border workers, 47% of all foreigners in Switzerland are permanent residents with a C permit. They are here to stay.

SECONDOS

Of the two million or so foreigners who live in Switzerland, about a fifth were actually born here. They are not automatically Swiss if neither of their parents is, so they grow up here as foreigners and have to apply for naturalisation. These second (and third) generation immigrants are known as Secondos and are usually the most integrated of all foreigners. In 2017 Ignazio Cassis became the first Secondo to be elected to the Federal Council – of course, he had become a Swiss citizen first.

WHO LIVES HERE

There are over two million foreign residents in Switzerland, representing almost every nationality possible. Below is the breakdown of the ten most common. The UK comes in at number 11 with over 41,000 nationals, or around half of all the resident native English speakers.

TOTAL: 2,081,169

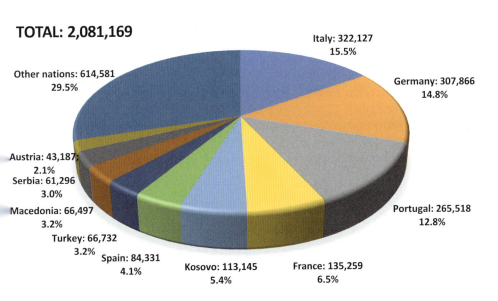

Other nations: 614,581
29.5%

Italy: 322,127
15.5%

Germany: 307,866
14.8%

Portugal: 265,518
12.8%

Austria: 43,187
2.1%

Serbia: 61,296
3.0%

Macedonia: 66,497
3.2%

Turkey: 66,732
3.2%

Spain: 84,331
4.1%

Kosovo: 113,145
5.4%

France: 135,259
6.5%

Source: State Secretariat for Migration

FAMOUS NAMES

For many foreigners, trying to name a famous Swiss person is quite hard, partly because the Swiss are modest by nature and don't really go in for hero worship. You won't see many statues to the great and good here but that doesn't mean Switzerland hasn't had its share of notable names. These are some of the more important figures from Switzerland's past, with the lack of women's names largely reflecting Swiss society until recently:

History: no monarchs or presidents but normal people and their achievements.
- **Guillaume Dufour:** victorious general who also mapped the country in detail.
- **Henri Dunant:** founded the Red Cross and won the first Nobel peace prize.
- **Alfred Escher:** Credit Suisse founder who started the Gotthard railway.
- **Henri Guisan:** Second World War general who resisted the threat of invasion.
- **Ulrich Zwingli:** Zurich pastor who brought the Reformation to the Swiss.

Arts: as the birthplace of Dada, Switzerland has made its mark in the world of arts.
- **Max Frisch:** writer whose book *Homo Faber* found a global audience.
- **Alberto Giacometti:** sculptor famous for his very tall, very thin figures.
- **H. R. Giger:** creator of the creatures in *Alien*, which won him an Oscar.
- **Paul Klee:** artist from Bern who became Swiss a few days after his death.
- **Johanna Spyri:** author of possibly the most celebrated Swiss book, *Heidi*.

Science: per capita the Swiss have won the most Nobel science prizes in the world.
- **Albert Einstein:** born German, died American but was Swiss for his $E=MC^2$.
- **Leonhard Euler:** 18th-century Basel man who transformed mathematics.
- **Albert Hoffmann:** discovered LSD while researching a cure for migraines.
- **Carl Jung:** renowned psychiatrist who founded analytical psychology.
- **Hermann Rorschach:** Zurich psychiatrist who created the inkblot test.

DID YOU KNOW?

Both Roger Federer and James Bond have one Swiss and one foreign parent, Whereas Roger's mother is South African, the (fictional) James has a Swiss mother and British father.

FOREIGN GUESTS

Switzerland has long been a favourite for famous foreigners, many of whom came for inspiration. Writers from Byron and Dickens to Mann and Tolkien were joined by likes of Wagner, Tchaikovsky and Turner in finding their Swiss muse. More recent guests have been seeking to escape the paparazzi or the taxman. But in decades past Switzerland was often a safe haven from persecution, revolution and war. A few of these exiles are rather well-known.

Jean Calvin: born in France, the reformer turned Geneva into the Protestant Rome.
Charlie Chaplin: escaped the McCarthy-era witch-hunts to find peace in Vevey.
James Joyce: found refuge from the First World War in Zurich, where he is buried.
Vladimir Lenin: revolutionary resident of Geneva, Bern and Zurich until 1917.
Benito Mussolini: avoided Italian military service by living here 1904–6.
Henri Nestlé: German pharmacist whose liberal views were unwelcome at home.

A STAR ABROAD

Sometimes it's the Swiss who leave their own country to find fame, fortune or simply a better life. Some of these well-known names might surprise you with their Swiss roots.

Ursula Andress: the first ever Bond girl was born in Canton Bern.
Louis Chevrolet: this car man swapped La-Chaux-de-Fonds for Detroit.
César Ritz: king of hoteliers left Valais for the lights of Paris and London.
Le Corbusier: star architect originally from La-Chaux-de-Fonds.
Jean-Jacques Rousseau: philosopher from Geneva buried in Paris.

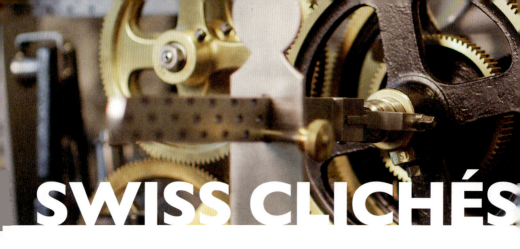

SWISS CLICHÉS

Every country has its stereotypical clichés and Switzerland seems to have more than its fair share. Ask almost anyone what Switzerland means to them, and most likely you'll hear one (or all) of these in reply: cheese, chocolate, cuckoo clocks, mountains, trains, watches. Let's have a look at each of those clichés.

Cheese: the Swiss don't eat as much as the world-champion Danes (22kg per head annually compared to 28kg) but they have made one sort synonymous with their country – cheese with holes. However, hardly any of the 450 different Swiss cheeses are holey, the main one being the classic Emmentaler. 'Swiss cheese' as a generic term for cheese with holes is something you'll never hear in Switzerland.

Chocolate: Switzerland is the chocolate capital of the world, thanks to the likes of Daniel Peter, who invented milk chocolate in Vevey in 1875, and Messrs Lindt, Tobler, Suchard and Cailler, who all became global chocolate brands.

Cuckoo clocks: on sale in souvenir shops but they're not originally Swiss. Cuckoo clocks came from the Black Forest, over the border in Germany, but most tourists don't seem to mind. Some are handmade in Switzerland these days.

Mountains: with 48 named peaks over 4000m, Switzerland is the Roof of Europe. Some summits stand out from the crowd, with the Matterhorn and the Eiger ranking as the two most famous, though neither is the tallest. That's Dufourspitze at 4634 metres.

Trains: the Swiss were late to embrace trains but have made up for it ever since. They now have the world's longest train tunnel (the Gotthard Base at 57.1km), the steepest rack railway (Pilatus with a maximum 48% gradient) and the steepest funicular (Stoosbahn with 110% gradient).

A CLOCKWORK COUNTRY

Swiss watches are world leaders, not in terms of quantity, where it's hard to beat China, but in terms of quality. And it's largely thanks to Calvin, the puritanical Protestant who banned jewellery in 16th-century Geneva, forcing craftsmen to turn to something else. Their new jewels were watches, permitted because they were functional. A Swiss stereotype was born. Today the Swiss watch industry is still going strong, having been resurrected by the creation of the Swatch in 1983.

- **Exports:** 23.7 million watches, worth 21 billion francs, with Hong Kong, the USA, China, Japan and the UK the main markets.
- **Price:** average price of an exported Swiss watch = $859; average price of an exported Chinese watch = $4.
- **Brands:** 230 brands listed by the Federation of the Swiss Watch Industry.
- **Bestsellers:** brands with a turnover of more than one billion francs a year – Rolex, Omega, Cartier, Longines, Patek Phillipe, Tissot.
- **Employees:** over 57,800 people directly employed in 500 companies mainly in cantons Neuchâtel, Bern, Geneva, Solothurn, Jura and Vaud.
- **Income:** the watch industry accounts for around 1.5% of Swiss GDP.

NEUTRALITY

Switzerland is famous for not taking sides. It has spent the last two centuries or so being officially neutral and is home to the UN and the Red Cross. But the Swiss were once as bellicose as anyone. Even when they abandoned that in the 16th century, they still hired out men as mercenaries. And today, the neutral Swiss have an army, with men having to do military service, and an arms trade, which exports war materiel to over 70 countries.

MEET YOUR EXPERTS

Christina Fryer arrived in Switzerland in 2007, originally for two years, but 13 years later she's still here. Since 2011 she has been running NewInZurich.com, the online magazine that informs expats and locals alike about events, exhibitions, festivals, travel and more.

Clive Greaves has been living in Switzerland since 1981, when he started teaching at a Zurich international school. With a Swiss wife from Ticino, he has a unique insight into the ways of the Swiss and often travels around the country writing articles for NewInZurich.com.

DAILY LIFE

From the moment you arrive in Switzerland and move into your new apartment only to find the light bulbs are missing, you get an inkling that daily life in Switzerland might be just a little bit different. From shopping and recycling to laundry and pets, this chapter covers the key aspects of everyday life.

There are certainly many rules to abide by but the upside is that everything in Switzerland runs so smoothly. From the clean, tidy streets to the supremely interconnected transport system, Switzerland really does merit the high scores it receives on a regular basis from worldwide quality-of-life surveys. Swiss friends tell us that you don't need policemen in Switzerland because everybody is one. It's nothing to be afraid of – it just shows how much everyone cares. But do remember, there will always be exceptions that prove the rule.

Settling in to a Swiss routine can take a while. Opening hours seem antiquated, it feels as if there are rules governing everything and your new neighbours might keep their distance at first. But get used to all that, and you'll find that life in Switzerland is a bed of roses with only a few annoying thorns.

THE LOWDOWN

- What your municipality can do for you
- Household tips on rubbish, recycling, laundry and neighbours
- Practical advice on driving licences, parking and road rules

THE MUNICIPALITY

At the centre of the community in every town and village in Switzerland is the municipality. Crucially, it is where you first register when you arrive but it's also where you pay the bulk of your income tax (though you pay cantonal and federal income tax too). They literally know (almost) everything about you. It's also where you de-register should you move to a different town or leave the country.

As the glue that holds the community together, the municipality holds the keys to many aspects of daily life. Not only is it responsible for the everyday workings of the community, but also schools, rubbish, recycling, leisure facilities, library, parks and general amenities all come under its jurisdiction. It usually organises a number of social events and festivals throughout the year as well as childen's activities, clubs, adult education and cultural programmes. In short, this is the most important hub of Swiss daily life.

The municipality is there to help and provide assistance, so it's a good idea to get to know the people who work there. They can point you in the right direction if you need information and they're also the ones responsible for issuing residence permits. If you have any questions about your locality, this is the place to go. You can search online for information too, though note that most local websites are not in English.

Switzerland's municipalities are responsible for town planning as well as for running local schools, the fire service, and social services. Larger municipalities have elected parliaments and regular referendums but smaller ones (which make up 80% of the total) are run by communal assemblies of voters. Foreign residents have voting rights at a municipal level in only eight cantons, mostly in the French-speaking part.

CHURCH TAX

When you first register, in most cantons you will be asked if you are Catholic or Protestant. If you are liable to pay a church tax, which varies but is typically around 2% of your salary. In certain cantons, businesses are also liable. If you want to stop paying this tax, you have to resign officially from your church, informing it in writing.

THE END OF THE WORLD?

Every year on the first Wednesday of February your peace and quiet will be disturbed by an earsplitting noise. No, it's not the end of the world – simply the the national sirens being tested. Switzerland's network of around 7,200 sirens stands ready to be used as a public warning system in the event of a national emergency, such as major flood or an imminent breakdown of a nuclear power plant. The general alarm is tested from 1.30pm to 2pm. In applicable areas, for example, where people live close to dams etc, a water test follows at 2.15pm.

The sirens are sounded once every five minutes with a regularly ascending and descending tone, each time for one minute. If you hear sirens and it's not the first Wednesday in February, you should listen to the radio, follow the instructions from the authorities and inform your neighbours. More information: ch.ch/en/alarm-signals

OPENING HOURS

If you're not from mainland Europe, one of the first things you notice when living in Switzerland is that shops still have opening hours from a few decades ago. Late-night shopping is once a week, if that, and Sunday shopping does not really exist, although as with every good rule, there are a few exceptions (see below).

Even if you are not religious, Sunday in Switzerland is special. It's part of the Swiss work-life balance. This is the one day of the week when you see families and friends out together, hiking in the mountains, skiing or swimming, visiting exhibitions, or simply going out for a meal. Just remember not to mow the lawn, use loud machinery, do any DIY or visit the bottle bank on Sundays – they are all too noisy.

Sunday shopping: most city centres and out-of-town malls are closed but there are some places where you can indulge in retail therapy on a Sunday.
- The main airports are open 365 days a year and have many shops landside that are open to everyone and not just to passengers.
- Most large railway stations have a shopping centre with a supermarket and a host of other shops, often even a hairdresser.
- Petrol stations and motorway service stations have small convenience stores with longer opening hours than usual.
- During Advent there are designated Shopping Sundays (which vary according to region) when shops are open prior to Christmas.

General hours: shop opening hours vary depending on the business and location. However, over the past 10 years shops have gradually been opening for longer and fewer close over lunch, except in small villages or residential suburbs. But it's still the case that 24-hour shopping is almost unheard of (except in large train stations) and even in big cities like Zurich, shops close at 8pm Monday to Saturday.

TOP TIP

Avoid calling businesses – including government offices – over lunchtime as they are often closed for an hour or more.

SHOPPING TIPS

Even once you're used to the idiosyncratic opening hours, there are still a few things worth bearing in mind when shopping in Switzerland.

- Always have a few coins for parking (even at the supermarket), and keep a one-franc coin for the supermarket trolley.
- Take your own shopping bags with you to avoid excessive use of plastic bags (which are usually not free).
- The two main Swiss supermarkets, Migros and Coop, both have loyalty cards (Cumulus and Supercard respectively), so it makes sense to sign up and collect points for discounts.
- Additional family loyalty cards – Famigros and Coop Family – give families with children even more discounts and offers.
- Online food shopping can be a convenient option with Coop@home or Migros' Le Shop service.
- In the high street, cash is king. Although plastic (or contactless cards and payment apps) have become more popular, it's still advisable to have cash on you, especially in the countryside.
- Charity shops are rarely found on the high street, though the Salvation Army has 20 retail outlets across the country.
- Don't convert prices back into those from your home country! Switzerland is expensive but hopefully your salary is higher than back home.

PUBLIC HOLIDAYS

Official public holidays vary depending on the canton and even municipality, but there are four days a year when the whole country is off: New Year's Day, Ascension Day, Swiss National Day (1 August) and Christmas Day. Other religious holidays are widely observed, eg Good Friday is a public holiday in 24 cantons and St Stephen's Day (Boxing Day) in 21. In addition to national holidays, there are also cantonal and local ones, so that if you live in Ticino you get 15 holidays a year but in Vaud it's only nine. Check feiertagskalender.ch or publicholidays.ch for the holidays in your area.

If any public holiday falls on the weekend (or when you are on holiday from work) you are not entitled to that day off in lieu.

RUBBISH AND RECYCLING

Almost a religion in Switzerland, getting rid of your rubbish or unwanted stuff is easy when you know how – but you have to be aware of the various regulations and disposal points to get it right. Every municipality sends out an annual Rubbish Disposal Calendar which explains when you can dispose of various items, and includes dates for special collections of more unusual things like paint, oil and Christmas trees.

Household waste: for your everyday rubbish you need to buy either special municipal rubbish bags or normal black bags plus the official rubbish stickers; which version you have to buy depends on your local municipality. Both the official bags and stickers can be bought from supermarkets or the post office – just be sure to buy them only in your municipality as those from another town may not be valid.

Official bags usually come in four different sizes, with the 35-litre one the norm for most kitchen rubbish bins. The cost is based on the capacity, so that, for example, in Bern a 35-litre official municipal bag costs 1.40Fr. You can usually separate raw food waste for collection, and supermarkets sell small food bins for this purpose. However, check the situation with your neighbours or your municipality.

Textiles: Texaid and other charities accept used clothes and shoes as long as they are fit to wear. Texaid bins are located widely across Switzerland and the company is the leading textile recycler. In 2017 they collected around 140 million items of clothing in Switzerland, generating approximately 7.8 million francs for charitable purposes

TOP TIP

Look for these symbols on everyday household items like yoghurt pots or olive oil bottles:

 This must go in the household rubbish.

 This can be recycled.

RECYCLING

In Switzerland residents sort their own recycling and dispose of it according to type. Nearly all supermarkets accept old batteries, lightbulbs and plastic bottles (either PET or detergent/shampoo containers). Most other plastic packaging cannot yet be recycled in Switzerland. Paper and card are typically collected for free from the doorstep, as long as you make a neatly-folded bundle tied up with string.

In the streets you find larger recycling containers which usually take glass, tins and sometimes paper. Remember these can't be used on Sundays or evenings as it's too noisy!

Alternatively, go to a recycling centre which normally has facilities for almost everything including aluminium coffee capsules, oil, paint, wood, plastic bottles, metal, etc. Check your local recycling centre as rules vary, and note that you may be charged for the disposal of metal or wood. You can also dispose of large items such as furniture and mattresses, again for a fee based on weight – or you can donate them to charities such as the Salvation Army.

You can take electrical items to your local recycling centre or to any shop selling electrical appliances, as the price of purchasing electrical goods always includes a disposal tax.

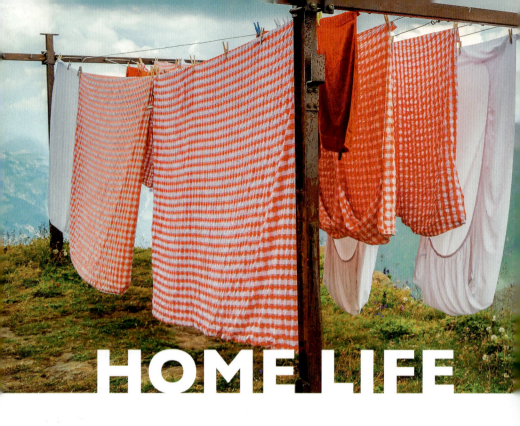

HOME LIFE

In Switzerland many people live cheek-by-jowl in apartment buildings; in fact, apartment living is more common than house ownership, though that situation is changing. Therefore, it is important everyone respects the other's private sphere, and to encourage this there are house rules that exist to foster peaceful and comfortable living.

Relationships with your neighbours are very important and these can be established early on in your stay. Be proactive – have a welcome Apéro when you move in to introduce yourself and your family. Use this opportunity to ask about the local rules. Be sure to make early contact with the building's caretaker or janitor and say hello.

Should you decide to have a cleaner, he or she will need to be registered, and paperwork will have to be filled out. This is one of the areas where the local municipality will be able to help you out. Alternatively, you can use a cleaning agency that does all the paperwork for you.

TOP TIP

There may be a building residents' committee that meets on regular occasions to discuss developments and problems. Find out who is on this committee and which meetings you are expected to attend.

HOUSE RULES

Most buildings also have unwritten rules.

- The Swiss usually take off their outdoor shoes inside the house – so don't be offended if you're asked to leave your shoes on the mat.
- There may be a quiet hour at lunchtime when, in theory, people might be napping so noise should be kept to a minimum.
- After 10pm is usually the quiet time for the night, so peace should reign from then on.
- Always let neighbours know (or invite them!) if you're having a party that's likely to be noisy or go on late.
- In some old apartment buildings you may be prohibited from flushing the toilet after 10pm.

LAUNDRY

If you live in an apartment, chances are your washing machine and tumble dryer won't be in your flat but in a designated laundry room shared by all the other building occupants. It's usually in the basement. Some buildings have no laundry rules but often you're allocated a day or a specific time when you can use the room. This can take some getting used to. However, it is important not to stray from this without the prior permission of others as this can really damage neighbourly relations!

Laundry rooms also have their own sets of rules, often written on a notice. This means not just leaving the room clean and tidy after use, but cleaning out the lint from the dryers and various other tasks. It might also be the case that the laundry room is closed on Sunday, so as not to disturb the peace.

You might have to pay per load of laundry, using a charge card or even coins, or the machines could be free, which in fact means included in your share of the communal utility bills.

If in doubt, ask the caretaker or neighbours what is expected.

PETS

The most common pets in Switzerland are cats and dogs. There are no special requirements for cats but it is a good idea to microchip them. Dogs however need to be registered with your municipality and you have to pay an annual dog tax (not applicable for guide and rescue dogs). See ch.ch/en/dog-tax for more details.

It is no longer compulsory for new owners to take a dog training course but it is highly recommended, so contact your municipality for details. Also ask about any regulations in relation to dangerous or banned dog breeds. All dogs should be microchipped by the age of three months and those coming from outside Switzerland must be taken to the vet within 10 days of entering the country.

If you take your dog or cat over the border you will need the animal's pet passport showing that all its vaccinations are up to date. Most importantly your pet needs to have had the rabies vaccination, so that you can bring it back into Switzerland, as the country is rabies – free. Please consult your vet for information as regulations vary depending on which country your pet is visiting.

All across Switzerland you'll find green Robidog bins for dog dirt (with plastic bags supplied).

DID YOU KNOW?

Social animals, such as rabbits, guinea pigs, hamsters and parakeets, can only be bought in pairs as they are deemed to suffer on their own. The Federal Veterinary Office (blv.admin.ch) or your local vet will have more details.

TECHNOLOGY

Depending on where you live there are normally four main providers for TV and internet – Swisscom, Sunrise, Salt & UPC – as well as some local providers. They all offer a number of packages at different prices with a variety of options to purchase alone or bundled with landlines and/or mobile phones.

For mobile phones there are the same four providers plus various reseller options, such as Migros M-Budget (via Swisscom) or Yallo (via Sunrise) and many others. Before committing to any provider speak to your immediate neighbours to find the most reliable network for your area, as mobile phone reception can vary widely outside the main cities.

In order to take out an annual contract you will need your permit. Study all the options carefully as it is a very competitive market and there are new offers appearing weekly! If you travel widely, consider plans which include a certain amount of roaming in the countries you visit often.

Check out the best deals for mobile handsets on toppreise.ch and compare the best mobile phone subscriptions on comparis.ch. There are a huge number of options and the market is particulary competitive for the 18–26-year-old age group.

TV LICENCE

The now-defunct Billag radio and TV licence has been replaced by Serafe, which costs 365Fr a year. Even if you don't have a TV, you will need it to cover the radio in your car or on your smartphone. If you are unable to access TV or radio at all you can apply to Serafe for a dispensation (serafe.ch).

BUYING A CAR

When buying a car the choice is whether to buy direct from a car dealer or privately. Using a dealer is easiest as they take care of the paperwork and can organise your number plates. More vigilance (and paperwork) is required when buying privately, so be sure of what you're buying and that you trust the seller. Autoscout.ch is probably the largest marketplace for private sellers but you will find local ones too.

Car number plates are personal to you and your address (not the car). You transfer your plates from car to car if you change vehicles so long as you live in the same canton. Move cantons, and you'll need to re-register at your new road traffic department, and get a new number plate.

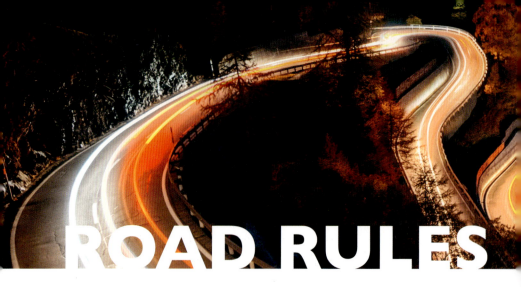

ROAD RULES

Apart from the obvious – drive on the right! – there are various other road rules specific to Switzerland.

- To drive on Swiss motorways, you need an annual vignette (40Fr); this must be stuck to the windscreen (not propped against it) and clearly visible.
- Always drive with dipped headlights during daylight hours. It's the law.
- You should have a red warning triangle in your car, plus a first aid kit and fire extinguisher.
- You need winter tyres from October to May (roughly), but in the mountains chains may be necessary in heavy snow if you don't have a 4×4 vehicle.
- The blood-alcohol limit is 0.5 milligrams per millilitre.
- Traffic coming from the right has priority, and trams have right of way.

PARKING

Beware of parking in the street where there are no marked spaces, as you are likely to be fined.

White zones: usually free but may be time-limited during the week. Sometimes designated specifically for visitors.

Blue zones: keep a blue parking disc in the car for short-term parking in blue zones. Paid parking is also permitted in most blue zones, or you can buy a residents' pass from your municipality.

Metered parking: often coins only, though car parks normally accept credit cards. In non-numbered spaces, put the ticket in the windscreen but in numbered spaces, keep the receipt from the machine. Note that some spaces can be quite tight!

DRIVING LICENCES

Within 12 months of arriving, you must apply to exchange your national <u>driving licence</u> for a Swiss one. Miss this deadline and you'll need to take the full written and practical Swiss driving test. To exchange your licence, you have to:

*   fill in the required forms at an optician and undergo a simple eye test.
*   send the forms to the road traffic department, with a colour photo and your current driving licence; you will need to pay a fee.
*   wait a week or two for your Swiss driving licence.

For those from EU countries, your original licence is sent back to your own country. For certain other countries, you'll receive your old licence back with a sticker stating that it's not valid in Switzerland.

Countries where no test is needed to exchange a licence within 12 months include:

*   all EU members, including the UK after Brexit
*   EFTA members (Iceland, Liechtenstein, Norway)
*   Andorra, Australia, Canada, Israel, Japan, Monaco, Morocco, New Zealand, San Marino, Singapore, South Korea, Taiwan, Tunisia, USA

If you hold a driving licence from any other country, you must undergo a driving assessment with an examiner. It's not the full driving test but lasts around an hour, so it's a good idea to hire a local instructor beforehand. You must complete the assessment by the time you have been in the country for 12 months.

Always carry your driving licence with you when driving, plus have your car registration documents in the car, in case you're stopped.

TOP TIP

Pedestrians usually have right of way on crossings; use designated crossings and wait until the red man turns green, – otherwise you could get a fine for jaywalking.

DISABILITIES

There are many Swiss associations, both professional and voluntary, offering help and support for people with disabilities. The first stop should be your municipality to find out what services are available locally.

For general advice and help, the best resource is Pro Infirmis (proinfirmis.ch), the umbrella organisation for the disabled in Switzerland. Despite the Disability Discrimination Act of 2004, recent surveys have shown that disabled people still face problems with access to employment and accommodation.

Public transport: the transport network is relatively sensitive to those with mobility issues. In cities, many tram stops have been adapted to help wheelchair users, while trams usually have folding ramps and newer buses can 'kneel' down. Outside larger towns, travel can be more of a challenge, though resorts such as Zermatt have online information for disabled guests, including which hotels have wheelchair access.

People with disabilities are entitled to buy the national annual travel pass (GA) with a 35% discount in either first or second class. SBB has a free helpline for disabled customers (0800 007 102), where you can ask about the most suitable options for you or request assistance getting on and off trains.

Mobility International Switzerland (mis-ch.ch) specialises in collecting travel information for people with handicaps around the world. For example, it details barrier-free accommodation, restaurants and excursions in Switzerland.

Taxis: for those who are wheelchair-bound, Tixi Taxi (tixi.ch) offers an invaluable service with vehicles specially adapted to carry wheelchairs. They can be booked individually, and fares roughly match public transport include a door-to-door service.

Home help: the Spitex organisation (spitex.ch) provides all sorts of practical help at home for people who are unable to look after themselves, such as help with cleaning and bathing.

DISABILITY BENEFIT

ONLINE RESOURCES

There is a lot of information available online, though not always in English:

- general disabled organisation: inclusion-handicap.ch
- for disabled friendly holidays: denkanmich.ch
- for people with hearing disabilities: sgb-fss.ch
- for people with eyesight disabilities: blind.ch
- disabled sport information: plusport.ch
- Federal Social Insurance Office: bsv.admin.ch

The main form of state benefit is the Disability Insurance, which covers adults living and/or working in Switzerland. Under federal law a disability is defined as 'a full or partial earning incapacity that is likely to be permanent or persist in the longer-term' (Federal Social Insurance Office), regardless of whether its cause is medical, accidental or congenital.

The aim of the insurance scheme is to achieve the integration of disabled people into the workplace through training, therapy and job schemes. If this rehabilitation is not possible, and the disability results in an income loss of at least 40% for more than one year, then you can apply for various benefits:

- **iInvalidity pension:** applicable once your inability to work has lasted for more than a year. A sliding scale applies depending on the degree of disability, and there is a monthly maximum payment.
- **helplessness allowance:** for those who need regular help with daily tasks such as bathing, dressing and eating.
- **personal assistance allowance:** for those who have a helplessness allowance but live at home so need to hire someone for the necessary help.

Those on low incomes can get extra help. Once you reach the official retirement age, then the pension system takes over. Disability Insurance is a compulsory deduction of 1.4% from your monthly wages, with employer and employee paying half each; the self-employed must pay the full amount. The unemployed are covered by the minimum state benefit.

Each canton has its own insurance office, so address any queries to the one in your canton.

MEET YOUR EXPERT

Diccon Bewes is a British travel writer and author of five books on Switzerland, including the number one bestseller, *Swiss Watching*. He fell in love with Switzerland after arriving back in 2005, and his first Swiss job was working in Stauffacher bookshop in Bern for six years. After all these years, he has just about got used to the shops being shut on Sundays. You can follow him via his website dicconbewes.com, on Twitter (@dicconb) or on Facebook (facebook.com/SwissWatching).

SHOPPING

Shopping in Switzerland can sometimes feel like it is stuck in 1989: almost no shops open on Sundays, 24-hour shopping non-existent, credit cards not universally accepted and no Swiss Amazon. True, it might be a bit of a retail shock if you're used to shops open past midnight and free internet deliveries. But once you get over that, you'll rediscover the joy of more relaxed browsing and buying, and settle into the Swiss retail rhythm.

To help you navigate the Swiss high street, this chapter looks at the two main supermarket chains, Coop and Migros, with tips on using them as Swissly as possible. Plus we recommend our favourite markets around the country, be they every week or once a month or purely at Christmas. There's nothing quite like buying local seasonal produce or home-made jams and cheese.

It's certainly true that Switzerland is more expensive than its neighbours for almost everything – electronics are a notable exception – but some products are only slightly pricier, while for others you'll be paying significantly more. So we also look at hopping over the border to shop as well as buying online – in Switzerland and abroad – and highlight the rules and pitfalls.

THE LOWDOWN
- Discover the main supermarkets with tips on making the most of them
- Explore our favourite markets, including the magical ones at Christmas
- Navigate your way around Swiss online shopping and importing goods from abroad

SUPER FOODS

The two main supermarket chains, Coop and Migros, dominate the Swiss food market, accounting for almost 70% of all purchases (or if you include the cheaper chain Denner, majority-owned by Migros, then it's almost 80%). German discount chains Aldi and Lidl have made some inroads recently but together barely account for one in ten shoppers. Many Swiss define themselves as a Migros or Coop shopper, so don't be surprised if you're asked which one you prefer.

Coop or Migros: there isn't actually much difference between the two, with both offering local produce as well as imports. Coop tends to have more international brands on sale, while Migros doesn't sell any alcohol or tobacco (though its sister-shop Denner does).

Fruit & veg: you normally have to weigh these goods yourself, tap in a code number (displayed beside the produce) and then stick on the printed price label. Cheaper chains, like Aldi and Denner, use a simpler system of produce being weighed and priced at the till by the cashier.

Loyalty cards: both Migros and Coop have a loyalty card (Cumulus and Supercard respectively) so sign up to collect points for discounts or special offers. They can be used in shops from the supermarkets' own retail group, eg Melectronics with Migros and Interdiscount with Coop. There are also family schemes (Famigros and Coop Family) that offer additional discounts.

Online: food shopping online can be convenient but be wary of delivery fees. With Coop@home, delivery is free if the order is over 500Fr, otherwise there's a sliding scale based on the order value. With Migros' Le Shop, the lowest charge is 2.90Fr for orders over 200Fr. Both supermarkets offer free pick-up at specified locations.

TIPS

Even once you're used to the idiosyncratic opening hours, there are still a few things worth bearing in mind when shopping in Switzerland.

- Always have a few coins for parking (even at the supermarket), and keep a one- or two-franc coin for the supermarket trolley.
- Take your own shopping bags with you as neither plastic nor (larger) paper carrier bags are free.
- Both big supermarkets have their own brand products (Prix Garantie in Coop and M-Budget in Migros) which are cheaper than famous brands but usually just as good quality.
- Self-checkouts have become more common in recent years but not all of them accept cash (eg Migros has card-only payment).
- In the high street, cash is usually king. Although cards (or contactless and payment apps) have become more popular, it's still advisable to have cash on you, especially in the countryside.
- Shops are generally closed on Sundays and public holidays. For more on opening hours in general, see the Daily Life chapter.

MARKETS

The weekly market is part of town (and country) life all across Switzerland. What in other countries is called a farmers' market is usually a normal market here, with farmers and producers – both local and from further afield – coming into town to sell their wares. The concept of market traders buying from wholesalers and then selling from a stall is less common. More likely you'll find locally-grown fruit and vegetables (very often organic), home-made jams and cordials, bread, cheese and meat. Cut flowers and pot plants are often there too, along with some handicrafts.

While there are weekly markets in almost every town (usually on a Saturday), larger places have one twice a week and are well worth a visit. Some are twice-weekly only between Easter and October, and others will have a smaller market on weekdays, so always check. These are some of our favourites for their location and choice of stalls:

- **Bellinzona:** colourful market in the old town, Wednesday and Saturday
- **Bern:** right in front of federal parliament, Tuesday and Saturday
- **Carouge (near Geneva):** pretty Italianate town, Wednesday and Saturday
- **Lausanne:** hilly streets and cobbled squares, Wednesday and Saturday
- **Lucerne:** along the riverbank between the bridges, Tuesday and Saturday
- **Vevey:** one of the largest market squares in Europe, Tuesday and Saturday
- **Zurich (Bürkliplatz and Helvetiaplatz):** in the city centre, Tuesday and Friday

SECOND HAND

Flea markets are surprisingly popular and pop up in almost every town at some point during the year. Larger regular ones include Plainpalais in Geneva (twice weekly), Kanzlei in Zurich and Petersplatz in Basel (both every Saturday), and the market on the last Sunday of each month in Nyon.

However, charity shops are rarely found on the Swiss high street, unlike in many English-speaking countries. The Salvation Army does have 20 retail outlets nationwide, very often quite large places selling furniture as well as clothes and crockery. More common are second-hand shops run as businesses rather than charities, which sell the whole range from bric-a-brac to antiques.

ADVENT

Christmas shopping may not be as manic as elsewhere but it's atmospheric with the window displays, lights and sometimes snow. This is one time of year when shops can open on Sundays, though the number of Sundays and which ones in particular vary from town to town; some places allow shopping on two or three Sundays in Advent, others none at all, so check locally. Even if the shops are shut, the Christmas markets are open, with some running for the whole month and smaller ones for a few days in December. Most have stalls serving mulled wine to warm you up, while the gifts on sale cover everything from hand-carved wooden toys to woollen hats from near and (very) far away.

Christmas markets can be found all over the country, but these are the ones we like best. Dates vary each year but can be found online.

- **Basel:** one of the largest, with stalls spread over two central squares
- **Bern:** traditional stalls set in the heart of the old town
- **Einsiedeln:** great monastery setting and the world's largest crib
- **Montreux:** picture-perfect location along the shore of Lake Geneva
- **Murten:** only on for three days but one of the prettiest choices
- **Stein am Rhein:** fairy-tale town with a magical market full of lights
- **St Urbanne:** one weekend only but worth it for the medieval village
- **Zurich:** weather-proof market in the main hall of the railway station

RETAIL THERAPY

Most everyday products the Swiss use – from shampoo to computers to running shoes – are the same as everywhere else. So deciding where to shop mostly comes down to price and convenience. While Swiss prices are generally higher than in France and Germany (around 25% more for clothes, and 50% for cosmetics, though electronics are generally about 10% cheaper), local shops often win on convenience.

Remember to save your receipts: all goods purchased in Switzerland are guaranteed for two years against defects. If you still have proof of purchase, shops must either give you a replacement or a full refund, unless they can show it was your neglect that caused the breakage.

SHOP ABROAD?

Neighbouring countries might look tantalisingly cheap but with higher VAT, import limits and strict paperwork, your attempt to save a few francs can quickly backfire. Here's what you need to know.

Limits (per day, per Swiss resident): coming into Switzerland, you can bring 5 litres of beer or wine, 1 litre of spirits (above 18%), 1kg of meat, 1kg of butter, and 250 cigarettes. Everything else is duty-free with a limit of 300Fr per person. If the value exceeds 300Fr you must pay VAT on the entire sum.

Your 19% German VAT back: to get a refund (only for purchases of at least €50), you need export papers from the shop that are stamped by German customs as you export the goods from Germany. Only then can you return to the original shop (without the goods) for your refund. It sounds complicated but VAT can quickly add up and many German shops near the border know refunds are one of their USPs.

Your 20% French VAT back: it's much more difficult to get a French refund. First off, you can only ever reclaim 12% of your original purchase, and that purchase must be at least €175. Only some shops offer tax refunds.

Import by post: there's no 300Fr duty-free limit unless you cross the border with your goods. If you order something by post, you must pay VAT on any amount, though you may be exempt if the final VAT amount is less than 5Fr (gifts from abroad are exempt up to a value of 100Fr). However, if the package isn't correctly marked, the Swiss may charge a 13Fr inspection charge.

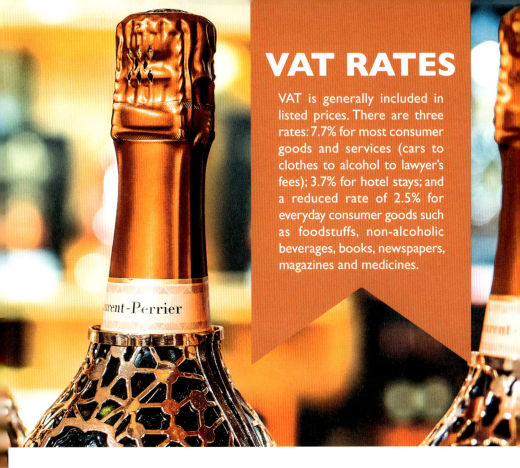

SHOP SWISS?

Many of your best online shopping options are in Switzerland, largely thanks to no border being involved. Here are our favourites:

- **Galaxus** and **digitec**: while the former sells household and sporting goods and the latter electronics, they are actually one company. Both offer free next day shipping (or same-day pick-up at the 10 digitec outlets).
- **Ricardo**: forget eBay – the Swiss prefer their homegrown version, where you can buy and sell everything from antique fondue caquelons to new cars. Most of the communication is in French or German.
- **Toppreise.ch**: technically not a shop, but its price comparison tool will point you in the cheapest direction.
- **Zalando**: this clothing retailer wasn't the first to offer free returns but it perfected the process. Simply repack anything you don't want back inside the box and return it at Zalando's cost.

Lastly, don't underestimate the potential of online outlets for international workers coming and going. Facebook groups for buying and selling (eg 'Basel buy and sell') or expat forums (eg englishforum.ch) have plenty of people desperate to unload furniture, cars, clothes – or everything they own.

MEET YOUR EXPERT

Isobel Leybold-Johnson grew up in Oxford, UK, and moved to Switzerland as a postgraduate student. She never really left, apart from a short stint to do her journalism diploma in the UK. Isobel is a senior journalist at SWI swissinfo.ch, the international service of the Swiss Broadcasting Corporation, where she covers the Swiss school system, higher education and apprenticeships. At home, she is the mother of twin boys who are going through the Swiss local education system, so she has direct experience of the highs and lows of being a parent of Swiss school pupils.

FAMILY

Switzerland is an excellent place to raise children. It's safe and the standard of education and healthcare is very high. It's also quite traditional in some respects, which is more difficult for working parents, especially mothers.

Uppermost on your mind when you have a family is likely to be finding the right school and settling in. There are many excellent international schools in Switzerland, but it also has very good local schools, with pupils regularly doing well in international surveys, especially in maths. Some aspects of the local system take some getting used to, such as the school hours, but it is not all bad. The Swiss are very big on giving their kids independence and children generally thrive on this.

After compulsory school finishes, around two thirds of young people opt for an apprenticeship under Switzerland's much-admired dual – track system, which combines classroom theory with on-the-job training. Pupils at the country's baccalaureate schools, in contrast, set their sights on Switzerland's excellent universities, which have lower fees than in many other countries.

Overall, while there may occasionally be challenges along the way, children growing up in Switzerland are given a good start in leading healthy and successful lives.

THE LOWDOWN
- Choosing a school or childcare for your children
- Navigating the local school system
- Facing the financial and bureaucratic challenges of having a baby and raising children in Switzerland

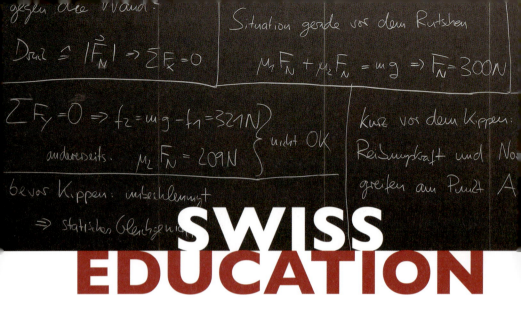

SWISS EDUCATION

In Switzerland, every child must go to school. Most pupils go to local schools. Cantons are in charge of educational matters in Switzerland. This explains why there are some educational variations between the cantons, although an attempt has been made to harmonise the different systems. Only around five percent of children attend private schools, and home schooling is very rare. A key difference from international norms is the emphasis given to apprenticeships after leaving school – approximately two thirds of pupils go down this route.

THE BASICS

In Switzerland, compulsory education generally lasts 11 years. This includes primary level (eight years including two years of kindergarten or first learning cycle) and lower secondary level (three years). Children usually start kindergarten at age four and move on to school at age six, although there are a few cantonal variations in the German- and Italian speaking parts regarding how long a child should or can attend kindergarten – so do check local regulations.

TOP TIP

Many universities and universities of applied sciences offer programmes that are taught entirely in English. For more information in English on studying in Switzerland, including entry requirements, head to studyinswitzerland.plus.

The language of instruction is the local one, and most children have begun learning another national language as well as English by the time they finish primary school.

At around the age of 12, pupils are streamed in all or some subjects according to aptitude. At this time, parents have to help their children begin to decide what they want to do once they leave school at age 15–16. Most opt for an apprenticeship, which is highly respected in Switzerland (see information overleaf for more details). Most of those aiming for university go to baccalaureate schools, which offer a general education with a final exam, but have strict entry criteria. Note: there is generally no national final school exam at age 15–16, although some cantons have introduced a school-leaving certificate.

The Swiss Baccalaureate, obtained at the baccalaureate school, allows pupils to enrol directly at any Swiss university (but some courses, like medicine, have limits on enrolment).

UNIVERSITIES

Switzerland has 12 public universities, including the top-ranked Federal Institutes of Technology in Zurich (ETH Zurich) and Lausanne (EPFL). Most have low fees of 1,000Fr to 4,000Fr a year, although living costs can be expensive, which is why many Swiss students still live at home, at least at the beginning. There are also eight public and one private universities of applied sciences and arts, which take a more practical, skills-based approach. Trainee teachers can apply to universities of teacher education. Note: university students tend to be older when they graduate than in many other countries – in their mid- to late-twenties, with 25.8 years the average age for starting a master's degree.

THE SWISS EDUCATION SYSTEM

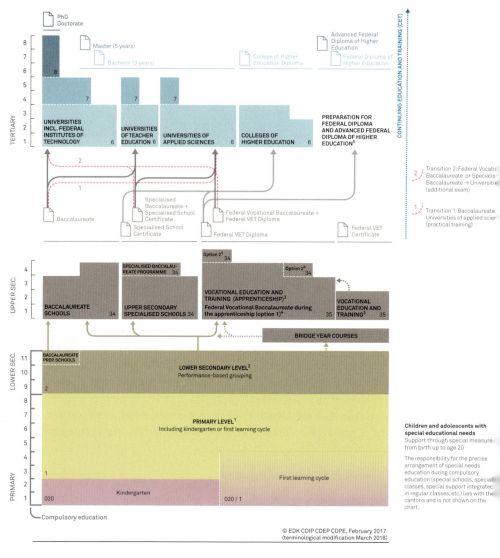

© EDK CDIP CDEP CDPE, February 2017
(terminological modification March 2018)

Children and adolescents with special educational needs
Support through special measures from birth up to age 20

The responsibility for the precise arrangement of special needs education during compulsory education (special schools, special classes, special support integrated in regular classes, etc.) lies with the cantons and is not shown on the chart.

ISCED | International Standard Classification of Education 2011

- ISCED 8
- ISCED 7
- ISCED 6
- ISCED 4
- ISCED 34 + 35
- ISCED 2
- ISCED 1
- ISCED 020

[1] Two years of kindergarten or the first two years of a first learning cycle: included in compulsory education in the majority of cantons

[2] Lower secondary level: 4-year scuola media in the Canton of Ticino (pursuant to exception clause in Art. 6 HarmoS Agreement)

[3] Vocational education and training (apprenticeship): training company + VET school + intercompany courses; full-time school education possible

[4] Federal Vocational Baccalaureate: combined with an apprenticeship (option 1) or after an apprenticeship (option 2); duration option 2: full-time 1 year, part-time 1.5 – 2 years

[5] Federal examination / Federal diploma of higher education = ISCED 6 Advanced federal examination / Advanced federal diploma of higher education = ISCED 7

A DUAL SYSTEM

Many foreigners are surprised by the emphasis on vocational training in Switzerland, but around two thirds of pupils opt for this route and it is highly respected. There are over 230 professions to choose from, but there's lots of careers advice at school. Pupils are expected to do short trial apprenticeships to gain work experience.

Switzerland's dual-track system combines vocational school with on-the-job training at a company, during which apprentices earn money. An apprenticeship usually lasts three to four years and results in a diploma. Options for afterwards include higher vocational diplomas, focusing on expertise and managerial skills. It's also possible to take the Federal Vocational Baccalaureate, which allows direct entry to universities of applied sciences. Students who pass the University Aptitude Test (UAT) can also study at a regular Swiss university or university of teacher education.

ACADEMIC ROUTE

Entry conditions for baccalaureate schools vary, but may include having the right grades, a teacher recommendation or even passing a tough exam. It's best to check with your canton. Only around 20% of students go to these schools. Some German-speaking cantons, like Zurich, also have long-cycle baccalaureate schools that begin after primary school, starting at age 12.

Some adolescents find the whole process of deciding about their future difficult, but don't worry: there are bridge courses that act as interim solutions, which can be done in the year after finishing school. The different tracks are also pretty permeable, meaning you can change course later on – going on to study, for example, after completing an apprenticeship. Note: there are also specialised schools that prepare for tertiary education in certain occupational professions, such as social work or primary school teaching, as well as IT- and business-oriented schools. Check with your canton what is on offer. You can find a good graphic of all the options on the preceding page. Margaret Oertig's *Going Local: your guide to Swiss schooling*, also published by Bergli Books, presents an excellent overview of the Swiss education system.

Generally, the Swiss Baccalaureate is accepted by universities abroad, although anecdotal evidence suggests that in the UK in particular, it is not as well-known as the International Baccalaureate (IB) and you may be required to show very high marks. As ever, it is best to check directly with the university about entry requirements.

GO LOCAL?

A big consideration for many parents is whether to send their children to a local or an international school. There are also private bilingual schools, which fall somewhere between the two, offering both a local and an international outlook.

International schools: Switzerland has a large number of international schools, many of which – but not all – are clustered around the main expat hubs of Zurich, Geneva and Basel. The country is also famous for its more exclusive boarding schools, many of which can be found in alpine resorts. Overall, international schools have a good reputation. Many institutions offer the International Baccalaureate (IB), but some follow the UK, US or other systems.

For admission procedures, it is best to check with the school directly. Bear in mind that some schools may have waiting lists. A trip to look at the school is a good idea to get a better feeling for the learning and curriculum options available. To find a school, a good first stop is the Swiss Group of International Schools, whose members are listed at sgischools.com (this does not include all international schools). These schools generally cost around 25,000Fr to 35,000Fr per child per year. A year at a more exclusive school can cost up to three times as much.

Bilingual schools: there are also plenty of bilingual schools in Switzerland. These schools generally combine elements of the cantonal curriculum with international ones, with tuition in English and a local language. Older pupils may have the opportunity to take the Swiss Baccalaureate (school-leaving certificate that opens the door to a Swiss university) and/or the IB. Bilingual schools may be a good option if you are unsure about how long you will stay in Switzerland. Fees start at around 20,000Fr.

Note: some Swiss local baccalaureate schools offer bilingual education programmes – for example, there are 16 schools in canton Zurich offering a bilingual baccalaureate in German and English. It's worth checking with your canton about this.

Other types of private schools: you will find a list on the official Private School Register. These schools are extremely varied: some have alternative schooling philosophies (eg Steiner, Montessori), and/or offer different structures such as smaller classes and more pupil freedom. Officially registered private schools must generally offer a curriculum that is similar to the local cantonal one.

LOCAL SCHOOLS

Pros	Cons
Good, all-round education, particularly for maths	Many foreigners find that the decision about whether a child will follow a vocational or academic track is made rather early – usually around age 14–15.
School is nearby	Schools send children home for lunch and can have varying afternoon hours, so extra childcare may be needed (see School Life and Childcare sections for more details)
Integration with local community, having local friends	Very good on special needs and weaker pupils, less so on gifted kids
Immersion in local language, younger children will pick up language easily	Communication with the teacher and school will be in local language, though in many municipalities translation is available
Free	Native-language proficiency will have to be maintained at home, especially if planning later study abroad

INTERNATIONAL SCHOOLS

Pros	Cons
Ensures educational consistency and maintains access to UK, US or other education system; may be better for older children	Generally longer travel time needed to reach school
English or other main language is maintained	Fewer local friends; high turnover of pupils at school due to short expat stays
Internationally recognised school leaving certificate, like the IB	Children may not learn the local language
International community and outlook	Admittance depends on availability of places; there could be waiting lists.
School days generally longer than local schools, easier for working parents	Expensive

SCHOOL LIFE

If you opt for the local primary system, there are a few aspects that might take some getting used to, but there are many positive sides too. However, working parents beware.

Kindergarten: the curriculum does not contain much emphasis on formal learning – including reading and numeracy. Forest kindergartens, where the kids are outside whatever the weather, are popular, especially in the German-speaking part.

Eligibility: you cannot normally choose your local school, nor are there any school rankings. Instead, you will be allocated a local kindergarten or school by the school authority in the municipality in which you are registered (see Arrival Chapter for how this works). Cantons set the enrolment age, but generally, children must reach four by a certain date (usually 31 July) to be admitted into kindergarten the next school year, which generally starts between mid-August and early September. Parents can apply for their children to start early or delay a year.

Walking to school: in German-speaking Switzerland especially, young children are expected to walk to school on their own, and being taken by car is frowned upon. It is argued that walking to school fosters independence. Children are generally provided with a reflective band or vest.

School hours and lunch: there is a long break over lunch, during which children usually go home rather than stay in school. Many schools and local authorities offer a cooked lunch club service (against payment) as well as an out-of-school club in the afternoon. Children don't have afternoon school every day, and they may not have the same timetable as their siblings. There is generally no school on Wednesday afternoons.

School community: teaching is a well-respected profession and children are generally expected to shake hands with their teachers at the beginning and end of the school day. With Switzerland's high rate of immigration, most schools are multicultural, and respectful of this, although there have been some reported incidents of racism.

Language help: there is extra language help for pupils who don't speak the local language well, such as intensive language courses or extra language classes during the school week.

SPECIAL NEEDS

Switzerland has an inclusive approach to education and many children with special needs are taught at regular schools. There are also special needs schools for children with more severe disabilities or learning and behavioural difficulties.

Schools are generally quick to see if children need some sort of therapy for speech, learning or motor difficulties. It is commonplace: in Canton Zurich, for example, statistics show that at least half of pupils have had some kind of therapy during their school careers. Repeating a year is also fairly common in Swiss schools and generally accepted as part of school life.

Parents have reported that help for gifted children is still a bit patchy, though existing measures range from skipping a year and mentoring, to after, school classes and special schools. According to swissinfo.ch, part of the problem is that the inclusive approach to education, which is supposed to cover gifted kids as well, focuses more on children with special educational needs. To be recognised as gifted, a child will first need to undergo an assessment.

TWINS

If like me you have twins, check your local school authority's policy. Some schools prefer to put twins in separate classes, but as a parent you have a say in this. You may need to put your request in writing.

CHILDCARE

The lack of affordable childcare is often a concern in expat surveys. It can cost up to two thirds of an average salary in Zurich, for example. There are however tax breaks and subsidies (the amount that you are entitled to varies depending on where you live and your salary). A good tip is to think about organising childcare early. Here's a rundown on what's on offer.

Pre-school: crèche/day care is available, either half- or full-day, usually for a minimum of three half-days a week. It can be expensive, with private ones costing around 60Fr–150Fr a day in the big cities, according to swissinfo.ch. Finding a place can sometimes be difficult and there may be waiting lists. Hours are generally 7:00 to 18:30. Some companies offer their own day care.

Child-minders: child-minders look after several children at their own home, generally for 5–12Fr an hour per child. This arrangement can continue during school years and costs less than day care. It is usually organised by local associations, which also take care of the billing.

Out-of-school clubs: clubs cover the gaps in the Swiss school day: before school starts, over lunchtime, and in the late afternoon. At midday, lunch clubs offer children hot meals (there are generally no school lunches in Swiss schools), for a fee of around 80Fr for a half day with lunch or 25Fr for lunch only.

Au pairs: there are certain conditions for employing au pairs from EU/EFTA states, so check with your canton first. For au pairs from outside EU/EFTA states, like the US and Canada, you must go via the State Secretariat for Economic Affairs (SECO) website of approved agencies at avg-seco.admin.ch (in German, French, Italian). Expect to pay the au pair around 700–800Fr a month. Qualified nannies are also an option. A good idea is to go through an agency, with salaries around 4,000 to 5,000Fr a month.

Less-formal arrangements: many Swiss parents rely on friends, often in a reciprocal arrangement when working part-time, or on grandparents, to provide childcare.

Attitudes: it is not uncommon for Swiss mothers to work part-time; in fact, the country has the second highest rate of part-time working in Europe, after the Netherlands. This is partly practical, due to the school day, and partly cultural. A word of warning: mothers of young children working longer hours may attract a few negative comments. Part-time employment by men is becoming more socially acceptable.

FINDING CHILDCARE

- Best overviews in English: swissinfo.ch's 'Children and Childcare' or ch.ch: 'Childcare'
- Best childcare resources: kibesuisse.ch (in German, French and Italian)
- Best parenting and childcare checklists: swissmom.ch (in German)
- Best nanny and babysitter platforms: babysitting24.ch and liliput.ch (or check with your local parents' association)
- Best babysitting course provider: Swiss Red Cross

HAVING A BABY

Switzerland is generally an excellent place to have a baby as the standard of care before, during and after delivery is very high. Basic health insurance will cover the cost of pregnancy check-ups, the birth, post-natal care and breastfeeding advice.

There is no legal time limit for informing your boss about a pregnancy, although most Swiss wait until at least the 12-week mark. Women are guaranteed relatively little maternity leave, just 14 weeks (at 80% of wages), but are protected from dismissal during pregnancy and maternity leave, and some employers offer additional leave. Note: maternity leave starts from the birth; to stop work earlier, you'll need a doctor's note. At the time of press, parliament has approved two weeks of paternity leave, but it is unclear when this will be implemented. In practice, many employers have begun offering at least that much.

Many foreigners are impressed by the quality of post-natal care. Mothers are generally not sent straight home after the birth and get advice on breastfeeding, if wanted. Very useful are the mostly free drop-in health consultation services, where parents can get baby-related advice from qualified experts. Consult muetterberatung.ch (in German, French and Italian).

You must register a birth within three days. Home births must be registered personally at the local civil registry. You will need: proof of address and identity, and a report/birth certificate issued by the doctor/midwife, and you may need to prove the civil status of the parents. Unmarried parents wanting to establish joint parental authority, which includes custody, should consult ch.ch's 'Parental authority for unmarried parents'. Paternity also needs to be acknowledged at the registry, either before or after the birth, if the couple is unmarried. Note: your child will not automatically be Swiss if born here (see 'Becoming Swiss' chapter).

It is best to register your child for health insurance before the birth as insurers may not grant supplementary insurance afterwards if, for example, the child has a medical condition from birth.

CHILD BENEFITS

Switzerland provides <u>child benefits</u>, which are direct payments to the parents in addition to their income. They are known as family allowances. They are not automatic; you have to put in a claim. Here's the lowdown on the three types of benefits (some cantons offer higher rates of family allowances), according to the Federal Social Insurance Office.

Child allowance: 200Fr a month per child, up to age 16, or 20 if the child is ill or has a disability and is unable to work.

Education allowance: 250Fr a month per child, from age 16–25 for children studying or in vocational training.

Birth and adoption allowances: not all cantons. See ch.ch's article on 'Family Allowances'.

Those eligible to claim include:
- employees earning at least 592Fr per month, in which case the allowances are normally paid by the employer along with the salary
- the self-employed living in Switzerland earning 592Fr per month and the non-gainfully employed up to a certain taxable income threshold (42,660Fr), but in both cases only if connected to a cantonal family compensation office.

Not eligible: those receiving unemployment benefits, but they may apply for a similar supplementary benefit at their unemployment insurance office.

NAMES

First names: there is no list of forbidden names, but according to the Swiss Ordinance on Civil Status, a civil registrar's office has the right to reject a name if it 'harms the interests of the child'.

Surnames: if the parents are married, the child takes the couple's joint surname. If a married couple have different surnames, the parents may choose (conditions apply). If the parents are not married, the child will normally take the mother's maiden name, but in cases of joint parental authority, the child can have the father's surname if wanted. See 'What will my child's surname be?' at ch.ch.

OVER THE BORDER

Cross-border commuters from an EU or EFTA country are entitled to Swiss family allowances even if their children are living in another EU or EFTA country. However, if you receive an allowance from another country, Switzerland will only make up any difference between this payment and the Swiss family allowance, if higher.

FAMILY LIFE

If you have small children, an excellent way to integrate is to take your child to your local <u>playgroup</u>. Contact your local authorities to find the nearest one. There is a wide range of family meet-ups, in many languages, all across the country, and many clubs and activities for older children, but mostly in the local language.

The Swiss expect children to behave well and be polite. Don't be surprised if a young Swiss child greets you with a handshake. At other times, like in playgrounds, Swiss parents tend to employ a hands-off approach, which is aimed at fostering children's independence. Children are often expected to try to resolve their differences first before an adult steps in.

Traditions are celebrated enthusiastically, so your local school, or school, may hold events in the run-up to Christmas, Easter or for <u>carnival</u> (usually in February). The main Christmas celebration is on 24 December in Switzerland. Children get a visit from St Nicholas and his sidekick Schmutzli (Père Fouettard) on 6 December.

Hiking: there are many family-friendly trails – a personal favourite is the Schellenursli trail in Guarda in the southeastern canton of Graubünden – with scenic spots for picnics and grilling sausages, an activity which is much loved by the Swiss.

<u>Lakeside recreation areas</u> and outside pools are sometimes free of charge, but not always. For rainy days, many municipalities have <u>toy libraries</u>. For a nominal fee, these allow children to borrow several toys for a couple of weeks.

TRAVEL DISCOUNTS

The Swiss Federal Railways offer excellent discounts for families. Kids under six travel free, and at half-price up to age 16. The annual Junior travelcard (30Fr per year) allows kids aged 6–16 to travel free of charge on public transport when accompanied by a parent with a valid ticket. There is also the Children's Co-travelcard, also 30Fr, for age 6–16, for which another adult, like a grandparent or friend, can be designated.

HEALTHCARE

Paediatric care is generally excellent in Switzerland. Check-ups and appointments take place at your local children's doctor. Many speak English. Ask around to find a good doctor or click on your canton on: doktor.ch/paediatrics.

Swiss experts generally recommend check-ups at the following ages: 1 week, and then at 1, 2, 4, 6, 12 and 18 months; age 2, 4, 6, 10 and around 14 years old. These check-ups include a physical exam and an assessment of the child's development and are covered by the basic health insurance.

Vaccination is not mandatory in Switzerland, though 95% of children aged one in Switzerland have had the anti-measles jab. The standard Swiss vaccination plan recommends basic vaccination against diphtheria, tetanus, whooping cough, Hepatitus B, pneumococcal infections, haemophilus influenzae type b, polio, measles, mumps and rubella. There is also a vaccination for the human papilloma virus (HPV) for teenagers.

GOOD TO KNOW

Switzerland has a tick problem. These pesky bugs can cause serious illnesses, such as the bacterial Lyme's disease and the tick-borne encephalitis (TBE) that can affect the central nervous system. In February 2019, the Federal Office of Public Health recommended the TBE vaccination from age six for people living in all areas of Switzerland, apart from Geneva and Ticino, who do regular outdoor activities. There is no Lyme's disease vaccine, but it can be treated with antibiotics, if caught early. It's important to see a doctor immediately if you suspect it. A key symptom is a ring-shaped rash around the bite site.

MEET YOUR EXPERT

Day and night, the world of Dimitri Burkhard revolves around tourism. At Swiss Travel System, he ensures a seamless digital journey for tourists using public transport in Switzerland. And as the founder of Newly Swissed Online Magazine, he has built a loyal community that likes to feel the pulse of Switzerland. Dimitri grew up near Zurich and then spent nearly a decade in the United States where he graduated with a BA in communications. Visit the magazine at newlyswissed.com or follow it on social media: facebook.com/newlyswissed, Instagram/ Twitter @newlyswissed.

TRAVEL

Can you name a landlocked country with a primarily alpine terrain that fits in California ten times? You guessed it: Switzerland. What continues to fascinate me is the fact that this dwarf of a nation has limitless activities waiting to be tried out, scenic spots waiting to be discovered and hiking trails waiting to be walked. There are 12 Unesco World Heritage sites, countless train and mountain railway lines, as well as accommodation ranging from Mongolian yurts to five-star design temples. In short, those who visit Switzerland for the first time or those planning to settle might want to add a blank page to their bucket lists.

As a basis for all explorations, this chapter outlines the best public transport passes for your needs. I'll let you in on unique Swiss experiences – be they on water, on land or in the air. I've listed creative and wallet-friendly ways of exploring Switzerland. And just when you think you have seen it all, I'll tell you where to spend those saved francs on worthwhile upgrades.

THE LOWDOWN
- Swiss public transport explained, from passes to the best train rides
- Savings, upgrades and unique tips
- Road trips, scenic hikes and Switzerland's Walk of Fame

SCENIC TRAIN RIDES

If your idea of scenic includes lakes, mountains and valleys, then any train ride in Switzerland is scenic by definition. But there are some über-scenic rides you should not miss. Besides, there's no better way of exploring Switzerland than from behind a panoramic train window.

The barrier of entry is low, as most scenic train journeys simply require a regular ticket. The only exceptions are the Glacier Express and Bernina Express lines – both of which need seat reservations. A majority of scenic trains are regular lines that also offer fantastic views. My favourites are the Luzern–Interlaken Express and the Voralpen Express between St. Gallen and Lucerne, with the latter featuring luxurious coaches and a family section.

When the summer weather is nice some lines attach open-air coaches to their regularly scheduled trains. Feel the fresh air on Appenzeller Bahnen between Appenzell and Gais. Or hop onto a yellow convertible carriage of the Bernina Express between Davos and Filisur, St. Moritz and Tirano, Chur and Arosa or Landquart and Ilanz.

With all this choice, it is a good thing there is the Grand Train Tour of Switzerland, combining the best panoramic train lines in one continuous journey. Along roughly 1,280km there are no less than eleven lakes, numerous famous landmarks and even glaciers. For a quick train adventure, try the shorter themed routes: Hidden Treasures or Stunning Waters, each requiring three days and two overnight stays.

BUCKET LIST TRAINS

- The Bernina Express runs along the Albula and Bernina lines, a Unesco World Heritage site, with 55 tunnels and 196 bridges, plus the Landwasser Viaduct and emerald Lago Bianco. (rhb.ch)
- Known as the 'slowest express train in the world', the Glacier Express is a must-do for any railway enthusiast. Eight hours fly by with the changing scenery, on-board food service and bonus stops for photographs. Reservations are mandatory. (43Fr reservation fee – included in the Swiss Travel Pass; glacierexpress.ch)
- The Schynige Platte railway still uses the original carriages from the Belle Époque with a cogwheel train. Climb through forests and across alpine meadows to the summit, with its panorama of the Eiger, Mönch and Jungfrau.

THE BEST SEATS

This list is for those on a quest to fill their holiday albums or Instagram feeds with memorable photographs. Seat recommendations presume that you're facing the front of the train.

Trip	Where to sit	What to see
Bern to Lausanne	Upstairs on the left-hand side	Around Puidoux, the train will enter the Unesco World Heritage site of Lavaux. Lake Geneva and the vineyards are on the left-hand side.
Chur to Tirano	At the back on the right-hand side	The curves across the Landwasser Viaduct, the Morteratsch Glacier as well as Lago Bianco are on the right-hand side.
Flüelen to Bellinzona	On the seasonal Gotthard Panorama Express, reserve a seat on the right-hand side.	Thanks to two helical tunnels, the church in Wassen appears three times from different perspectives. Be ready the third time for that perfect photograph.
Zermatt to Gornergrat	On the right-hand side – hands down!	The Matterhorn in its full glory.
Zurich to Lucerne	Upper level on the left-hand side	Lake Zurich and Lake Zug

LAKES AND MOUNTAINS

With 48 named mountain peaks above 4000 meters, Switzerland is the ultimate vertical playground. The majestic Alps run right through this small country, offering some of the best mountaineering, hiking, biking, paragliding and skiing.

Another main pastime of the locals is sightseeing on mountain tops. (You know you're Swiss when you check live webcams during breakfast to find the best mountain views.) Ascending a peak on one of the 345 chair lifts, 245 cable cars, 123 gondolas or 53 funiculars offers an instant change of perspective. The flatlands below turn into a miniature railroad set and it becomes apparent that Switzerland truly is a land of water.

Glaciers, snow fields, waterfalls, rivers and no less than 1500 lakes altogether hold six percent of Europe's water reserves. With all that H_2O, a wealth of opportunities from canyoning to river cruises, from mineral spas to natural ice-rinks, and from steamboat rides to waterfall hikes are waiting to be explored.

Travelling back in time on a historic paddle-steamer is memorable during any weather. On Lake Geneva, a fleet of Belle Epoque steamers will take your breath away as you cruise by the Unesco World Heritage vineyards with snow-capped mountains in the distance.

UNIQUELY SWISS

- Cable car hiking in Engelberg along the Buiräbähnli Safari ("Farmer's Cable Car Safari") involves meeting local farmers who will open up their homes for overnight stays. Then they will send you off across the valley floor in a hanging box.
- An overnight stay on the summit of the Brienzer Rothorn starts with the rack railway journey of your life. Within one hour, the historic open-air coaches will chug you from 566 to 2244 meters above sea level. There, stay in the modest Berghaus Alpine Lodge and watch the sunrise before the first day trippers arrive.
- One of Switzerland's most impressive rock faces is located in the Jura mountains. Count on 4:35 hours for the roundtrip hike from the Noiraigue station to the Creux du Van. There is no telling how long you will marvel at this natural monument once you get there.

MUST-DO MOUNTAINS

Jungfraujoch, Titlis and Pilatus: some of Switzerland's tallest peaks reachable by public transport should most definitely be on your bucket list. But doing it like the locals means also visiting smaller but just as spectacular mountain tops.

Must-do mountains	What to expect
Jungfraujoch (3454m) Schilthorn (2970m)	Bernese Oberland: on top of Europe at Jungfraujoch, walk on a glacier and touch snow year-round. Just across the valley is the Schilthorn, a peak once featured in a James Bond movie. Both offer breath-taking vistas.
Pilatus (2128m) Titlis (3238m) Stanserhorn (1898m)	Central Switzerland: the "Golden Round Trip" from Lucerne to Pilatus combines a boat ride with the steepest cogwheel railway in the world, while Titlis has a glacier. Stanserhorn is in a different league but the ascent in the open-deck CabriO cable car comes with serious bragging rights.

TRAVEL PASSES

The Swiss travel system is one of the densest in the world, with a tight-knit web of rails, waterways and roads reaching even the smallest hamlets. Public transport runs on highly synchronised timetables, guaranteeing smooth transfers by co-ordinating all forms of transport down to the exact minute.

Many first-timers to Switzerland are surprised by the lack of gates or ticket validators on station platforms. Swiss public transport runs mostly on an honour system, so passengers can hop on and off but must produce a valid ticket or pass during random checks. There are on-the-spot fines for those who don't have a ticket.

Point-to-point tickets can be purchased at stations or online but all-inclusive travel passes provide the best experience. However, some are exclusive to visitors with a foreign address, such as the Swiss Travel Pass. This favourite all-inclusive solution covers most railways, boats and buses, with steep discounts on travel up mountain peaks.

For those who call Switzerland home, the annual GA travelcard offers unlimited travel on almost all public transport in first or second class. Discounts of 25–30% apply for young adults, students and seniors, while a child's GA or the family version can be even cheaper. A Duo Partner GA is great for two people living at the same address as the second GA is 25% cheaper. There is also a GA for bikes and one for dogs. The annual Half Fare travelcard is a set price for everyone but slashes all fares in half, paying for itself after only a few trips.

TOP TIPS

- Some great scenic rides are entirely covered by the GA and Swiss Travel Pass, eg the Glacier Express between St. Moritz and Zermatt (reservations mandatory), the seasonal Gotthard Panorama Express and the year-round GoldenPass Line.
- A great way to explore a new city is by bus, boat or tram. Hop on and off using a Swiss Travel Pass or GA, both of which cover city transport. For those without either, a city day pass will be most economical.

AT A GLANCE

There are numerous ways of taking advantage of Switzerland's public transport. Here's an overview of the most common travel passes:

Pass	Main benefit	Expert tip
GA travelcard: Residents 3860Fr per year for an adult in 2nd class	For a set annual fee, the GA offers unlimited travel on trains, buses, trams and boats. Most mountain railways and cable cars offer discounted fares to GA holders.	When travelling abroad for extended periods, snooze your GA for five to 30 days. You then receive a credit corresponding to the number of inactive days.
Half Fare travelcard: Residents 185Fr per year	Savings of 50% on tickets for most trains, buses, trams and boats. Valid for one year.	Visitors from abroad can also buy a Half Fare travelcard for one month (120Fr).
Swiss Travel Pass: Multi-day visitors 232Fr for 3 days 418Fr for 8 days	One pass for unlimited use of most trains, buses, boats and some mountain transport. Other mountain railways at 50% discount. Available for 3, 4, 8 or 15 days – either consecutively or individually in the time frame of a month.	The pass also includes the Swiss Museum Pass, Most economical for at least 8 days 15% discount for those under 26 years
Day Pass: Residents or visitors 75Fr with Half Fare travelcard	One pass covers almost all transport companies and forms of transportation	Saver Day Passes available in advance SBB, the postal office, Coop and Interdiscount regularly run promotions
Regional Passes: Residents or visitors	More or less unlimited use of trains, buses and boats. Some regions extend free transport for the entire duration of the pass, while others restrict free days but grant discounts on remaining days.	Great for those staying in one region. Some popular passes that cover lots of ground: Tell-Pass for central Switzerland, Regional Pass Bernese Oberland, graubündenPASS, Easy Card in Valais, Lake Geneva-Alps Pass.
City Passes: Residents or visitors	All transport modes within city limits for a pre-defined duration.	Many places offer free passes when staying overnight: one night minimum in Basel, Bern, Geneva or Lausanne; two night minimum in Davos/Klosters, Engadin, Interlaken or Montreux, among many others.

SAVING MONEY

Switzerland is a premium destination but it doesn't have to strain your wallet. If you're flexible with time, location or comfort levels, there are ways to save a franc while enjoying the best of Switzerland.

It pays to avoid rush hours when travelling by train. On sbb.ch, or in the SBB app, look for the red % symbol for Supersaver tickets, which offer discounts of up to 70% for specific lines and times. If you prefer to stay flexible, download the FAIRTIQ app, which automatically calculates the lowest fare based on that day's travel patterns.

On trains and most local transport, children aged 6 to 16 travel free with a parent or designated adult having a valid ticket, if the child has a Junior Card (30Fr annually for travel with either parent) or a Children's Co-travelcard (30Fr annually for travel with a single designated adult). Children under six travel free.

Budget travellers with more time can use the Flixbus coach network that connects around 40 destinations in Switzerland. For instance, Zurich to Bern is less than 12Fr if booked in advance on flixbus.ch. Be aware that bus terminals, unlike train stations, are not always centrally located.

Over 500 museums are part of the Swiss Museum Pass, an attractive key to unlock highlights such as the Olympic Museum or Zentrum Paul Klee (166Fr annually, museumspass.ch). Even better value is the family pass (288Fr annually), valid for two adults and up to three children under 16. All Museum Passes are up to 30Fr cheaper with a Half Fare travelcard or GA.

FREE STUFF

It might be hard to believe but some things in Switzerland are free.

- Pack a picnic lunch and a set of matches for mountain hikes. More than 500 *Schweizer Familie* outdoor fireplaces are pre-stocked with chopped wood and communal grills.
- Carry a water bottle with you as public drinking fountains can be found everywhere in Switzerland, from big cities to alongside hiking paths. Signs are required on fountains with water that isn't safe to drink.
- Slow down and explore a city by bike. In Zurich daily rentals are free, while in other places such as Bellinzona, Geneva or Thun, up to 30 minutes are free. Bring an ID and some cash for the deposit (velospot.ch). More geared towards locals is Publibike, a subscription-based bicycle rental network (publibike.ch). Cheap rides during daytime and free rides from 22:00 to 8:00 are offered by carvelo2go.ch.
- Why book a tour when you could join a free walking tour? Cities such as Basel, Geneva and Zurich offer these informative walks at no upfront cost (freewalk.ch – tips are encouraged).

CHEAP SLEEPS

- Reka villages are geared towards families, offering low-budget apartments with shared amenities including indoor pools (reka.ch).
- Campgrounds offer budget options in some of the best scenery. Expect to pay 25–80Fr per night for a family of five in a tent. Extras might include parking, showers or a larger tent. Use tcs.ch for an excellent search portal of 350 of the best sites.
- Stay at a Swiss farm in a bed of straw. Prices are as low as 30Fr per person (myfarm.ch).
- Youth hostels offer beds in prime locations for less. For example, a night in Zermatt costs from 50Fr in a shared room or 120Fr in a private room – breakfast included. Anyone can stay but members enjoy a 7Fr discount per night (33Fr annually, youthhostel.ch).
- Switzerland is known for luxurious hotels but what if you could buy your way in for half the price? A Hotelcard subscription lets you book hundreds of Swiss hotels at a 50% discount (hotelcard.com, 79Fr annually for unlimited bookings).

WALK OF FAME

After her dentist appointments in Zug, a charming actress would stop by the Treichler pastry shop to eat a slice of *Zuger Kirschtorte*. It was Audrey Hepburn, and one of her silk dresses is on permanent display in the shop. Other cherry tart lovers included Pope Francis, Winston Churchill and Charlie Chaplin.

When she was not on a *Roman Holiday*, Hepburn's home was in Tolochenaz, near Morges, where she treasured the idyllic town's privacy and chose its cemetery as her final resting place. Tolochenaz is not too far from Corsier-sur-Vevey, where Charlie Chaplin is resting in peace. The British actor also left quite a mark on Switzerland. His statue stands by the lake in Vevey, and his former mansion is one of my favourite museums: Chaplin's World.

Switzerland has not only been home to many actors – it's also been featured in various Bollywood and Hollywood productions. James Bond fans should head to the Schilthorn, the hideout of arch-nemesis Blofeld, then drive the infamous Furka Pass road from *Goldfinger*, passing by the now-closed Hotel Belvédère. Or step into Pierce Brosnan's shoes and jump off the Contra dam in Ticino, as he did in *GoldenEye*.

Fans of Bollywood will rejoice when they visit the dozens of filming locations. For more than half a century, famous productions have highlighted pristine alpine backdrops. And in case you were wondering, the bridge from *Dilwale Dulhania* does exist: it is located in Saanen near Gstaad at N 46.48811° E 7.25964°.

STAR-STRUCK

Grab your camera and head off for some star spotting. You'd be amazed how popular it is to seek out famous graves and statues.

Statues for selfies:
- Charlie Chaplin (Lake promenade, Vevey)
- Yash Chopra (Casino, Interlaken)
- Albert Einstein (Rosengarten, Bern)
- Sherlock Holmes (town square, Meiringen)
- Freddie Mercury (Lake promenade, Montreux)
- Empress Sissi (Quai du Mont-Blanc, Geneva)

Star graves:
- Coco Chanel, French designer (Lausanne)
- Charlie Chaplin, British actor (Corsier-sur-Vevey)
- Audrey Hepburn, Belgian actress (Tolochenaz)
- James Joyce, Irish author (Zurich)
- Paul Klee, Swiss & German artist (Bern)
- Thomas Mann, German author (Kilchberg)

ALP FICTION

The scenery of the Bernese Oberland has inspired many writers, such as Arthur Conan Doyle, who visited the Reichenbach Falls near Meiringen and used them as the backdrop for the death of his hero, Sherlock Holmes. Or the lush Lauterbrunnen Valley, the blueprint for the Elven home of Rivendell in J.R.R. Tolkien's fictional world of Middle-earth.

SLEEP WELL

There once was a zero-star hotel in Switzerland – a bed under the starry alpine skies. On the other end of the spectrum are the luxury hotels where Swiss hospitality management was born. And in between, there are campgrounds, youth hostels, mountain lodges and mid-range hotels.

Wild camping regulations are complex, though it is widely practised at higher altitudes; consult the Swiss Alpine Club's free online pamphlet 'Camping and Bivouacking in the Swiss Mountains'. At lower altitudes there are numerous campgrounds, however. Some will not only rent tent space but also small chalets or RVs. Before booking, make sure you know what's what: is it a safe location without the risk of flash floods? Is there a view, a noisy road? Reliable directories are available at tcs.ch and camping.ch.

Surrounded by nothing but alpine beauty, Switzerland's mountain inns and huts offer the ultimate retreat. Expect mostly simple amenities such as shared bathrooms, some single rooms but often dorms, and hot meals served in a dining hall. These basics are compensated by the beautiful views out your window.

Step back in time in a Swiss historic hotel, most of which have two or three stars, and thus offer affordable lodging in an authentic setting. For example, the Atrium Hotel Blume in Baden is in a 15th-century building, with the rooms opening up to an inner courtyard. Or the Hotel Saratz in Pontresina, featuring an Art Nouveau hall for meals. The grandest hotel experience can be had in one of the opulent Belle Époque hotels, such as Le Montreux Palace. You will feel like a modern-day time-traveller.

TOP TIP

Book your bed in a mountain hut in advance as most sell out in high season, especially on Saturday nights. Many are bookable via the Swiss Alpine Club (sac-cas.ch). Be aware that most huts only have mixed dorm rooms.

AUTHOR'S PICKS

Type	Reasons why
Campgrounds	Fischer's Fritz for instant vacation feeling (Zurich), Vidy for live music and Lake Geneva views (Lausanne), Bella Riva for river swimming (Gordevio)
Mountain inns	Berggasthaus Seealpsee for its easy access and alpine vibes (Wasserauen)
Youth hostels and guest houses	wellnessHostel4000 is a youth hostel with a full-blown spa (Saas-Fee); Pension für Dich is modern and neat (Zurich).
3-Star hotels	Hotel Gloria for its views and gourmet kitchen (Beatenberg) Hotel Rothorn Kulm where the ibex graze at dusk (Brienz)
4-Star hotels	Wellnesshotel Golf Panorama – it's in the name (Lipperswil) Hotel Cresta Palace as a vantage point for sports activities (Celerina) – Hotel Schweizerhof for the interior design (Zermatt)
5-Star hotels	Castello del Sole for utmost privacy and a farm-to-table menu (Ascona) – The Chedi Andermatt for the pools and spa

UNIQUE STAYS

- At the remote Alp Flix in Graubünden, stay in an authentic Mongolian yurt (agrotour.ch).
- Cuddle up in a giant wine barrel near the Rhine Falls. They're way more spacious than a Japanese capsule hotel (rueedi-ferien.ch).
- Nestle into the Whitepod Eco-Luxury Hotel in Valais. It's built with sustainability in mind, so you'll only be leaving a small ecological footprint (whitepod.com).
- Transparent bubble hotels are scattered in some of the most scenic locations throughout Thurgau (himmelbett.cloud).
- Every winter igloo hotels are carved out of the snow in Davos, Gstaad and Zermatt. Bonfires, fondue and hot tubs are included (iglu-dorf.com).

SPOIL YOURSELF

There is no need for rose-coloured glasses in Switzerland. It's a country of tremendous beauty, good hotels and reliable infrastructure. But to lift your experience to the next level, here are a few worthwhile upgrades.

Why not switch from a deluxe room in a four-star hotel to a standard one in a five-star? You'll reap all the rewards, from complimentary pick-ups to breakfast buffets from heaven. Or splash out on the view when staying by a lake: treat yourself to an upgrade at Hotel Beaulac in Neuchâtel, Hotel des Trois Couronnes in Vevey, Hotel Walter au Lac in Lugano or Art Deco Hotel Montana in Lucerne. Hands down, they offer some of the most breath taking lake vistas in Switzerland.

Maybe you don't want to think twice about going certain places: most attractions offer annual memberships with unlimited visits. For example, the countless historic trains and planes at the Swiss Museum of Transport in Lucerne require more than one visit – an annual pass is worth it (70Fr). At the Ballenberg Open-Air Museum near Brienz, sponsor an animal, such as a duck (200Fr) or a donkey (600Fr), in exchange for a season ticket. Or simply flash your Swiss Museum Pass (166Fr) to gain admission to 500 museums.

Five-star concierge services for the masses: SBB offers door-to-door luggage service within Switzerland. They pick up your luggage at home, a hotel or the airport and take it to your destination. For only 12Fr apiece (minimum 40Fr if door-to-door, though no minimum station-to-station; max weight 25kg), this service quite literally takes a load off your shoulders.

DELUXE TRAVEL

Line	Reasons why
Glacier Express (1st class)	Oversized panoramic windows and table service, including hot meals
Gotthard Panorama Express (1st class)	Upper deck views on the paddle-steamer and personal travel concierge on the train
GoldenPass MOB Panoramic	Between Zweisimmen and Montreux, treat yourself to a VIP seat with front-row views (15Fr).
Brienzer Rothorn and Schynige Platte	Train lovers can pay extra to ride in the driver's cab of these steam trains – it's less comfortable but most memorable!

GOOD TO KNOW

There are some places that do not offer upgrades per se, but you are getting a better experience no matter what.

- Some Bernina Express and GoldenPass coaches in 2nd class still have windows that open. This is an advantage over 1st class as you can take stunning photographs without the glare.
- Anyone with some extra francs to spare can have a drink at the lakeside Park Hotel Vitznau or on the rooftop of Hotel Savoy in Lausanne – both are five-star hotels.
- Spending a day at a spa will make you feel like a millionaire: Rigi-Kaltbad (37Fr), Tamina Therme (40Fr) or the Dolder Grand Spa (210Fr lunchtime special, including 1-hour massage).

HIKING

There's nothing more Swiss, or more wonderful, than hiking through the spectacular landscape, breathing in the mountain air and soaking in the views. Luckily, everyone can enjoy this national pastime as there are hiking paths for all levels.

HIKING PATHS

There's an official rating system for hiking paths, so you know how difficult they are. Harder paths and signs are colour-coded: red-and-white stripes for difficult-but-doable mountain paths, and blue-and-white for expert level alpine paths.

T1 (yellow)	Hiking path	Well-cleared trail and flatter terrain doable with trainers
T2 (red & white)	Mountain hiking	Sometimes steep, hiking boots recommended
T3 (red & white)	Demanding mountain hiking (rocky path)	Some hazards (eg exposed rocks, scree) require good boots
T4 (blue & white)	Alpine hiking (path not always visible)	Solid trekking boots and alpine experience needed
T5 (blue & white)	Demanding alpine hiking (often no path, some climbing)	Mountaineering boots and equipment plus climbing experience needed
T6 (blue & white)	Difficult alpine hiking (no path, climbing sections)	Technical mountaineering equipment and experience needed

St.ne di Pazzallo 🚋 1h
Pazzallo 🚌 1h 10 min
Paradiso 🚆🚌⛴🚋 1h 35 min

The trail network is both vast (over 65,000km) and efficiently organised. Yellow signs show the destination and usually the time needed to walk there; harder hikes are colour-coded (see box). Check out wandern.ch for interactive maps and route tips.

If you're really into the outdoors, join the Swiss Alpine Club (SAC), which organises guided hikes and runs 153 mountain huts that are essential for multi-day hikes. Some offer food and showers, others just a place to sleep in dorms. Covers and pillows are normally provided but don't forget your sheet sleeping bag. Bring a battery pack to recharge your phone as there's often only solar energy.

Biking is another Swiss favourite, with nine national routes and countless local ones (all on schweizmobil.ch). If you're into road cycling, an e-bike helps with the hills, especially on the beautiful *Herzroute* (aka Route 99) that cuts across the whole country. Or get the ultimate adrenalin kick with downhill biking in the mountains. To be taken on a train, bikes always need a ticket, which is the same price as a standard half fare ticket. Or you can buy a Bike Pass for 14Fr for a day or 240Fr annually.

FIRST STEPS

The Swiss are experts when it comes to hiking, so others often struggle to keep up. Here are six great hikes for beginners, all accessible at both ends by public transport.

- **Bernese Oberland:** Männlichen to Wengen via Kleine Scheidegg. A grand panorama trail with some of the best Swiss scenery that isn't too hard on the legs.
- **Graubünden:** Muottas Muragl to Alp Languard. Stunning views of the Upper Engadin valley are the reward for this hike, which is steep in places but worth it.
- **Lake Geneva:** the Swiss Wine Route. A lovely walk through the terraced vineyards of the Lavaux, which are stunning in autumn. The easiest of these suggested hikes.
- **Lake Lucerne:** the Swiss Path. Too long to do in a day so choose historic Rütli for a dramatic hike, up or walk the old Axenstrasse between Sisikon and Flüelen.
- **Ticino:** Monte Tamaro to Monte Lema. From the striking Botta church at Alpe Foppa it's a long but wonderful hike along a panorama ridge with great views.
- **Valais:** Bettmerhorn to Fiescheralp via Märjelensee. Get up close to the longest glacier in the Alps on this hearty, slightly harder, hike beside the river of ice.

AUTO
MOBILITY

<u>Car hire</u> works much like anywhere else but there are a few important things to note. Given all that mountainous terrain, it's not surprising that many Swiss cars are manual, so be ready to pay more for an automatic. Rental cars are generally insured for France, Germany and Austria, but Italy may be excluded. Some countries, like Croatia, may be off limits so always check before you rent.

For residents, the Mobility car sharing platform (mobility.ch) offers instant access to cars located at nearly 1,500 pick-up points. You pay per hour and per kilometre when using the car, but this pay-per-use pricing includes fuel, servicing and insurance. Here's how it works:

Select and reserve a vehicle in the app, then unlock it by tapping your membership card on the windscreen. If the tank falls below one-third full, fill it up using the prepaid fuel card before returning the car to its original space or parking at a new location.

The Click&Drive plan is perfect for infrequent use of Mobility cars as there is no annual fee. And it is open to anyone, as is the annual subscription plan with lower usage rates. Instead of owning a car, you could combine Mobility with a public transport pass, giving you full flexibility without the high overheads of ownership.

Since you pay by the hour, Mobility is good for shorter trips, such as runs to the DIY store or moving house. For example, a standard-size car under the Click&Drive plan costs 4Fr per hour and 0.90Fr per kilometre. In Geneva, a comparable rental car starts at 50Fr per day, so it pays to do the maths. Generally speaking, rental cars are economical for trips longer than one day or if you are planning to go across the border.

TAXI TIP

In a country where regular taxis charge a premium, it's good to know that Uber can give you a lift. With strongholds in Lausanne, Basel and Zurich, Uber is a legit choice.

DID YOU KNOW?

The first traffic lights in Switzerland were installed in 1935 in Geneva, while the first parking meters followed in 1952 but in Basel.

SPEED LIMITS

A Swiss millionaire garnered a ticket of 299,000Fr and an entry in the Guinness Book of World Records for speeding through a village at 90km/h. This goes to show that speeding fines may be based on the income of the driver. Stay on the safe side of the law by following these speed limits, but pay attention to special signals indicating a decrease due to bad air quality or a construction site. Note that Swiss traffic cameras usually flash vehicles from the front.

- **Motorway:** 120km/h
- **Expressway:** 100km/h
- **Outside built-up areas:** 80km/h
- **Within built-up areas:** 50km/h
- **Go-slow areas in cities:** 30km/h
- **Interaction zones:** 20km/h

GOOD TO KNOW

Blowing the horn is admissible when there is a safety issue or the driver in front fails to notice that the lights have changed. But leaning on the horn like a New Yorker is strictly not permitted here. The jury's still out on the legality of dashcams so you're better off not using one.

ROAD TRIPS

Narrow winding roads among impressive rock faces, service areas located next to glittering lakes, and alpine passes desired by secret agents like James Bond: there are many good reasons for discovering Switzerland on a road trip.

The Swiss road network spans 71,000km. It is inevitable that you will pass some of Switzerland's most beautiful parts as you roam around, but not every stretch provides scenic views. With more than 200 tunnels, you'll enter the side of a mountain about every 6.5km.

Crossing an alpine pass is surely on many a car enthusiast's bucket list. And with some clever planning, you could be negotiating three passes in a single day. Start with the Susten Pass, followed by the Grimsel Pass and the Furka Pass, thereby crossing from Uri in central Switzerland to the Bernese Oberland and on to Valais, and then back to where you started.

If this is going to be your first time snaking up a mountain on a narrow cobblestone street, why not pick a weekday? There will be less leisure traffic, such as slow road bicycles that need to be passed or motorbikes coming your way after sharp curves. In any case, check the road status of the alpine pass prior to your trip – it may still be snow covered in May or even June.

BOOST YOUR TRIP

- It would not be Switzerland if there weren't road trips by public transport. Postal buses provide a vital link for remote places that cannot be reached by train. Between June and October, hop on a yellow Swiss PostBus in Andermatt or Meiringen for a trip across the Alps. Seat reservations are highly recommended.
- Approximately 300 charging stations along the Grand Tour of Switzerland allow for an emissions-free road trip by electric car.
- Photo spots reachable by car: the vast landscape atop the Albula Pass, the Lugano sunset from Monte Brè, or the Roman bridge across the emerald Verzasca River in Lavertezzo.

THE GRAND TOUR

The Grand Tour of Switzerland (myswitzerland.com/grandtour) is the ultimate road trip covering Switzerland's diverse landscapes and cultures. It combines 1,600km of the most scenic roads, including these five Alpine passes:

Where and when	Why cross it	Good to know
Flüela Pass (2383m) May to December	During summer, share the scenic road to the Lower Engadin Valley with a historic mail carriage pulled by six horses.	Alternatively, load your car onto a train between Selfranga and Sagliains.
Furka Pass (2436m) June to October	Relive the James Bond car chase from *Goldfinger* while descending to the Rhône Valley.	The road is open for RVs but not trailers. Car shuttle train between Realp and Oberwald.
Julier Pass (2284m) Open year-round	Enjoy alpine vistas on this pass connecting Engadin with the rest of Graubünden.	Summer sunsets at the top are especially beautiful.
San Bernardino Pass (2065m) May to October	Showcase your driving skills as you negotiate the hairpin curves to the top of the pass.	Make a stop at the summit's 15th-century chapel dedicated to Saint Bernhardin of Siena, Italy.
St Gotthard Pass (2108m) June to November	From the top, descend 900 meters on the ancient *Tremola* cobblestone road.	Learn about the significance of the main European watershed at the St Gotthard Museum.

EXPERT'S CHOICE

One of the things I love most about Switzerland are the countless transportation options. Whether on rail, on water or in the air, the Swiss have figured out how to negotiate the alpine terrain. Here I've chosen all kinds of record-breaking or otherwise unique experiences for your Swiss bucket list. Trust me: you simply cannot leave Switzerland before doing these!

Here's a trip for you to try: ride Switzerland's only metro from the Lausanne train station to Ouchy by the lake. There, embark on a Belle Époque paddle-steamer to Chillon Castle. As you coast alongside the Lavaux vineyards first built by monks in the 12th century, look out for a giant fork in the lake. This is the sign that you are getting close to the impressive island castle that inspired Lord Byron's *The Prisoner of Chillon*.

Or spend a day in Solothurn, a city that tourists often overlook. For centuries, it was the seat of the French ambassador to Switzerland, so it has Baroque architecture throughout the old town. The views from the top of the St Ursen cathedral are reminiscent of Florence. And Solothurn has a playful side, too: from 11 city gates to 11 fountains and even a clock with only 11 hours, it challenges you to discover ever more instances of 11. My recommendation: visit on a Wednesday or Saturday when the market takes place. And for lunch, try the traditional white wine soup at Zunfthaus zu Wirthen.

SWISS RECORD BREAKERS

Aletsch Glacier: from the valley floor glide up to the car-free villages of Riederalp, Bettmeralp or Fiescheralp by cable car and enjoy a panorama of the longest glacier in the Alps. Better yet, hike to Bettmerhorn or Eggishorn and really appreciate this river of ice.

Rhine Falls: Europe's largest waterfall is not only impressive but also immersive. For one, a boat will drop you off at a rock in the centre of the falls. And on the observation platform, you will feel the raging river Rhine with all your senses.

Saas-Fee: if chasing extremes rings your bells, how about embarking on Metro Alpin, the world's highest underground train? In three minutes, it will zip you to the Mittelallalin summit at 3456m. And while you're there, check out the world's highest revolving restaurant.

Stoos: Switzerland has the world's steepest funicular, the Stoosbahn. This marvel of technology, with a maximum incline of 110 degrees, has round cabins that appear to climb nearly vertically. From Stoos hike to the top of Fronalpstock for marvellous views of Lake Lucerne.

I DARE YOU!

- Walk high above the treetops at the *Baumwipfelpfad* in Neckertal, Mogelsberg.
- Soar like a bird above Ascona-Locarno as part of a tandem paragliding flight. You'll take off from Cardada at 1671m and land in Switzerland's lowest spot at 196m (flyticino.ch).
- The world's longest suspension bridge for pedestrians is a two-hour hike from Randa. Are you ready to cross 494 metres with nothing but the deep valley floor underneath?

MEET YOUR EXPERT

Felix Schneuwly is a health insurance expert for the internet comparison site comparis.ch AG, and holds an Executive Master of Business Administration (MBA). Following an apprenticeship as a plumber, he studied journalism and psychology in Fribourg. From 2008 to 2011, he worked as a Delegate of Public Affairs for health insurance provider association santésuisse. He has also served as Secretary General for the Swiss Association for the Blind and Visually-Impaired and for the Swiss Federation of Psychologists.

HEALTH

The Swiss are healthy. So healthy, in fact, that they have the highest life expectancy in the world, at 83.7 years. This longevity might be due to the fresh mountain air or the consumption of chocolate, but the excellent healthcare system probably also plays its part.

Coverage is universal because health insurance is compulsory for every resident and no one can be refused basic standard cover. After moving to Switzerland, you have three months to take out a policy offered by one of the many health insurers – and you must be accepted. It is a regulated private system, with free choice for the consumer and open competition; however, there are also state controls to limit the excesses of a competitive market. Overall it works well, but it's expensive: after the USA, Switzerland has the highest per capita health costs in the world.

Some companies might contribute towards your costs as part of an employment package but it's unusual for healthcare to be linked to a job. It's far more common to have your own health insurance, so in this chapter we'll take a look at how the system works, including tips on how to reduce those painful costs and what supplemental insurance is available.

THE LOWDOWN
- Explaining Swiss health insurance
- Reducing costs and adding benefits
- Seeing a doctor

LIFE AND DEATH

When it comes to quality of life, Switzerland regularly tops the polls, thanks to a healthy work-life balance, active lifestyles and the wonderful natural environment. But death comes to everyone, even the Swiss, who live longer and are more prosperous than the citizens of many other nations. On average 183 people die in Switzerland every day, which sounds like a lot until you learn that 239 babies are born each day. To put all of that into perspective, here are a few vital statistics about health in Switzerland (all from the Federal Statistical Office).

Facts of life: a huge 96% of babies in Switzerland are born in hospital, with about a third coming into the world by caesarean section. The average age of the mother is 31.9 years, with only 30% of babies born to women under 30. Infant mortality stands at 3.5 per 1,000 live births, below the EU average of 4 and far better than the USA at 5.9.

Medical care: typically, 81% of the population visit a doctor at least once a year, with men aged 25-44 predictably the ones to go least often. In comparison, only 60% of the population visit the dentist once a year. If a stay in hospital is needed, there are 281 of them to choose from, with the average stay in acute care lasting five days at a cost of 2,235Fr a day.

Smoking kills: over a quarter of the population smokes, though the national average of 27% rises to 32% in the 15-24 age group. That's higher than the EU average and much more than countries like the UK (16%) or the USA (14%). Smoking causes 26 deaths a day, or about one in seven fatalities in Switzerland.

DID YOU KNOW?

Foreigners make up 25% of the population of Switzerland but only account for 10% of deaths. That's because they are younger, and also less likely to die from cardiovascular diseases or accidents.

CAUSES OF DEATH

There are around 65,000 deaths a year, with well over half due to two main causes, cardiovascular diseases and cancer. Between ages 16 and about 34 the majority of deaths are caused by accidents and suicide, but from around age 40 cancer is the most common cause. From about age 80 it's cardiovascular diseases.

Total deaths per year ranked by cause:

- cardiovascular diseases: 20,712
- cancer: 17,201
- dementia: 5,764
- respiratory diseases: 4,108
- accidents: 2,552
- diabetes: 1,274
- suicide: 1,016
- assisted suicide: 928
- infectious diseases: 752
- alcoholic liver cirrhosis: 441

Source: Federal Statistical Office

ASSISTED SUICIDE

Under Swiss law assisted suicide is legal as long as patients commit the act themselves and helpers have no vested interest in their death. Organisations such as Exit and Dignitas help people organise their own death under certain conditions (note that Exit is only for Swiss citizens and residents in Switzerland, whereas Dignitas is open to anyone): the person wishing to die must know what they are doing, not be acting on impulse, have a persistent wish to die, not be under the influence of any third party, and commit suicide by their own hand. They do not have to have an incurable disease, although cancer is the reason for 42% of assisted suicides. Overall, assisted suicide remains rare, accounting for fewer than 1,000 deaths a year in Switzerland, which is lower than the number of other suicides

HEALTH INSURANCE

Basic health insurance is obligatory for every resident in Switzerland. It's as simple as that. Your age, gender, nationality or medical condition make no difference: you must have insurance and you cannot be refused basic coverage. That's the founding principle of the Swiss healthcare system, as defined by the Health Insurance Act of 1994. Under that law, the health service is not funded by taxes, but is a regulated system of about 50 commercial health insurers. It's a free market but with controls in place to ensure full coverage and limit excessive medical bills for the consumer.

Health insurers must offer the same level of basic cover to everyone, with no exceptions no matter how sick they are (see box). But competition means that premiums vary and basic cover can be supplemented by cover for things like private hospital rooms. Customers have a free choice of insurers, and can change easily, but can also opt for higher premiums or extra coverage.

You pay a monthly premium and are then liable for the deductible or excess, known as a *franchise* in Switzerland. This is the amount you must pay each year if you have any medical bills, and all deductibles are set by law, with an adult minimum of 300Fr a year and a maximum 2500Fr (for children, 0 and 600 respectively). Once bills exceed your deductible, you're liable for a minimum 10% of any extra costs, up to a set annual maximum of 700Fr (350Fr for children). In other words, you're unlikely to go bankrupt or have to use crowdfunding to pay your medical bills.

Later in this chapter, we'll give you advice on how to reduce your premiums, plus examples of what supplementary cover is available. Note that people on lower incomes can apply for state help with premiums and bills.

PREMIUM PRICES

Your monthly premium is not allowed to be based on pre-existing conditions, medical questionnaires or even whether or not you smoke. It is calculated using four standard factors.

- **Age group:** children under 18, young adults 19–25 and adults over 26. Premiums for children must be lower by law but reductions for young adults are not compulsory. Senior citizens get no discounts (but get full coverage).
- **Deductible:** the lowest annual deductible of 300Fr for adults means a higher monthly premium, so you need to weigh up the overall costs.
- **Insurance model:** many insurers offer discounts for policies which require you to see your own family doctor first or contact a medical helpline, a health maintenance organisation (HMO) or even a pharmacy when you are sick.
- **Location:** premiums differ from canton to canton and even between rural and urban areas in the same canton.

BASIC COVERAGE

All insurers must offer the same standard benefits in a basic policy, as defined by law. Alongside free choice of doctor, these include many other benefits.

- **Hospital:** stay in a general ward in your canton of residence; emergency coverage and specialist care (eg transplants) in other cantons are included.
- **Outpatient:** examinations and treatment, including physiotherapy, nursing care, occupational therapy and psychiatric therapy (with some limits)
- **Coverage abroad:** emergency care up to twice the amount the same treatment would cost in Switzerland – enough for Europe but not for the USA or Japan
- **Emergency transport:** half the cost of medically-necessary rescue missions (up to 5,000Fr a year); also half the cost of transport in non-life threatening situations (maximum 500Fr a year)
- **Alternative medicine:** some traditional healing methods, including homeopathy and acupuncture, are now allowed under certain conditions.
- **Medication, tests and medical aids:** covered according to the official list under the Health Insurance Benefits Ordinance
- **Maternity:** minimum of seven pre-natal examinations plus costs of childbirth and post-natal care. Legal abortion is covered. For a 'normal' pregnancy there are no deductibles or percentage charges.
- **Prevention:** certain preventative tests and treatments, eg shots for tetanus and hepatitis B, mammograms, pre-school check-ups, child immunisations
- **Dental:** excluded except for severe and unavoidable diseases or after an accident (if not covered by another insurance)
- **Eyes:** glasses and contact lenses are excluded for adults, except for medical reasons, eg diabetes; children get 180Fr a year towards the costs.

CUTTING COSTS

Swiss healthcare isn't cheap and premiums go up most every year, with the national average at 374.40Fr a month for an adult (according to the Federal Office of Public Health). But there are three simple ways to reduce the cost: switching insurers, changing policies and raising deductibles. Use comparison sites like comparis.ch to shop around the various insurance companies and policies.

Switching insurers: given that all insurers have to offer same level of basic cover, you can easily compare standard policy premiums for your age and location. You can switch insurers even if you are receiving medical treatment. When switching, you must cancel your existing policy by 30 November so that your new insurer takes over on 1 January the following year. If you have a standard policy with basic cover and a 300Fr deductible, you can also switch mid-year but with three months' notice, ie by 31 March.

Changing policies: you can change your policy to a less expensive model and benefit from up to 25% off. Under the HMO and family doctor models, you choose your GP from the insurer's list of approved doctors, then agree to consult him first. With the Telmed model, you must call a consultation helpline for each new medical problem before seeing a doctor. Emergencies are exempt from these restrictions. Depending on your existing policy, you may be able to change models with the same insurer with one month's notice.

Raising deductibles: the levels of deductible are set by law, with all insurers required to offer the statutory minimum of 300Fr a year for adults. Choosing a higher deductible level, eg 1,000Fr a year, reduces your monthly premium – but you'll pay more if you get ill. Raising deductibles with your existing insurer must be done in writing before 31 December.

TOP TIP

Cancelling policies or raising deductibles must be done in writing, which is best sent by registered post. Your insurer must receive notice by the last business day before the relevant deadline; the postmark date makes no difference.

SAVING MONEY

Here's a worked-out example to give you an idea of how you could save money every month. Frédéric and Clémentine Rochat and their two young children have policies with the minimum 300Fr deductible (0 for the children). Each month they pay 1,267.40Fr to insure the whole family, or a grand total of 15,208.80Fr a year. Quite a lot – but they can save money with any of three changes.

- **Switching insurers:** keeping their existing basic level of cover and lowest deductible, they could still save by switching to the cheapest insurer. Annual saving = 1,670.40Fr.
- **Changing policies:** the Rochat family could save almost 200fr a month by staying with their current insurer but changing to the Telmed model. Annual saving = 2,284.80Fr.
- **Raising deductibles:** upping the adults' deductibles to the maximum 2,500Fr could pay off if neither is chronically sick and both rarely need a doctor. But as the kids see a doctor more often, they keep those deductibles at zero. Annual saving = 2,865.60Fr.

Combining all three possibilities produces the greatest annual savings of all: Total = 6,820.80Fr, or about 45%.

HELP WANTED

People on lower incomes may be eligible for state help in the form of a premium reduction. The minimum income thresholds and levels of support vary by canton, as does the application process, so check with your canton for more details. For example, in Bern adults earning under 35,000Fr a year are automatically eligible, based on their annual tax return; a sliding scale of reductions means that an adult with an income of less than 9,000Fr a year gets 221Fr a month, whereas an annual salary of 25,000 to 35,000Fr warrants 67Fr a month. This money is generally sent directly to the insurer to reduce the premium.

ADDING BENEFITS

While the standard level of basic coverage must be the same across all insurers, customers have the freedom to add to that in a number of ways. Of course, the more elements you add, the more your premiums increase – and there are also fewer controls. Unlike with standard policies, supplemental insurance coverage can vary according to insurer, and companies are freer to base supplemental premiums on your age, gender, weight or state of health. They are also allowed to impose restrictions on coverage or even turn you down without giving a reason.

Supplemental insurance coverage and prices can also be compared online so that customers can choose what extras they want and at what cost. As with standard policies, premiums for supplemental insurance vary – so make sure you compare all the benefits from any extra policy. For example, for 10Fr extra per month you might get 150Fr towards the cost of new glasses with one insurer, while for 14Fr a month with another insurer you might get that plus full medical coverage when abroad and money towards your annual gym membership.

For some supplemental insurance policies, you may have to fill out a medical questionnaire and apply to be accepted. Answer all questions about your state of health carefully and truthfully, and if in doubt ask your doctor or current health insurer. It's better to declare one health problem too many than too few.

TOP TIP

You can use different insurers for your basic policy and any supplemental ones but remember that supplemental policies can have different terms and conditions, eg minimum of three months' notice to cancel, or even a five-year minimum term.

PIMP YOUR POLICY

Supplemental insurance can cover almost anything you want, but generally falls into two categories, outpatient and inpatient.

Popular outpatient supplements:
- contributions towards gym membership or fitness classes
- alternative therapies such as massage
- glasses and contact lenses
- home nursing services and domestic help
- full medical coverage abroad, including travel vaccinations
- dental treatment and corrective dentistry
- emergency transport

Popular inpatient supplements:
- general ward hospital care (for non-emergencies and non-specialist treatment) outside the canton of residence
- free choice of hospital outside the canton of residence
- semi-private hospital care throughout Switzerland, eg a two-bed room instead of a ward
- private hospital care throughout Switzerland, eg a one-bed room with free choice of hospital doctor

CANTONAL COSTS

One additional cost factor is your place of residence. As most people can't realistically move to another canton purely to reduce health costs, this is an unavoidable extra. Which canton you live in helps to determine monthly premiums, so that the lowest, in Appenzell Innerrhoden, are 45% cheaper than the highest, in Basel Stadt.

Five cheapest cantons:
Appenzell Innerrhoden, Uri, Nidwalden, Zug, Obwalden

Five dearest cantons:
Basel-Stadt, Geneva, Vaud, Neuchâtel, Basel-Landschaft

ACCIDENTS

By law anyone working at least eight hours a week with the same employer must be covered for accidents by that employer's insurance, no matter when or where in Switzerland the accident occurs. This saves you around 5-10% on your premiums, as you can remove accidental cover from your own policy, and gives you better coverage, eg emergency transport costs are included.

If you don't qualify for this, then you must include accident cover in your basic policy but there are some restrictions. For example, calling an ambulance could be expensive, as basic policies need only cover half the costs (up to a set maximum level) even if it is a medical necessity; if you could have travelled by car or public transport, ambulance costs are not covered. You may want to add supplemental insurance for emergency transport.

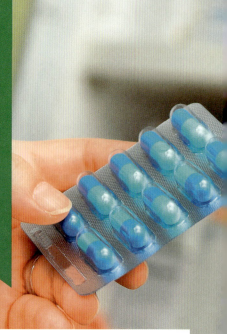

TOP TIP

Aside from personal recommendations, you can also search for doctors online, even filtering by language:
- Comparis Medical Directory: comparis.ch
- Medicine & Health Switzerland: doctor.ch
- Swiss Medical Association: doctorfmh.ch

BILLS EXPLAINED

Claudia Jung's health insurance policy has a 300Fr annual <u>deductible</u>. Let's see what she would end up paying after treatments during one calendar year.

Doctors' bills

Dr Müller (family doctor)	1,300
Dr Meier (specialist)	700
Generic medicine	200
Branded medicine	200
Total	**2,400**

Health insurance statement

Medical bills	2,400
minus deductible	-300
Sub-total	2,100
minus 10% of doctors' bills	-170
minus 10% of generic medicine	-20
minus 20% of branded medicine*	-40
Claudia's health insurer pays	**1,870**

* the percentage for branded medicine is 20% if a generic product is available and not taken (unless there is a medical reason).

At some point you may need to use your health insurance and see a doctor. In an emergency you can go straight to a hospital or, in larger towns, to a minor accident clinic near the train station. Otherwise your first stop will be your family doctor, or GP, which means you should register with one as soon as you arrive in Switzerland.

You have free choice of doctors, unless you have a cheaper insurance policy that restricts your choice, and you'll probably have a few to choose from: Switzerland has 4.1 doctors per 1,000 people, well above the EU average. To find a GP, start by asking friends, neighbours, colleagues or other parents at school, or search online via the websites listed in the box. Registering is relatively simple once you have health insurance, as most insurers issue customers with a credit-card-style insurance card that you can use at the doctor's and the pharmacy.

Seeing your GP is usually by appointment only, but waiting times are normally short, with the same day often possible. Many practices also carry out blood tests, minor surgical procedures and even x-rays, as well as fill out prescriptions. Consultations are typically billed per minute, with every test, tablet, plaster and procedure itemised so you know exactly what you're paying for. Some doctors now send bills directly to your insurer (who will in turn charge you for any deductible); if not, then you have 30 days to pay and later reclaim the money from your health insurer.

If necessary, your GP will refer you to a specialist doctor or a hospital department, but be prepared to wait a few weeks for an appointment. If your health insurance allows it (check carefully first) you can go directly to specialists without a referral but you'll still have to wait for an appointment.

House calls are not common, especially at night, so expect to pay a hefty surcharge if you do need one; it will be included under the basic coverage of your health insurance.

TAKE YOUR MEDICINE

The market for medicine in Switzerland is strictly controlled so that, unlike in countries such as the UK or USA, you cannot buy medicines anywhere except pharmacies or from a doctor. That applies to simple items like painkillers, cough mixtures or hay fever remedies as much as to prescription drugs, so you can't get your ibuprofen at the supermarket, newsagent or 'drugstores' like Müller.

Many over-the-counter (OTC) medicines, such as headache pills or flu remedies, can be bought at a pharmacy without seeing a doctor first. Compared to other countries, OTC prices are high, so consider getting them on prescription next time you see your doctor. You can only get drugs requiring a prescription, eg antibiotics, after seeing a doctor, though some surgeries can fill the prescription rather than you having to go to a pharmacy. Expect to pay the full market price, so ask if there's a generic version available as they are cheaper than branded medicines.

MEET YOUR EXPERT

Daniel Dreier is senior editor at moneyland.ch, Switzerland's unbiased online comparison service. Having moved here after decades as part of the Swiss diaspora, he has first-hand experience with the potential mix-ups and rip-offs that newcomers face while finding their way in Switzerland. In addition to interactive telecoms, banking, insurance and credit card comparisons, moneyland.ch also provides a free Q&A service. If you have any questions that are not answered here, just submit them on the forum to get straightforward answers at no cost.

MONEY

Switzerland has been referred to as the land of milk and money. While the lactose-intolerant will find plenty of alternatives to milk, money is something that you will not be able to escape. From the time Google first sniffs out your interest in Switzerland, you will likely be bombarded with advertisements from Swiss insurance companies and credit card issuers. Banks are a steady fixture in the Swiss landscape. Over-insurance is practically the Swiss way of life. From bank-sponsored school materials to insurance-sponsored hiking trails, there are few places in which the business of money is more deeply engrained in everyday life.

Once you learn to ignore the advertising, you can appreciate the facts that make Switzerland a safe bet for your money. GDP per capita is currently more than 50% higher than the average for EU countries, while household savings are more than five times the EU average. Property rights rank among the soundest in the world. The Swiss franc has a long track record of holding its value. In this chapter we help you navigate the key elements of the complex and quirky, yet surprisingly straightforward Swiss personal finance landscape. Learn how living in Switzerland will affect your tax bill, retirement plan, business ambitions, peace of mind, home-purchase plans, and most importantly – your wallet.

THE LOWDOWN
- The Swiss tax system explained
- Understanding pensions and benefits
- Buying property and getting a mortgage

THE SWISS TAX SYSTEM

Swiss government works on a bottom-up basis. The tax system reflects this setup, with most tax laws governed by municipalities and cantons.

Municipal taxes: these are voted on and levied on a municipal level, which means municipalities can easily adapt local taxes to suit their individual needs. For you as a newcomer, it means that the place you choose to live can make or break your taxes' piggy bank. In the most extreme cases, simply moving across the road can significantly reduce your tax bill. Municipalities can levy taxes on income, wealth, inheritance, capital gains, property and much more. In Switzerland, private investors do not pay taxes on stock market capital gains, but dividends are taxable income. Professional investors pay tax on capital gains but can deduct capital losses.

Cantonal taxes: most major tax laws are decided at the cantonal level. Cantonal governments levy taxes on top of municipal taxes and also determine what taxes may be levied by municipalities. So which canton you live in both directly and indirectly determines what you have to pay taxes on and how much you pay. Some cantons allow municipalities to offer flat-rate tax deals in order to 'onboard' high-net-worth taxpayers.

Federal taxes: the federal government levies a personal income tax, called direct federal tax. It applies to all of Switzerland's tax residents. This progressive tax is relatively modest, with an 11.5% rate for the highest tax bracket. The federal government also levies value added tax (standard: 7.7%; hospitality: 3.7%; groceries, medicines, newspapers, books: 2.5%) and customs duties. TV and radio fees – a form of tax for government-sponsored radio and television – are levied countrywide. A 35% withholding tax is applied to interest earnings and refunded based on tax returns.

THE SWISS TAKE

Government in Switzerland is seen as administrative and not authoritative. Tax laws are largely voted on by citizens and taxes have traditionally been seen as voluntary donations to the common good rather than the God-given right of kings. This makes sense from a historical perspective, because Switzerland is one of the only European countries which was never fully ruled by aristocratic governments. Tax evasion is a civil offence rather than a criminal offence. Tax offices are not allowed to inquire into taxpayers' bank accounts unless there is strong evidence of criminal activity. Delinquent taxpayers can declare their delinquency voluntarily and simply pay up the taxes owed without harsh penalties. Late payers are charged penalty interest but do not face legal action. Perhaps surprisingly, this arrangement seems to work very well.

PECULIAR TAXES

Church tax: when you become a resident in Switzerland, you will be asked whether you are a member of one of the officially recognised religious denominations. If you declare yourself a member of a Catholic, Protestant, Jewish or other denomination recognised in your canton, you will be required to pay a church tax. If not, you won't. Even as a Catholic you can choose to opt out but still attend mass. A papal decree states that services cannot be contingent on payment.

Fire brigade tax: this tax is levied in many Swiss cantons. What makes it peculiar is that in some cantons you can avoid paying it by becoming a voluntary firefighter – if you meet the criteria.

YOUR TAX RETURN

The Swiss tax year is based on the calendar year. Your annual income determines income tax liability, and the value of your assets on 31 December determines your taxable wealth for the tax year. You have until 31 March of the following year to submit your tax return (or tax deduction claims if you pay withholding tax, see below). You can often extend that deadline, depending on your canton.

You receive your tax bill after your tax return has been processed. If possible, pay it promptly to avoid paying penalty interest. In many cantons, tax offices send you provisional tax bills based on your estimated income and wealth up to one year ahead of tax season. Some cantons (like Aargau) require you to pay provisional tax bills, while in others (eg Zurich) it is voluntary. Some cantons pay interest on tax advances which can make paying provisional taxes worthwhile (overpaid taxes are refunded).

Temporary residents do not file tax returns. Instead you pay withholding tax which is deducted directly from wages, but you can claim refunds. Exceptions to this rule: you earn more than 120,000 francs per year (500,000 in Geneva); you are married to a Swiss citizen or permanent resident; you own property in Switzerland (you must file returns even if you do not live in Switzerland).

Taxation in Switzerland is based on residence, not nationality. Residents must declare their global income and assets. Switzerland has double taxation agreements with more than 100 countries (including the UK and the US) that help you avoid paying tax twice for the same assets.

WEALTH TAX

Switzerland is one of a few countries where wealth taxes are levied. Cantons and municipalities levy this tax on your personal assets which exceed a threshold (each canton has its own). Swiss wealth taxes are progressive, so wealth is taxed at different rates in tax brackets. All cantons have exemptions, but thresholds vary: wealth taxes in the least favourable cantons (Basel, French-speaking cantons) can be more than five times higher than in the most favourable cantons (Nidwalden, Schwyz). A childless married couple with one million francs of assets could pay anywhere from 1,000 to nearly 7,000 francs per year in wealth tax, depending on where they live.

TAX DEDUCTIONS

Whether you pay withholding tax or submit returns, you can claim tax deductions. There are nearly 100 tax deductions on the federal tax level alone, plus hundreds more cantonal tax deductions. Here are current federal figures for the most broadly-applicable deductions.

Alimony and child support: fully deductible (these count as the recipient's income)

Children: 6,500Fr per child

Childcare: up to 10,100Fr

Commuting: cost of public transportation up to 3,000Fr

Donations: deductions vary between cantons, but as a general rule, tax-free donations cannot exceed 20% of your annual income.

Home maintenance: the costs of maintaining the value of real estate can be deducted. In most cantons, homeowners can choose between a flat deduction (even when no renovations are made) and actual costs.

Home office: if you work from home. Deductions vary between cantons.

Insurance premiums: up to 1,700Fr

Interest charges: interest paid on debt (not including car leasing) can be deducted in full.

Medical expenses not covered by insurance: if they surpass a certain threshold (typically 5% of your income). Threshold varies between cantons.

Professional education: up to 12,000Fr

Voluntary pension fund contributions: fully deductible

Voluntary retirement savings: currently up to 6,826Fr (employed) or 34,128Fr (self-employed) for pillar 3a contributions (see 'Pensions')

Workplace meals: up to 3,200Fr

Work-related expenses: cost of special work clothes or equipment, or use of private car for work up to 4,000Fr

PENSIONS AND BENEFITS

Standard retirement age in Switzerland is still different for men and women, with women being able to claim full pensions at 64 and men at 65. Retirement planning is based on three levels (called pillars), two of which are compulsory.

Pillar 1: or OASI: every adult living in Switzerland has to contribute to this government pension scheme, with contributions based on income. At retirement age you can claim a pension based on your contributions, but never more than the highest possible pension (currently 2,370Fr per month).

Pillar 2: or occupational pension funds. If you are employed with an annual salary over 21,330Fr, you have to join your employer's pension fund. Mandatory contributions are based on the portion of your salary between 24,885 and 85,320Fr, and are paid by you and your employer. You can make voluntary contributions if your salary exceeds this level. Pension funds must pay interest on mandatory benefits (current minimum: 1% per year).

Pillar 3: or voluntary private retirement savings. Pillar 3a savings are tax-privileged, and contributions are tax-deductible up to certain limits (see: 'Your Tax Return'). You can only withdraw pillar 3a savings when you reach standard retirement age (see 'Self-employment' and 'Buying Property' sections below for exceptions). Pillar 3a savings can be invested in retirement accounts, retirement funds or life insurance. You can compare pillar 3a accounts and retirement funds on moneyland.ch and other comparison sites.

The term pillar 3b denotes non-tax-privileged retirement savings. There are no legal limitations on how much you can save or when assets can be cashed out.

PENSION PILLARS

Pillar 1	Pillar 2	Pillar 3a
Old Age and Survivors Insurance	**Occupational Pension Funds**	**Tax-privileged private savings with banks, life insurance, funds and life annuities**
Mandatory contributions for all residents aged 20 (18 if employed) to 64 (women) or 65 (men)	Mandatory contributions for employees with annual salary above 21,330Fr	Voluntary

Contributions		
Unemployed: 482Fr p.a. **Self-employed:** 8.4% of income **Employed:** 4.2% of salary (employer pays remaining 4.2%)	**25 to 34:** 7% of salary **35 to 44:** 10% of salary **45 to 54:** 15% of salary **55 to 64/65:** 20% of salary	Maximum annual contributions: **Employed:** 6,826Fr **Fully self-employed:** 20% of income, max 34,128Fr Limits are subject to change.
Contributions are based on your full salary or income. A minimum annual contribution is required.	Contributions are based on the portion of your salary between 24,885Fr and 85,320Fr	You decide whether you want to contribute and how much.

Taxes		
Contributions are tax-deductible. Pension is taxed as income.	Contributions are tax-deductible. Pension is taxed as income.	Contributions and capital gains are tax-deductible. Assets are taxed upon withdrawal.

Pensions		
You can claim a pension up to 5 years before or (if you remain employed) 5 years after standard retirement age.	You can claim a pension as early as age 55 or (if you remain employed) up to 5 years after standard retirement age.	You can withdraw assets up to 5 years before or (if you remain employed) 5 years after standard retirement age.
Highest possible lifelong annual pension: currently 2,370Fr per month. Low-income residents can claim supplementary OASI benefits.	Lifelong annual pension equal to 6.8% of accrued benefits if you participate in a Swiss pension fund when you reach retirement age. Otherwise cash out.	Lifelong pension only possible with life annuities. Otherwise assets must be cashed out at retirement.

Inheriting		
No inheritance of unused benefits. Eligible dependents can claim a survivor's pension.	Inheritance rules vary between pension funds.	Priority: spouse, children, legal heirs.

LEAVING SWITZERLAND

Pillar 1.

Swiss and EU/EFTA citizens who move outside of the EU or EFTA can voluntarily continue to contribute to the OASI after 5 years of contributing in Switzerland. If your country of citizenship does not have a social security treaty with Switzerland, you can claim a pension if you live in an EU/EFTA country or cash out benefits if you move outside of EU/EFTA . If your country has a social security treaty with Switzerland, you can claim your pension no matter where you live.

Pillar 2.

If you move to a country which is not an EU/EFTA member, you can cash out your pillar 2 benefits and take them with you. If you move to an EU/EFTA country, you can cash out voluntary contributions but compulsory benefits must be transferred to a Swiss vested benefits solution. If you already receive an occupational pension, you continue getting your pension after you move.

Pillar 3.

You can cash out and take pillar 3a assets with you, but this is not obligatory. Pillar 3b plans can be maintained when you leave.

BENEFITS

Compared to other countries, Switzerland seems both generous and stingy with social benefits. Rather than relying on taxpayers, the Swiss system largely relies on insurance schemes to fund employee benefits.

Unemployment insurance: you'll pay a premium equal to 2.2% of the portion of your net salary up to 148,200Fr, and 1% of the portion above that limit – deducted from your salary by your employer. You have to have been employed for at least 12 months in the past 2 years in order to claim benefits. If you become unemployed, you receive a benefit equal to 70% or 80% (with dependents) of your salary below 148,200Fr. Depending on how long you were employed, you can receive benefits for between 90 and 640 days. You can continue making pension contributions (see table on previous page) and the unemployment office pays the half of contributions which would normally be paid by your employer. You also remain covered by accident insurance. The downside of this social unemployment insurance is that there are strict conditions for receiving benefits. You have to be willing to participate in employment programs and accept jobs offered to you even if they are less than ideal. You also have to be resident in Switzerland. In addition, if you lose an employer-sponsored residence permit along with your job, you may have difficulty claiming unemployment benefits. An exception is made if you move to EU/EFTA countries to look for work, in which case you can continue to receive Swiss unemployment benefits for up to 3 months.

Accident insurance: this is mandatory in Switzerland. Swiss employers must provide occupational accident insurance to all employees. If you are employed more than 8 hours per week, you also receive non-occupational accident insurance through your employer. The premiums for the non-occupational accident insurance are typically deducted from your salary. If you have an accident at work or in your free time, this insurance covers medical expenses and loss of income (80% of salary, max. 406Fr per day). If you are not insured by an employer, you have to get accident insurance through your compulsory health insurance (this does not include loss of income coverage).

Paid sick leave: this varies between cantons, with 20 (including Geneva and Bern) having annual paid sick leave entitlements between 3 weeks (first year) and 26 weeks (21st to 40th year). Paid sick leave must be covered by employers, so many employers take out insurance to cover this risk.

For details on maternity and paternity leave see 'Family' chapter. For details on public holidays and paid leave see 'Work' chapter.

SELF-EMPLOYMENT

Becoming your own boss is relatively easy if you live in Switzerland. If you come from an EU/EFTA country and hold a Swiss B or C permit, you can establish any type of company in Switzerland. If you come from another country, you will need a C permit to open certain kinds of companies. You must register for VAT once business revenues hit 100,000Fr or more per year.

The rules and requirements for founding a company in Switzerland depend on the type of company you want to set up.

GmbH/Sàrl: similar to a UK private limited company or a US limited liability company. It must have at least one founder to whom it is directly linked (though liability is limited). You must place 20,000Fr of capital into a capital payment account and enter the company in the canton's commercial register to found a GmbH.

AG/SA: similar to a UK public limited company or a US corporation. You must place 50,000Fr of capital into a capital payment account and enter the company in the commercial register. The company is a legal entity. As its employee you enjoy most employee benefits (executives are generally excluded from unemployment benefits).

Limited partnership: you need a minimum of two partners to found a limited partnership. General partners bear full liability while limited partners bear partial liability. Limited partnerships must be entered into the commercial register.

Simple partnership: you need at least two partners who share full liability. You have no obligation to enter the company into a commercial register or even create a contract to open a simple partnership.

Sole proprietorship: this is the simplest form of company. To open a sole proprietorship, you just need to register your company in your cantonal commercial register. You cover social security premiums in full yourself and do not benefit from unemployment insurance. Creating a sole proprietorship can be beneficial if you become liable to charge VAT (annual turnover of 100,000 francs or more). You bear full liability personally.

ANOBAG

This curious-sounding designation is reserved for people who live in Switzerland but work for non-EU/EFTA employers. If you as a resident work for a foreign employer, you have to register as ANobAG at the social security office. You can use a plan from the Substitute Occupational Benefit Institution to continue building your pillar 2 pension benefits, but you pay the full contributions. As a whole, this setup is a lot less attractive than working for a Swiss employer.

FREELANCING

Switzerland has no special social security status for freelancers. If you earn more than 2,300Fr a year freelancing, you must register as self-employed with the social security office – effectively founding a sole proprietorship. The 2,300Fr social security exemption doesn't apply to artists and people who work in private households. For tax purposes, on the other hand, you have to declare all income. If you pay withholding tax through your employer but earn additional income freelancing on the side, you have to submit tax returns.

When you become self-employed, you can withdraw occupational pension fund and pillar 3a assets (see 'Pensions') if you choose to. You can voluntarily participate in one of the few occupational pension funds which cater to the self-employed (namely the Substitute Occupational Benefit Institution and the pension funds offered by some industry associations). If you do not use an occupational pension fund, you can take advantage of the higher pillar 3a limit for self-employed persons.

THE PROFESSIONALS

Certain professions are regulated in Switzerland, and can only be practised if your qualifications are recognised by the relevant cantonal authority. That medical professions fall under this category goes without saying, but even limo drivers, chimney sweeps and ski trainers have to be recognised as such before they can practise. Specialised professional liability insurance is mandatory for many regulated professions.

INSURANCE

If there was a global prize for risk-aversity, the Swiss might well win gold. Residents are born with two compulsory insurance policies (health insurance and social security). Life insurance for kids is a thing. Insuring unborn children's teeth is not uncommon. There are few limits to what you can insure and how much you can spend on insurance.

Essential: the only voluntary insurance you can't do without is <u>personal liability insurance</u>, which covers your liability for physical or financial injuries to third parties. If you rent a home, this insurance covers the cost of damages you inflict on it. If you cause an accident in which another person is injured for life, this insurance covers your liability for their lifelong loss of income. Most policies cover your dependents as well, which keeps things friendly if your kids scratch a neighbour's car. Priced between 100 and 200 francs per year for between 3 million and 10 million francs of coverage, this insurance is a good deal.

Maybe: <u>personal property insurance</u> (called household insurance locally) is usually bundled with personal liability insurance, but is a lot more expensive. This insurance is only worth getting if you own personal property valuable enough to pay several hundred francs per year to insure. You can add coverage for theft away from home for an extra premium. Be aware that you can get personal liability insurance as a stand-alone policy if you do not need personal property insurance.

    <u>Third-party liability car insurance</u> is mandatory if you use a car, and coverage is legally mandated, but premiums vary between insurers so take time to compare. Fun fact: If you own more than one car or motorcycle but only use one at a time, you can simply take the <u>number plates</u> off one car and put them on the other before driving it. You can even get special easy-access

number plate holders for this purpose. You only pay liability insurance for the more powerful vehicle.

Comprehensive car insurance can be added to mandatory liability car insurance to form what is known as partial casco car insurance. Collision car insurance can be added to this bundle to form full casco car insurance. Comprehensive car insurance is highly recommended due to Switzerland's frequent hailstorms (expect at least one per year) and cable-hungry martens. Collision car insurance is far more expensive and is generally only worth getting for cars up to eight years old.

Major Swiss motor clubs TCS and ACS offer paid memberships which entitle you to roadside assistance. But many Swiss car insurance policies include roadside assistance as a complimentary service. Unless you need two tow-trucks to move your car, only join an auto club if you don't get roadside assistance from your car insurance.

Term life insurance is offered by many Swiss insurance companies. It is relatively cheap and consumer protection laws for policyholders are solid. Exclusions are few (even suicide is covered after a qualification period) and insurance companies must meet stringent financial strength regulations. If you have dependents whom you want to protect financially, term life is an affordable way to do it. You can compare Swiss term life insurance on moneyland.ch or request quotes directly from insurance providers.

Not recommended: if you enter the Swiss pension system later in life or bring retirement savings with you when you come, you will be a prime target for the retirement saving solutions offered by Swiss life insurance providers. Cash value insurance products are offered in pillar 3a and pillar 3b varieties (see 'Pensions'). Permanent life insurance is a big business in Switzerland, but in most cases is not an optimal retirement saving tool.

PROPERTY

You need at least a B permit to buy a primary residence in Switzerland and a C permit to buy a secondary residence (EU/EFTA citizens: B, C or G permit). Swiss real estate has, historically, done a good job as a store of value against inflation. Switzerland also has sound property rights, tight building regulations and well-defined laws governing ownership. Add the excellent infrastructure and beautiful scenery, and it isn't surprising that price tags for both property and all forms of maintenance are (very) high. See 'Homes' chapter for tips on finding property to buy, but remember Switzerland has its own peculiarities:

Location: where you live will determine your building's insurance costs, whether or not your children can inherit your home tax-free, whether or not you pay property taxes and many more factors. Location also determines the risk of natural hazards such as avalanches, flooding, freezing damage, landslides and earthquakes.

Apartments: special rules apply to co-owned buildings. Jointly-owned property is divided into co-ownership stakes which are based on many factors such as the size, accessibility and orientation of apartments. Your co-ownership stake determines what portion of joint expenses you have to cover and how high your imputed rent (see 'Taxes and Fees' section) is, as well as your share of joint income and insurance benefits, if applicable. Walls, floors, balconies and other parts of the actual structure are jointly owned by all co-owners. This means all are jointly responsible for structural maintenance. It also means structural changes need the agreement of all co-owners.

Holiday homes: a popular initiative voted through in 2012 limits the legal number of secondary residences to no more than 20% of total residences in a municipality. Primary vs. secondary ratios for all municipalities are listed on the Federal Office for Spatial Development's website.

Insurance: property insurance against fire and other hazards is mandatory in all but four cantons. Nineteen cantons have compulsory cantonal insurance schemes. Three cantons require insurance but let you choose your own insurance provider. Seventeen cantonal property insurance schemes participate in a joint earthquake insurance pool and Zurich operates its own. However, these pools offer relatively little financial protection, so insurance companies offer stand-alone earthquake insurance. Personal liability insurance (see 'Insurance' section) covers liability to third parties in connection with your primary residence if the building contains no more than three apartments. If you own an apartment, all the building's co-owners should take out joint liability insurance. If you own property other than what is covered by personal liability insurance, getting property owners liability insurance is highly recommended.

Cooperative housing: this provides a possible alternative to buying or renting. You buy shares in a non-profit housing cooperative and in exchange, you pay rent that is well below the market rate.

MORTGAGES

In Switzerland you only have to pay off one third of your home, and can wait on repaying the other two thirds indefinitely as long as you pay interest and meet ongoing affordability requirements. Mortgages are offered by banks, insurance companies and pension funds. Swiss mortgage lenders offer fixed-rate mortgages (one to twenty years), variable-rate mortgages and LIBOR-linked mortgages. The SARON index will replace the LIBOR in 2022. Mortgages are available for new purchases, refinancing and construction/renovation. Reverse mortgages are offered by a handful of Swiss banks. You can compare mortgage guide rates on moneyland.ch and other comparison sites.

It is more difficult to qualify for a mortgage in Switzerland than in many other countries. The following are guidelines and not laws. Exceptions can be made.

Collateral value: Swiss banks use the lower of the price you pay and the estimated market value as per a valuation to determine the collateral value. Valuations are typically based on data alone without physical inspections. Unless you get an exceptionally good deal, expect the estimated market value to be lower than the price you pay.

Down payment: 20% of property's collateral value for a primary residence. Down payments as low as 10% are acceptable as per banking conventions, but few banks offer this outright. Down payments for holiday homes range between 30% to 50% of collateral value. Down payments can be made up of cash, securities, pension fund and pillar 3a assets.

Imputed interest rates: lenders currently use a 5% imputed interest rate to calculate mortgage costs in relation to your income. That is much higher than actual interest rates (currently just over 1% for a 5-year fixed-rate mortgage).

Income: total home and mortgage maintenance costs cannot exceed 33% of your income over the entire life of the mortgage. Holiday homes: Costs cannot exceed 20% of your income.

Insurance: life insurance is not normally a requirement. Buildings insurance is required.

Location: most Swiss lenders only finance properties in Switzerland and in some cases Liechtenstein. It is possible to get or maintain a mortgage for a Swiss property even if you do not live in Switzerland.

Terms: the first third of the property's collateral value must be paid off within 15 years. Generally, half the value of holiday homes must be paid off in that time.

TAXES AND FEES

Aside from federal income tax on imputed rent, the taxes and fees in connection with owning a home vary between cantons.

- **Imputed rent:** nothing portrays the peculiar Swiss take on fairness like imputed rental value. Because renters have to tax the income which they spend on rent, it is deemed to be fair that as a homeowner, a percentage of your property's book value should be added to your annual income for tax purposes. Percentages and rules vary between cantons. In some cantons, the imputed rent is used even when the actual rent you receive from tenants is lower (though this is seldom the case).
- **Inheritance tax:** your spouse or registered partner doesn't pay inheritance tax. Parent-to-child inheritances are taxed in five cantons. Two cantons (Schwyz and Obwalden) do not levy inheritance taxes at all.
- **Notary fee**: one-off fee shared by you and the seller. Varies between cantons. Examples: Zurich (0.1% of property value), Bern (0.5%).
- **Ownership transfer and land registry fees**: one-off fee charged in all cantons but Schwyz.
- **Property capital gains tax**: levied if you make a capital gain when you sell. In Zurich and Zug property capital gains tax is levied by municipalities but not the canton.
- **Property tax**: levied annually by the property's municipality whether or not you live in Switzerland. All but seven cantons levy property tax.
- **Property transfer tax**: one-time tax levied by all but eight cantons. Taxes vary between cantons. Examples: Basel-Landschaft (1.25% each for buyer and seller), Bern (1.8%).
- **Wealth tax**: the property's taxable value minus mortgage debt counts as personal wealth for annual wealth tax purposes.

DOWN PAYMENT

You can withdraw pillar 2 and pillar 3a assets (see 'Pensions') to buy a primary residence as often as every 5 years. This includes a primary residence co-owned by you and your spouse and/or located outside of Switzerland. You cannot use these to buy secondary residences. Assets become taxable upon withdrawal. Both pension funds and pillar 3a assets can be pledged as collateral against loans rather than withdrawn. Pledging assets lets you take advantage of tax deductions for retirement savings and interest charges (see 'Your Tax Return' section), and helps you avoid withdrawing assets and paying tax on them.

- Pillar 2: up to 90% of your down payment can be covered by your pension fund benefits. The minimum withdrawal is 20,000Fr. Only half of benefits accumulated from age 50 can be withdrawn. You must return benefits if you sell your home and don't buy another within 2 years. You can claim a tax refund if you make voluntary repayments to top up your pension fund.
- Pillar 3a: no additional limitations.

HAZARDS

Leaseholds are common in Switzerland and give you ownership of the building, but not the land under it, for which you have to pay rent (and rents can increase over time). Listed buildings are another potential hazard. The approximately 75,000 historically listed buildings in Switzerland might have a lot of charm, but come with many restrictions and obligations. I would only recommend buying one if you have deep pockets and love paperwork.

BANKING

A very liberal approach has helped make Switzerland a global financial hub. Around 250 banks operate in Switzerland, but only five of these have branches nationwide. Bank deposits are guaranteed by the Esisuisse depositor protection scheme up to 100,000Fr per customer and bank, up to a cap of 6 billion francs. Most Swiss banks require you to visit a branch in person to open an account, but some (like UBS and Bank Cler) now let you identify yourself via video chat to open accounts remotely. All Swiss banks offer standing orders, direct debits and transfers. Many Swiss banks do not charge fees for international transfers within the Single Euro Payments Area (SEPA). Some Swiss banks charge a fee when you withdraw money at ATMs operated by other banks. Note: many Swiss banks and life insurance companies tend to avoid doing business with US citizens because of the added administration demanded by the U.S. Foreign Account Tax Compliance Act (FATCA).

With a few exceptions, the 24 cantonal banks offer the most affordable private accounts (current accounts). Fully app-based accounts with no monthly account fees (namely Neon and Bank Cler's Zak account) have appeared in recent years. These provide very good value for transactions within Switzerland. The downsides are: international transfers are generally limited to SEPA countries; the amounts you can transfer or withdraw per day or week are limited.

Each bank has its own fee schedule. Using the account with the lowest fees can save you hundreds of francs in fees per year. moneyland.ch currently offers the only interactive online Swiss private account comparison which lets you compare costs based on your specific needs.

GOOD TO KNOW

Deposit slips are being updated. The new slips will be introduced in 2020.

PAYMENT METHODS

The popular expression *nur Bares ist Wahres* translates into something like 'only the physical is real' and indicates the attitude of many Swiss towards money. Recent surveys show that cash is the payment method which Swiss are least willing to forego. Nearly 87 billion Swiss francs in cash (around 10,000Fr per resident) is in circulation. You can settle payments up to 100,000Fr in cash without hassle and take any amount of money in or out without customs declarations. Accepting physical Swiss francs as payment is required by law. But that doesn't mean the Swiss haven't embraced other ways to pay.

Cheques: these were never popular in Switzerland and have only become less popular over time. Instant mobile transfers between customers are offered by most major banks.

Credit cards: most Swiss credit cards have annual fees, but there is little reason to pay for a credit card. No-annual-fee cards like the Cashback American Express from Swisscard, the Coop Supercard credit card and the Migros Cumulus Mastercard have strong reward programs and offer excellent value. Almost all Swiss credit cards have foreign transaction fees so using them abroad is best avoided. Low-cost international payment cards (like Transferwise and Revolut) are available in Switzerland and provide a cheaper alternative for international payments.

Cryptocurrency: Switzerland has become a blockchain hub in recent years, and popular cryptocurrencies can be purchased at ATMs in major cities. The municipality of Zug was the first government to accept payments in bitcoin, and bitcoin can actually be used to pay at some restaurants and shops.

Deposit slips: another distinctly Swiss financial trait is a strong love for deposit slips. Even Swiss online businesses offer this form of billing in addition to credit cards and e-billing simply because it is so popular. Many Swiss banks now include deposit slip scanning in their banking apps.

Digital wallets: giants like Apple Pay, Google Pay and Samsung Pay and homegrown alternatives like Swatch Pay and Twint can be used at many locations. Alipay is accepted but not available locally.

International transfers: I recommend using monito.ch to compare the costs of Swiss money transfer services based on your specific needs.

MEET YOUR EXPERT

Nicolas Mossaz is a partner at Ochsner & Associés, a well-established Geneva law firm. He has developed a specific area of expertise helping expatriates and foreign companies in Switzerland. He is the founder of the information hub Legal Expat (www.legalexpatgeneva.com). Nicolas has extensive experience representing clients in front of Swiss civil courts. He advises Swiss and international clients mainly in complex family law disputes, employment litigation and cross-border litigation.

LAWS

The Swiss legal system falls into the category of civil law, as opposed to common law. This means that Swiss law is very largely codified. Legal matters are integrated in several levels of competence divided between the Confederation, the cantons and the municipalities. Each canton has its own courts of first instance in its jurisdiction. The Federal Supreme Court is the highest legal authority in Switzerland, and the court of last instance on the cases submitted. It ensures the uniform application of federal legislation, while ensuring the protection of the constitutional rights of citizens.

In this chapter, after briefly reviewing Swiss judicial institutions and how they function, we focus on a few legal topics we believe to be relevant to foreigners to Switzerland.

While Switzerland's codified legal system presents some challenges, in general you can expect to be treated fairly and without the excessive waiting periods common in other countries. Swiss society is not especially litigious and you'll find that most disputes are settled outside of the courts. There are bureaucratic hurdles, as everywhere, but you can expect to complete basic legal matters without undue cost or frustration.

THE LOWDOWN
- Understand Switzerland's unique legal system
- Learn how to avoid legal trouble – and get out of it if the worst does happen
- Get acquainted with basic family law: marriage, divorce, adoption and inheritance

LEGAL SYSTEM

The Swiss political system is based on the separation of powers, namely independence between the judiciary, the executive and the legislature. The Swiss Supreme Court embodies the judiciary power, alongside the Federal Assembly (legislative power) and the Federal Council (executive power).

There are three normative levels in Switzerland: federal, cantonal and municipal. Federal law takes precedence over cantonal and municipal acts. This principle is known as the 'derogatory force of federal law'. It is the Swiss constitution that defines the competences of the Confederation, leaving to the cantons sovereignty in areas that are not governed by federal law. Federal law frequently sets minimum rules, leaving to the cantons the task of regulating a particular subject in accordance with the established framework.

Except for some areas such as military or international relations, the Confederation does not apply or execute federal laws directly. Thus, cantons are responsible for the implementation of federal law; this principle is called 'executive federalism'.

The Federal Supreme Court is the supreme judicial authority, ensuring the uniform application of federal law within Switzerland as well as the conformity of cantonal law with federal law.

SWISS CONSTITUTION

The current Federal Constitution is a revised version of the 1848 constitution, which gave birth to the Swiss Federal State. It was inspired by the US constitution and the ideas of the French Revolution. The constitution sets the principle of subsidiarity, in which the cantons are sovereign as long as their sovereignty is not expressly limited by the constitution.

At the top of the Swiss legal order, the constitution takes precedence over all other legislative acts (eg laws, ordinances, etc.) of the Confederation, the cantons and the municipalities. It guarantees the fundamental rights of citizens, such as the protection of private and family life, religious freedom and property rights.

As Switzerland is a member state of the European Convention on Human Rights, the fundamental rights of the Swiss constitution are interpreted in line with the case law of the European Court of Human Rights. Unlike other foreign constitutions (eg the US constitution), the Swiss constitution is regularly amended by the Swiss people through popular initiatives. Since 1891, Swiss citizens have voted on 216 initiatives but only accepted 22 amendments.

INDEPENDENT JUDGES?

While in some countries judges cannot be members of a political party, the opposite situation applies in Switzerland: judges here usually are members of a political party. This is due to the fact that in Switzerland, parliament usually elects judges, and so political parties divide the posts between them according to their political strength. The idea behind this is that different opinions should democratically influence the way the law is interpreted. However, this raises the question of judges' independence, especially knowing that judges are required to divert part of their income to their affiliated party.

COURT SYSTEM

The cantons oversee cantonal courts, meaning that the court system is characterised by marked variety. Decisions of these courts may, under certain conditions, be appealed to the Federal Supreme Court, which is based in Lausanne (with two social security divisions in Lucerne).

The role of the Federal Supreme Court is to ensure the uniform application of federal law throughout the country and a protection of citizens' constitutional rights. As a general principle, the facts of the case cannot be reviewed unless they are patently false or are based on infringement of federal law. According to statistics for 2017, only one out of every eight appeals wasadmitted by the Federal Supreme Court.

SWISS LEGAL TROUBLES

If you find yourself in legal trouble, you'll most likely need legal advice. A distinction is drawn between lawyers, who are registered in a cantonal register, and other professionals, such as legal agents, professional representatives and licensed representatives. Only lawyers can represent parties in all legal proceedings, while other professionals may, under certain conditions, assist clients in some specific cases.

In Switzerland, many associations aim to defend the rights of their members. For instance, the tenants' association provides guidance about tenancy law, while consumers' associations strive to protect consumers' rights. These associations provide free individual legal advice for their members but a small membership fee is sometimes required.

Should you need a lawyer, the websites of the bar associations in each canton will give you details of specialised lawyers in each field. Most of the cantonal bar associations have legal consultation desks, where lawyers provide initial legal advice at a reduced rate. As legal fees can quickly rise to significant amounts, it might be useful to obtain legal insurance, which covers legal fees in case of litigation.

The best approach is always to ask your lawyer directly about their hourly charges and other fees you will be expected to pay. These are largely calculated based on the complexity of the case and on the litigation value, combined with necessary expenses. A client who cannot afford legal fees can benefit from free legal aid, if their case requires legal representation and if at first glance it seems likely to succeed in court.

Domestic workers: if you wish to hire a nanny or other house workers (eg cleaning staff or a cook), make sure you respect the standard employment contract for domestic workers (see 'Collective employment agreement' at ch.ch), which applies even if the parties are not aware of it. It sets mandatory rules regarding employment, such as a minimum wage, social security contributions, overtime and the termination period.

Debt recovery: under Swiss law, if a person or business believes another person owes them money, there are two ways they can attempt to recover these funds. They can either file a request for conciliation in civil court, or start debt enforcement proceedings.

A conciliation request is filed through the Federal Department of Justice, with the names of the creditor and debtor, plus the reason for filing the request (grounds for payment). The creditor pays an advance on judiciary fees before a conciliatory hearing is held with the aim of finding a compromise. If no compromise can be found, the creditor can move on to civil proceedings and be granted a judgement on the merits.

But creditors can also submit a request for debt enforcement, provided that the debtor lives in Switzerland. Without verifying the existence or rectitude of the debt, the cantonal Debt Enforcement office will issue a payment summons to the alleged debtor. Upon notification, the debtor has to pay the claimed amount within 20 days or oppose the debt obligation within 10 days. No specific reasons have to be mentioned, and some safeguards exist if it was not possible to react in the time allotted. It's important to underline that the debt enforcement office doesn't act ex-officio; the burden to react is on the creditor's shoulders at every step of the procedure.

MINIMUM WAGE

In Switzerland, the principle of contractual freedom also governs wages. Though there is no federally mandated minimum wage, it is sometimes fixed by collective agreements governing specific professional fields, such as domestic workers. For example, in Geneva, it is currently 19.51Fr per hour for non-qualified domestic workers, while in all other cantons, the amount is of 18.90Fr. Salary paid in kind (such as accommodation or meals) might be deducted. If the worker is paid on an hourly basis, a fee of 8.33% for vacation compensation must be added.

The rules can be bewildering, and several private companies can help you correctly hire and insure domestic workers (eg Chèque Service or quitt.ch). Be warned that some cantons investigate domestic workers' employment conditions. Non-compliance with the minimum wage might result in an administrative penalty and/or a criminal fine.

UNIQUELY SWISS

The Swiss are reputed to be very respectful of their laws; some laws, however, may surprise foreigners. Here are some of the best examples.

Animal welfare: many Swiss are very concerned about animal welfare and regularly try to amend the Federal Constitution in that regard. For example, sociable species may not be kept alone. Thus, species such as guinea pigs, goldfish and parrots must be bought in pairs. Take note that it is forbidden to shorten the tails of dogs, to catch fish with the intention of releasing them back into the water, or to transport live fish on ice.

Traffic laws: be aware of the traffic laws or you might be heavily fined! Drivers must always remain in control of their vehicle, and the authorities have wide authority to interpret what behaviour is considered careless. For instance, it is forbidden to eat while driving. In 2012 a Swiss woman eating a pretzel while driving was arrested and fined 250Fr. If you get a bit peckish, you'd better stop your car… and pay for your parking. A man in Aargau stopped his car in a parking space in order to eat an apple, and had to pay a 40Fr fine for not having paid for parking. As for traffic lights, not only should you pay attention to red ones but to green ones as well: in Geneva, the police fined a man 250Fr because he did not start quickly enough at a green light, causing a traffic jam.

Dress or be fined: Swiss people are known to be rather modest people. They do not necessarily appreciate being visually confronted by situations they have not experienced before, such as naked hikers. This is so true that citizens of Appenzell Innerrhoden voted in 2009 to ban nude hiking in public, and established fines to punish it. In a decision following this vote, the Federal Supreme Court ruled that the ban was not unconstitutional, saying that naked hiking in public could be considered a gross breach of decency and convention.

Neighbourhood laws: the peace and quiet of the Swiss are not to be disturbed. Article 257f of the Swiss Code of Obligations expressly states that residents must show due consideration for others who share the building – and for neighbours. More generally, residents must behave in relation to the rented house and neighbours as good 'parents', and even ensure the good reputation of the building.

Urban myths: the often-quoted 'ban' on flushing the toilet after 10pm is an urban myth. Similarly, though widely cited, cafés and restaurants have no obligation to provide a free glass of tap water.

LOVE AND
MARRIAGE

To get married under Swiss law, spouses must be of different sex, older than 18, and must have the legal right to stay in Switzerland until the date of the marriage.

Swiss residents will need to submit a marriage preparation application form to the civil registry in the municipality of residence of either person, along with legal birth certificates and documents certifying the end of any previous marriages. Once approved, the civil ceremony must take place within three months (but no sooner than 10 days), and must precede any religious ceremony. You can hold the ceremony in the municipality of your choosing, and you'll need two witnesses.

Non-EU citizens who are not already Swiss residents will need a D visa (also called the National visa, a type of visa valid for stays of longer than 90 days) from the Swiss consulate of their country of residence before entering Switzerland. Once the marriage is completed, the foreign spouse can apply for a B permit, provided the spouses live under the same roof.

EQUAL MARRIAGE?

Same-sex marriage is not allowed in Switzerland (See Gay and Lesbian chapter). However, registered partnership is possible and the same registration procedures as for a marriage apply, though no witnesses are required to establish a registered partnership. A same-sex marriage established overseas is recognised under Swiss law as a registered partnership.

ADOPTION

Cantonal authorities will examine the future parents' motivation, health, financial situation and capacity to provide for the child before delivering the authorisation for any adoption (see 'Family' chapter for registering a birth). In addition, the biological parents must agree to the adoption, and even after agreeing have six weeks to change their mind.

Most adoption cases take place overseas. The adoption procedure can take up to four years with no guarantee of success. The Federal Central Authority acts as the intermediary between the foreign country and Swiss authorities. Overseas adoptions must comply with the Hague Convention.

A married couple can jointly adopt only if they are at least 28 years of age and have been living together for at least three years (though exceptions can be made). Likewise, a single person over 28 is eligible to adopt. Only in rare cases can a married person (or one in a civil partnership) adopt on their own. However, registered partners and spouses can now adopt their partner's children if the couple has lived together for at least three years. Generally, those adopting must be at least 16 and no more than 45 years older than the child.

Once the authorisation is obtained from both Switzerland and the child's home country, the child is eligible for a visa to enter Switzerland. Children adopted by a Swiss parent can apply for a Swiss passport; others will receive the same residency permit as their parents.

Every adopted child has the right to obtain information about their biological parents' identity once they turn 18.

DIVORCE

There are three ways of getting a divorce in Switzerland.

- **By joint request with a comprehensive agreement**: the spouses jointly request a divorce and submit a joint comprehensive agreement.
- **By joint request with a partial agreement**: the spouses jointly request divorce and ask the court to decide matters on which they cannot reach an agreement.
- **At the petition of one spouse after having lived apart**: a spouse may petition for divorce if, at the time the petition is filed, the spouses have lived apart for at least two years.

It is not mandatory to remain in Switzerland during the complete procedure, but judges will insist on seeing each spouse at least once.

DIVISION OF ASSETS

In Switzerland, there are three matrimonial regimes: (a) participation in acquired property, (b) community of property and (c) separation of assets. Provided that no previously-signed marital agreement or property regime stipulates otherwise, spouses are subject to the provisions governing participation in acquired property.

According to the participation in acquired property regime, the assets owned by the parties before getting married or received during the marriage as an inheritance or gift are excluded, while all other assets acquired by the spouses during the marriage are regarded as "acquired property" and are to be divided in half.

Finally, regardless of the matrimonial regime chosen by the spouses, 2nd Pillar pensions are equally split between spouses, to ensure that each party receives retirement benefits post-divorce.

SPOUSAL MAINTENANCE

The underlying principle in Swiss divorce law is that after a divorce, each spouse should provide for themselves (the "clean-break principle"). However, if a spouse cannot reasonably be expected to provide for his or her own maintenance, including an appropriate level of retirement provision, the other spouse must pay a suitable contribution.

In deciding whether such a contribution is to be made and, if so, how much and for how long, various factors are considered by the judge, such as the duration of the marriage, the standard of living during the marriage, the age and health of the spouses, the income and assets of the spouses and the possibility for a spouse to reintegrate into working life.

CHILD CUSTODY

As of 2014, joint parental authority became the norm in Switzerland. This means, that even in case of a divorce, both parents will, in principle, continue to exercise parental authority, which includes the power to make important decisions on behalf of the children (eg place of residence, choice of school).

Should the parties disagree regarding custody, the judge will have to decide in favour of the child's wellbeing. Starting in 2017, it became mandatory for the judge to consider whether alternating custody would best serve the interests of the child, though judges will take into account parents' history and potential for cooperation as well as the child's own wishes.

The legal consequences of custody arrangements are diverse. The maintenance allowance depends on parents' respective capacities. The child also has the right to benefit from the 'same lifestyle' as the parents. If divorcing parents can't find an agreement on the level of the allowances, the divorce court will determine one based on several criteria such as the child's needs, the income and net wealth of the parents, the child's own net wealth (if any) and the degree of custody allotted to each parent.

INHERITANCE

If you die while living in Switzerland, Swiss judicial authorities have jurisdiction over your estate and any related disputes, though this won't necessarily override jurisdiction claimed by the countries where your property is located.

Upon death, the estate of the deceased passes to the heirs in its entirety. This means that the deceased's claims, rights and even debts pass to the heirs. The legal and named heirs are entitled to refuse the inheritance within three months. Taxation of inheritance is not governed by federal law but rather at the cantonal level, meaning that taxation varies from canton to canton.

In the absence of a will, estates pass to the direct descendants (eg children, including adopted children), shared equally with a surviving spouse or registered partner. If there is no spouse or children, other descendants inherit. If the deceased left no progeny, the heirs are the direct ascendants (eg the parents). If none of them survive, more distant relatives inherit, and if no relatives at all exist, the entire estate goes to the canton or the municipality.

WILLS

Under Swiss law, testators have the opportunity to make their own arrangements concerning the distribution of their assets, in whole or in part, but this is subject to statutory restrictions. These restrictions stipulate that certain relatives cannot be entirely disinherited even through a will. This means that any family member with a claim to inherit is entitled to at least a certain fraction of the estate (three-quarters children inherit, one half for parents, surviving spouse or registered partner). A person who is not survived by any such heirs may dispose of his or her entire property by testamentary disposition.

A will can be kept at home, held by a third party or registered at the Swiss Wills Register. A will can be established in three different forms:
- drawn up and certified by a public notary
- holographic wills. These are handwritten wills and, in order to be valid, they must be dated and signed.
- oral wills in cases of emergency

Testators may nominate an executor. The executor is tasked with administering the estate, collecting debts due to the deceased, paying the debts of the estate and ultimately distributing the estate. The executor must have an independent position with regard to the heirs, and may take any decision necessary to fulfil their mandate. Appointing an executor may be a wise decision, especially when the estate is disputed, or the beneficiaries live in other countries, or simply because of the complexity of the estate.

CHILDREN?

In case of shared custody, if one of the parents dies while the child is a minor (or if the child is disabled), the surviving parent assumes sole custody. However, the surviving parent will have to disclose certain information to the Child Protection Services in order to ensure preservation of the child's interests. In case of death of both parents (or of the parent who exercised sole custody), the same authority will decide who shall assume custody of the child. There is no way to automatically designate who your child should live with in the case of your death, though Child Protection Services will take deceased parents' wishes into account in their overall assessment of what is best for the child's wellbeing.

REGISTERING A DEATH

A death has to be declared to the Registry Office in the municipality in which it has occurred. In practice, hospitals register most deaths, but in cases of death outside a hospital, the next of kin should report the death within two days, providing ID of the deceased as well as a death certificate. There is no cost to register a death.

RIGHTS
AT WORK

In general, employers (and employees) are free to terminate a permanent contract without having to give any particular reason and without respecting any formal requirement. The legal notice period is governed by the length of employment (see box), unless good cause is shown. Fixed-term employment contracts end on the fixed date, unless the contract provides for an early termination or good cause can be proved. Contracts renewed to form a 'chain of contracts' aren't allowed if their intention is to elude the protections associated with a permanent contract.

NOTICE PERIODS

Unless the employment contract provides otherwise, the following notice periods apply.
- Seven calendar days during the trial period
- One month during the first year of employment
- Two months from the second to the ninth year of employment
- Three months from the tenth year of employment

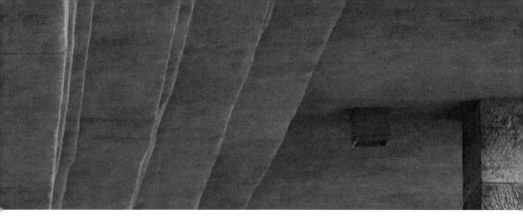

Non-compete: non-compete clauses are valid under Swiss law, provided that they meet the legal requirements: they must be in writing, the employee must have gained knowledge of the employer's clientele or trade secrets, and the use of such knowledge must be able to cause substantial harm. Non-compete clauses can be voided by a judge in some cases, and may exceed three years only in special circumstances.

Bonus: bonuses can be considered as true bonuses or as part of the employee's salary. The difference affects the employee's right to claim the bonus: an employer must pay a salary but enjoys complete latitude in paying true bonuses. Whether the bonus is mandatory or optional depends on many criteria: the existence of an agreement between the parties, the number of years a bonus was awarded, the the size of the bonus in relation to the fixed salary, and the total salary, among other factors.

Equal rights: according to the Federal Constitution, every person is equal under the law. Discrimination is not allowed on biological grounds (eg race, gender, age or disabilities) or cultural ones (eg national origin, language, class, religion, beliefs). However, the anti-racist criminal provision prohibits specific acts publicly made and directed against an individual or group of people on the grounds of their race, ethnicity or religion. See Gay and Lesbian chapter for a discussion of LGBT rights.

Gender equality: the Gender Equality Act ensures gender equality at work, protecting men and women against discrimination from the application process through to the termination of the contract, though it only covers the employer-employee relationship.

Beyond reporting any discrimination or harassment, you may a legal prohibition, injunction or declaration regarding the discrimination. Lost wages can be recovered in cases of wage discrimination. In addition, you may be granted three months' salary if you can show you did not receive a position due to discriminatory practices. Six months' salary is due in cases of discriminatory termination, and the same is also due when it comes to sexual harassment (in addition to any other damages you may be awarded). You only have to show a 'simple likelihood' of discrimination to be awarded damages, though in cases of discrimination in hiring or of sexual harassment, the burden of proof is higher. The act also protects employees against retaliatory firing in relation to any discrimination complaints.

MEET YOUR EXPERT

Diccon Bewes is a British travel writer and author of five books on Switzerland, including the number one bestseller, *Swiss Watching*. He arrived back in 2005 and fell in love with Switzerland and its people (and chocolate) so started writing about his life here. In doing so, he became an accidental expat expert and regularly speaks about the joys and trials of living in Switzerland. You can follow him via his website dicconbewes.com, on Twitter (@dicconb) or on Facebook (facebook.com/ SwissWatching).

12

TRADITION

Switzerland might be small but it has enough traditions and festivals to more than compensate for its size. Folk heroes like William Tell are famous far beyond the borders, as are the sounds of the alphorn and yodelling, but there's so much more to Swiss traditions than that. Almost every town has its own way of marking the passage of the seasons, very often involving scary flames or even scarier costumes, so we've picked some of the best festivals around the country.

It's quite normal to see people wearing traditional dress on high days and holidays, with each region having its own variations for men and women – for example, elaborate headdresses on Mother's Day or Sunday best for a yodelling competition. This isn't for show but simply part of everyday life, especially in rural areas.

Many aspects of traditional Swiss life have become popular with tourists, such as the annual descent of the cows from the mountains, but essentially none of the costumes or celebrations is there for Instagram. All have been facts of life for centuries, which makes them even more memorable to see in person.

THE LOWDOWN
- Where to find William Tell and Heidi
- How to play Jass, the national card game
- A calendar of the best festivals

FOLK HEROES

William Tell did not exist. That might come as a shock given how much the burly beardy man features on beer cans and book covers, stamps and statues. But the great Swiss hero is a figment of the national imagination, created to personify the resistance to tyranny. The story of Tell standing up to the Habsburgs became a play (written by a German, Schiller), an opera (written by an Italian, Rossini) and a foundation stone of Swiss national identity.

Arnold von Winkelried isn't a name too well-known outside Switzerland but he's a folk hero who died to save the nation – except that it's unlikely he ever lived either. At the Battle of Sempach in 1386 the Swiss couldn't break through the Austrian lines until Arnie (allegedly) threw himself on the enemy's pikes, resulting in a crucial Swiss victory.

Equally fictitious are the two national heroines, Heidi and Helvetia. The former was created by Johanna Spyri in a book first published in 1880, and this spirited little girl became an instant hit. She remains the archetypal Swiss miss fighting for what she loves, and is also used to sell anything from dairy products to the country itself.

Helvetia is all woman. She stands regally on Swiss coins, shield and spear in hand to defend her land. Of course, she isn't real and first appeared only in the 17th century. As for the man on the five-franc coin, he's not Tell but a generic Swiss shepherd.

THE SWISS SAINT

One hero who was real is St Nicholas von Flüe, also known as Brother Klaus. Born in 1417, he was a soldier, a judge and a father of ten before retreating from modern life to become a hermit. His wise counsel prevented a Swiss civil war in 1481, and he is venerated as the patron saint of Switzerland.

MEETING HEIDI

For anyone wanting to undertake a Heidi pilgrimage, there are three important stops – one where the book is set and two relating to the author:

Heididorf: the full-on Heidi experience near Maienfeld in Graubünden, with the house where Heidi 'lived' and other suitably rustic attractions.

Hirzel: village above Lake Zurich where Johanna Spyri grew up, and where the excellent little Spyri Museum shows the story of her life.

Zurich: Spyri lived at Zeltweg 9 until her death and is buried in a simple grave in Sihlfeld cemetery.

FINDING WILLIAM

The Tell legend is set in the heart of Switzerland. In case you've never heard it, here's his tale in brief: Gessler, the Austrian bailiff in Altdorf, sticks his hat on a pole and forces the locals to bow to it. Our hero refuses, and has to shoot an apple off his son's head as a penalty. Tell succeeds, of course, but if he had failed, he had a second arrow ready for Gessler. He's arrested and taken to prison by boat, but a storm on Lake Lucerne helps him escape, chase Gessler, and kill him. You can visit various places associated with the legend.

- **Altdorf:** scene of the apple-shooting incident and now site of the most-photographed statue of William and son Walter
- **Bürglen:** the tiny village in Uri was Tell's birthplace, so it naturally has a Tell Museum to tell the story.
- **Hohle Gasse:** a lane near Küssnacht where Tell killed Gessler with his second arrow
- **Interlaken:** definitely not part of the tale but home to the annual Tell Play, an open-air extravaganza with a cast of hundreds (including cows and horses)
- **Rütli meadow:** traditional birthplace of the nation and not actually part of the Tell story, though it's often mistakenly included.
- **Tell Chapel:** the spot alongside Lake Lucerne where Tell leapt from the boat taking him to prison, and escaped

FUN AND GAMES

That the Swiss excel at skiing, cycling and tennis won't come as a surprise to anyone who watches the Olympics, but Swiss traditional sports rarely get reported in the outside world. This is probably because almost no one else plays them, or understands them. Here are the main ones to watch out for.

Swiss wrestling: although it takes place outdoors in a sawdust ring, and in all weathers, Swiss wrestling is absurdly popular in the German-speaking regions. The wrestlers, or Schwingers, are nearly always big men (though some women do compete) who are farmers or truck drivers in the real world. They wrestle in normal clothes but with a huge hessian nappy over their trousers.

Stone throwing: shot-putting on a different scale. Instead of throwing a small ball, the challenge is to hurl a giant stone weighing either 20kg, 40kg or an enormous 83.5kg. That last is a special stone (called the Unspunnen Stone) that has been thrown competitively since 1808; the record is 4.11 metres. Stone throwing is not for the faint-hearted or weak-limbed.

Hornussen: possibly the most traditional Swiss sport, this weird mix of cricket and golf is played with teams of 16–18 people. One side launches a small puck into the air at speeds of up to 300km/h while the other team tries to knock it down with giant wooden paddles. A Hornussen playing field is 200 metres long and up to 15 metres wide, so it's not really a sport for the back garden.

SWISS OLYMPICS

Every three years there's a traditional Swiss version of the Olympics, with wrestling the main attraction and the victor being crowned king, winning a prize bull for his efforts. Stone throwing, yodelling, alphorn blowing and flag twirling are all thrown into the mix. The next festival, known as the *Eidgenössisches Schwing- und Älplerfest*, is in August 2022 in Pratteln (BL), with 300,000 spectators expected (esaf2022.ch).

JASS

One national obsession is the card game Jass (pronounced yass), which is similar to bridge or partner whist. It's played everywhere by almost everyone, and even has its own TV show. In the German-speaking part special Jass cards are used (with four suits: acorns, bells, roses and shields), while the rest of the country plays with a deck of regular suits. Both have no cards below the number six. Here are the basic rules.

- You play in pairs, always in an anti-clockwise direction.
- Each player gets nine cards.
- Aces are high, and worth 11 points, followed by the king (4 points), queen (3), jack (2) and ten (10 points). The cards nine down to six are all worth zero.
- For each hand, one suit is chosen as trumps, with the jack of trumps the highest card in the deck (20 points), followed illogically by the nine (known as the Nell and worth 14 points) and then the other trumps in the normal order.
- Tricks are won by the highest card played (trumps always beat other suits) and the value of the trick is equal to the total points of all four cards.
- Trumps can be played at any time, not only when you can't follow suit.
- You get extra points if your hand has a meld (three or more cards of the same suit), match (four identical cards) or marriage (king and queen of trumps).
- Variations include hands with no trumps, known as tops-down (where aces remain high) or bottoms-up (where sixes are high).

A YEAR OF FESTIVALS

Spring begins with the riotous colour of carnival, probably the only occasion the Swiss truly let their hair down. The biggest is in Basel, where it's a three-day holiday, starting with the pre-dawn ceremony on the Monday after Ash Wednesday. Many other towns celebrate in style, including Lucerne, Bern, Sion and Bellinzona.

Summer is a time to relax and enjoy the lakes and mountains, so there are fewer festivals. But there is one big public holiday: 1 August, or Swiss National Day, which is marked by barbecues and fireworks.

Autumn hosts the most famous of Swiss traditions, the return of the cows from the mountains. In many villages this is cause for celebration, with flower-bedecked cows being herded home to applauding crowds. This alpine descent of the cows can be found all over the country but popular ones are in Charmey (FR) and Schüpfheim (LU).

Winter sees all manner of weird and wonderful events, mostly aimed at warding off evil spirits or celebrating the turn of the year. Wrap up warm and enjoy the spectacles of fire, ice and some really freaky costumes.

FESTIVAL CALENDAR

January

Silvesterchlausen Urnäsch (AR)	Masked men in elaborate costumes celebrate the old New Year's Eve (pictured)
Epiphany Nationwide	The feast of the Three Kings is marked with a special cake, made for sharing
Vogel Gryff Basel	A griffin, a lion and a wildman of the woods dance through Klein Basel

Carnival time (February–March)

Hom Strom Scuol (GR)	Burning a giant straw man on the first Saturday in February to bring good harvests
Chienbäse Liestal (BL)	Procession of flaming carriages and torches through the old town (pictured)
Fasnacht Lucerne	The largest Catholic carnival begins on *schmutziger Donnerstag* just before Lent
Fasnacht Basel	The 'three most beautiful days', starting with *Morgestraich* at 4am Monday morning (pictured)

Tschäggättä Lötschental (VS)	Huge hairy beasts with scary carved faces roam around the villages
Chalandamarz Graubünden	Small children ring giant cowbells to scare away the evil spirits of winter (pictured)

Easter

Les Pleureuses Romont (FR)	20 wailing women veiled in black mark the Crucifixion of Christ on Good Friday (pictured)
Le Surrexit Estavayer-le-Lac (FR)	50 singing men walk through town at midnight to greet the start of Easter Sunday

April

Eierläset Cantons Aargau, Basel-Landschaft and Solothurn	Many villages hold egg races between two teams: one for winter, one for spring
Sechseläuten Zurich	The start of spring with the burning of the *Böögg*, or giant snowman (pictured)

May–June

Combat de Reines Aproz (VS)	Final of the Hérens cow fighting competition to decide the 'queen of queens' (pictured)
Maibär Bad Ragaz (SG)	The end of winter with a giant flower-and-foliage 'bear' sacrificed for spring
Herrgottstag Düdingen (FR) & Appenzell	Procession with military guards and women in elaborate dresses for Corpus Christi

July–August

Alphorn Festival Nendaz (VS)	Annual competition with over 100 players and folklore festivities on the side (pictured)
Swiss National Day Nationwide	Grilling *cervelats* speared onto sticks and watching the fireworks
Marché-Concours Saignelégier (JU)	Equine extravaganza with Freiberger horses and a grand procession

Chästeilet Various alpine villages	The division of the summer's cheese between the dairy farmers (pictured)	
Fête des vendanges Neuchâtel	Costumes, bands and parades to celebrate the successful wine harvest	
Knabenschiessen Zurich	Shooting competition for teenagers and a funfair for everyone	

September–October

Alpabfahrt/désalpe Various alpine villages	When the cows come home from their summer holidays in the mountains (pictured)	
La Bénichon Canton Fribourg	Harvest festival meets gourmet feast of eating and drinking	
Älplerchibli Cantons Nidwalden and Obwalden	Communal eating, dancing and flag-throwing to mark the end of summer	
Castagnata Ascona (TI)	Chestnuts galore: over 2000kg roasted or in jams, breads and cakes (pictured)	

November

Gansabhauet Sursee (LU)	A form of pin-the-tail-on-the-donkey using a sword, a dead goose and a sun mask
Rüeblimärt Aarau	In celebration of Aargau's signature vegetable – the carrot
Zibelemärit Bern	Everything you can possibly do to or with an onion (pictured left and above)

December

Samichlaus Nationwide	The Swiss St Nick has gifts for good kids but his evil sidekick punishes bad ones
L'Escalade Geneva	The victory over the Savoyards commemorated with chocolate cauldrons (pictured)
Klausjagen Küssnacht am Rigi (LU)	Vast paper head-dresses lit by candles and carried through town (pictured)
Silvesterchläuse Urnäsch (AR)	Masked men in elaborate costumes celebrate the new New Year's Eve

MEET YOUR EXPERT

Andie Pilot grew up near the Canadian Rockies, in Calgary, and now lives near the Swiss Alps in the Emmental. As a child, she came to Switzerland every summer to visit her grandparents in Eastern Switzerland, and to gorge on *Cervelat, Gipfeli,* Migros Ice Tea, and *Coupe Dänemark*.

After completing a degree in Humanities and training to be a pastry chef, she moved to Switzerland in 2010. In 2015 she started her blog, Helvetickitchen.com, which provides both traditional and modern Swiss recipes in English. The *Helvetic Kitchen* cookbook was published in 2017, followed by *Drink like the Swiss* in 2018.

FOOD AND DRINK

The Swiss excel at making cheese and chocolate, and even the least expensive supermarket versions are usually worth eating. But their cuisine goes beyond this, with different regions protecting and celebrating their own contributions to the Swiss culinary canon. Products like Gruyère cheese and the spirit kirsch have designations of origin (marked with the letters AOP/IGP), ensuring they are made to the highest standards.

Swiss food is a balancing act. The simplest raw ingredients, like pure Swiss milk, are processed by cutting-edge cheese- and chocolate-making technology. The culinary influences of Switzerland's neighbours – France, Germany, Italy and Austria – are seamlessly incorporated; for example, when dried pasta made it over the border, alpine herdsmen quickly began to bring this light, energy-dense foodstuff with them into the Alps, then used their abundant supply of milk and cheese to make their famous dish, *Älplermagronen*. This is served with apple sauce, balancing sweet and savoury as well. In Switzerland, even a strenuous day spent hiking in the Alps is complemented with a big pot of cheese fondue at the summit.

This perfect balance is what makes Swiss food such a joy to experience.

THE LOWDOWN

- Swiss eating is seasonal, corresponding with harvest or a holiday. You'll learn when to buy what.
- Swiss food is regional and we'll prepare you for both Appenzell and Geneva, and everything in between.
- You'll get a close look at those twin icons of Swiss cuisine – cheese and chocolate – and learn how to get an inside look at the production.

REGIONAL DISHES

Cheese and milk are as ubiquitous as the cows that dot the alpine landscape, and influence the cuisine of most of the country. Cheese fondue (melted cheese for dipping) and raclette (melted cheese for scraping) are enjoyed in all regions, as well as chocolate. *Birchermüesli, Zopf/tresse* (buttery, braided bread), and some form of *Wähe/ tarte* (a sweet or savoury quiche), can be found in most parts of the country too.

But there are plenty of regional favourites, and here's what you can expect.

BASEL

Try the *Läckerli,* Basel's famous spiced cookies, or the colourful *Mässmogge,* candy coated pralines. Carnival in Basel brings two more specialties, *Basler Mehlsuppe,* flour soup, and *Fastenwähe,* small breads often flavoured with caraway.

BERN

Rösti, Switzerland's famous fried potato dish, originated with Bernese farmers, as does their beloved bread, *Zopf.* The *Berner Platte* involves choice Bernese sausages, smoked pork, tongue, and other fine meats and is garnished with potatoes, sauerkraut, and dried green beans. The famous onion market in the city of Bern in November brings onion tarts and soups.

Geschnetzeltes, veal and mushrooms in a creamy sauce, is known throughout the country. For something sweet try *Tirggel,* Zurich's Christmassy honey biscuits, or Sprüngli's elegant Luxemburgerli, a smaller, chubbier macaron.

NTRAL SWITZERLAND

Cherry trees dot the landscape in Zug, leading to wonderful cherry dishes, not to mention the famous cherry spirit, kirsch, and, in cake form, the *Zuger Kirschtorte.* You'll find *Luzerner Chügelipastetli*, puff pastry filled with a creamy, meaty sauce.

STERN SWITZERLAND

When in Appenzell try the *Biberli,* or stuffed gingerbread. There is also Appenzeller cheese and Appenzeller *Alpenbitter,* a herby liqueur. Great sausages abound: *St Galler Bratwurst, Appenzeller Siedwurst, Schüblig, Glarner Kalberwurst,* and the dried *Appenzeller Möstbröckli* and *Pantli.* Glarus boasts the polarising, green *Schabziger* cheese, and *Glarner Pastete,* a plum- and almond-filled puff pastry tart.

RAUBÜNDEN

Try *Capuns,* meaty little dumplings wrapped in chard and poached in cream. *Maluns* are buttery potato niblets and *Pizokel* are buckwheat dumplings, both served with cheese. On the sweet side you have *Birnbrot* (pictured opposite page), a pastry loaf stuffed with dried pears, and *Tuorta da Nuschs,* a rich walnut and caramel pie.

REGIONAL
DISHES

GENEVA

The cardoon, a vegetable related to the artichoke, is beloved in Geneva, either served in gratin form or pickled. Chocolate cauldrons called *marmites* are available in supermarkets in early December as part of the *Escalade* festivities – break one and marzipan fruit might spill out. As for sausage, the fennel-flavoured *Longeole* is a favourite.

VAUD

The *saucissons* (sausages) of Vaud are among the finest the country has to offer. Some of the best are *Boutefas, Saucisson Vaudois,* and *Saucisse aux Choux Vaudoise,* typically prepared with leeks and potatoes in the dish *Papet Vaudois.* Don't miss *Pâté Vaudois,* little meat pies, and Gâteau du Vully, a bready cake topped either sweet with cream, or savoury with bacon and caraway.

FRIBOURG

Fribourg's famous saffron bread, *Cuchaule,* is often served with the sweet *Moutarde de Benichon.* Many regional dishes feature glorious double cream from Gruyères – or you can eat it straight, with meringues for dipping.

JURA

Another delicious sausage comes from Jura, the *Saucisse d'Ajoie*. Enjoy the savoury cream tart *Toétché*, and wash it all down with *Damassine*, the famous plum spirit.

VALAIS

This sunny region is famous for apricots (which also feature in their strong spirit, *Abricotine*), as well as some of Switzerland's best wines. It has famed rye bread, as well as dried meat, and the most famous dish is probably the unfortunately named *Cholera*, a delicious pie filled with cheese, potatoes, apples, pears, onions and meat.

TICINO

Polenta and chestnuts are on the menu, as well as wine, particularly Merlot, served in little ceramic cups called *Boccalino*. Try one of the canton's famous Grottos, rustic restaurants that serve hearty local fare.

A YEAR IN SWISS FOOD

Eating in Switzerland is a seasonal affair, with certain foods appearing with great fanfare at particular times of year, or coinciding with a specific holiday. Here's what you can expect in a typical year.

Spring: strawberries and asparagus mark the change to sunnier weather, with shops and restaurants proclaiming 'asparagus season'. Wild garlic shows up on many menus, flavouring everything from *Spätzle* to cheese. Easter means *Osterfladen*, a tart with creamy filling, as well as what the Swiss do best, chocolate, in bunny and egg form.

Summer: gorgeous Swiss produce rolls in throughout the summer. Cherry season starts in late May, and the cherry-producing regions of Basel and Zug have dishes and festivities to go along with it. Apricots from the Valais come in late July, with their famous 'red cheeks' the pleasing red speckling on the fruit. On 1 August, Switzerland's national holiday, most people have barbeques and you'll probably find *Cervelat*, Switzerland's national sausage, on the menu as well as celebratory milk buns with little Swiss flags.

Autumn: apples, and by extension apple juice and cider mark the start of autumn. The cows come down from the mountains sparking numerous regional markets that sell alpine cheese. Grapes are harvested in wine regions and many wine festivals are celebrated. Hunting season opens, and restaurants feature game (see box). The sweet smell of chestnuts greets you in most big cities, where you can buy a bag of the roasted nuts.

Winter: Christmas is on the way, and that means cookies. On 6 December, many Swiss eat *Grittibänz*, sweet boy-shaped breads, and children get little sacks of chocolate, nuts and oranges from the Swiss St Nick. During the festive period, many families eat raclette or fondue, both cheese and *Chinoise* (meat cooked in broth), though there is generally no set Christmas meal. On 6 January, there is the Three Kings' Cake (pictured opposite), a sweet, raisin-studded bread with a small plastic king figurine baked in – whoever finds it is king for the day. There are traditional foods for carnival as well, including fried *Fasnachtschüechli/Beignets de carnaval* and Berliners.

CHRISTMAS COOKIES

The most beloved Swiss Christmas cookies are the buttery *Mäilanderli/Milanaise*, chocolate *Basler Brunsli/Bruns de Bâle*, cinnamon-heavy *Zimtsterne/Étoiles à la cannelles*, and the jammy *Spitzbuben/Mirroirs*. Beyond these there are numerous others, including many regional favourites.

A characteristic of these cookies is their long shelf life. In many households, there will be a Christmas cookie-baking frenzy in early December, then they will be carefully packaged in tins—one variety per box—and served throughout the month at home, or carefully arranged on platters to bring to festive events.

CHEESE

The Swiss have been making cheese for centuries. Excellent Swiss cheese (and chocolate too) owes a debt to Swiss milk. Taking the cows up to the alps in the summer and letting them graze on fresh alpine meadows has a positive influence on the flavour of Swiss milk and cheese. According to Switzerland Cheese Marketing, almost half of all the milk produced in Switzerland is used to make cheese, and there are 750 varieties to choose from. Here are the most famous.

Emmentaler: the prototypical Swiss cheese, dotted with holes. The mild variants are great for cooking, and as they age they gain excellent flavour.

Gruyère: salty, firm but creamy, and crumblier with age, this quintessential Swiss cheese is equally suited for cooking or eating by itself. And don't miss its cousin, *L'Etivaz*, whose producers split off from regular Gruyère makers about a hundred years ago and continue to make their version of the cheese in the traditional way – in big copper pots over open fires.

CHEESE TOURISM

You can see cheese being made at:
- Appenzeller Show Dairy: Stein, Appenzell
- Emmentaler Show Dairy: Affoltern im Emmental, Bern
- La Maison du Gruyère: Pringy-Gruyères, Fribourg
- Maison de la Tête de Moine: Bellelay, Jura
- Show Dairy Monastery Engelberg: Kloster Engelberg, Obwalden

Appenzeller: another hard cheese, great for melting or eating plain. One of Switzerland's purported best kept secrets is the herby mixture that makes Appenzeller cheese taste so unique.

Vacherin: Vacherin comes in two varieties: *Vacherin Fribourgeois*, which is a hard cheese, excellent aged, and often paired with Gruyère for a fondue, and *Vacherin Mont d'Or*, which is soft and encased in spruce and is like its own little fondue, complete with pot. You wrap the whole thing in foil, then stick it in the oven and voilà, dippable cheese.

SWISS ARMY GRILLED CHEESE

A perfect showcase for any of the aforementioned hard cheeses is this Swiss classic, with a recipe adapted from the standard issue Swiss military cookbook.

100g hard cheese, grated
2 tbsp flour
1 egg
125ml milk

pinch of nutmeg, salt and pepper
2–3 thick slices of bread
knob of butter

- In a medium bowl, mix together the cheese, flour, egg, milk, and seasonings. Cover and let rest in the fridge for a couple of hours.
- After it has rested, give the cheese mixture a good stir and spread half on the bread slices, pressing it down a bit to make sure it sticks.
- Heat butter in a large frying pan on medium heat until it bubbles and splutters.
- Place the slices of bread *cheese side down* into the frying pan. Try not to move them around in the pan too much, just let them crisp up. As the cheese melts, it will adhere better to the bread.
- While the slices are frying face down, spread the remaining cheese mixture on their exposed side.
- After a few minutes (once you can smell the cheese) take a peek underneath and if it is golden brown, carefully flip the bread.
- Fry the second side for a few minutes, until golden brown.
- If you aren't so keen on frying, these can be baked (at 200° C / 400° F / gas mark 6) for about 15–20 minutes (cheese on one side only).

A DELICIOUS DAY

Unlike their cows, the Swiss are not prone to grazing throughout the day, instead limiting themselves to a few distinct mealtimes with an *Apéro* or two (see below) thrown in every other weekend. Throughout the country weekday breakfasts are generally light, with big spreads of baked goods like *Zopf/tresse* saved for weekend brunches. Lunch is the main meal of the day, served warm, with lighter fare at dinner.

The Swiss cocktail hour, *Apéro*, is an honourary Swiss mealtime and can be held to celebrate a wedding, a birthday, or simply the end of the working day. At the most basic *Apéro* there are glasses of cold white wine and bowls of paprika chips.

And make sure you don't drink too soon. Whether you say *Proscht, Zum Wohl, Santé, Salute,* or *Viva,* here are a couple of rules for raising glasses:

- once you receive your drink you must not take a single sip until the toast is over and everyone has clinked glasses with everyone else.
- make eye contact and say the person's name as you clink.

Likewise, before tucking into the plate in front of you, it is customary to wish other diners a good meal ahead. More musical than the standard German *Guten Appetit*, the Swiss (Germans) say *En Gueta*. The French and Italians keep the tradition, saying *Bon Appetit*, or *Buon Appetito* respectively, and it's *Bun Appetit* in Romansch.

EATING OUT

Eating out in Switzerland can be expensive, not chiefly because of food costs, but because the people serving you are making a living wage. Regardless of your budget, here are some things to remember.

- You are not required to tip in a Swiss restaurant, though it is customary to round up.
- You must ask for the bill. Servers will generally leave you alone until you do.
- Many restaurants only serve food during typical lunchtime (12–2pm) and dinner (6–9pm) hours.

DID YOU KNOW?

In German-speaking Switzerland, *das Morgenessen* (morning meal), *das Mittagessen* (midday meal), and *das Nachtessen* (night meal), simply get shortened to *Zmorge*, *Zmittag*, and *Znacht*. Additionally, there are two other smaller mealtimes, *Znüni* and *Zvieri*, which refer to the Swiss German words for nine *(nüni)* and four *(vieri)*, denoting the proper time of day to have them.

FONDUE

As part of the Christmas season, a work party, or a day of hiking or skiing, the Swiss love a good cheese fondue. Whether convenient supermarket vacuum-packed cheese or specialty mixes from local dairies, fondue in Switzerland is practically fast food. Even petrol stations sell bread and jars of pickles and onions.

What wine should I bring? White wine is a perfect match for fondue. People typically drink *Chasselas/Fendant,* but a nice *Amigne* or *Petit Arvine* from the Valais would also suit. Alongside wine, warm tea is often served, purportedly to help digestion.

One fork, or two? Most families dip and eat with one fork each, but if you don't know your fellow cheese eaters so well, or if you're sick, dip with one fork and use another for eating.

Help! I've lost my bread! Every family seems to have a different approach to lost morsels. Some threaten dish duties for those that lose their bread, others kisses.

The cheese is gone, now what? When you get to the end of the fondue, you will probably find *s'Grosi* or *la religieuse,* the bit of crispy cheese fixed to the bottom of the pot. Scrape this up and enjoy.

CHOCOLATE

Switzerland has been producing chocolate since the 17th century. The oldest chocolate producer still in existence in Switzerland is Cailler, founded in 1819 in Vevey, then the heart of chocolate production in Switzerland. It was also there, in 1875, where Daniel Peter helped revolutionise chocolate production by making milk chocolate using powdered milk.

Another revolution came in 1879 when Rodolphe Lindt (yes, of Lindt chocolate) invented the conching process. The chocolate of that time was gritty, but Lindt used a machine to press and grind the chocolate together into the smooth mass that we know today.

Although some of the smaller companies have now been bought up by huge conglomerates – Cailler is owned by Nestlé – there are still many independent Swiss chocolate factories that have been around for more than a century.

Swiss chocolate, or *Schoggi* as it is affectionately called in Swiss German, remains among the best in the world, and nobody knows it better than the Swiss themselves. According to Chocosuisse, they consume the second-highest amount of chocolate worldwide, averaging over ten kilograms of chocolate per person, per year.

DID YOU KNOW?

One of Switzerland's best-known chocolate exports is Toblerone. The pyramid-shaped chocolate was invented in Bern in 1908. In a tribute to the city of Bern's mascot, you can spot a 'hidden' bear in the face of the mountain on the packaging.

CHOCOLATE VISITS

Whether you go for the tours or tastings, these chocolate factories are bound to satisfy your sweet tooth.

- Chocolat Frey: Buchs bei Aarau, Aargau
- Camille Bloch: Courtelary, Bern
- Maison Cailler: Broc, Fribourg
- Chocolatiers Villars: Fribourg, Fribourg
- ChocoWorld: Root, Lucerne
- Maestrani's Chocolarium: Flawil, St Gallen
- Chocolate museum Alprose: Caslano, Ticino

KAMBLY

Tucked away in the charming Emmental town of Trubschachen is the Kambly cookie factory. The company started out making the buttery Emmental cookie, *Bretzeli*, and has now expanded to become one of the world's premier luxury cookie brands, while still using the same local suppliers for flour and butter that they did nearly a century ago. Entrance is free, and so is a sampling of dozens of different products.

DRINK LIKE THE SWISS

Despite their reserved manner, the Swiss do like to drink. According to the International Organisation of Vine and Wine, they drink 37 litres of wine per person per year, making them the fourth largest wine consumers in the world. As for beer, they boast the highest ratio of registered breweries to citizens. But it isn't just boozy drinks. According to CafetierSuisse, the Swiss are currently third in the world for coffee consumption, drinking around 1,110 cups per person, per year.

Wine: the Swiss have some truly excellent wine, but very little is exported, so do yourself a favour and drink domestic while in Switzerland. *Chasselas* (also know as *Fendant*) is the most popular Swiss white wine, and peppery pinot noir the most popular Swiss red. But the biggest surprises are to be found among the less-common grapes. Try some wonderful whites from Valais, like *Amigne, Petit Arvine* and *Heida,* pink *Oeil de Perdrix* from Neuchâtel, merlot from Ticino, and *Dôle*, a smooth blend of pinot noir and gamay grapes.

Beer: with so many breweries, Switzerland has a beer for everyone. Avoid the big brands that have been bought out by international conglomerates, and try something local. For something more traditional, try Appenzeller Beer, which incorporates local products like honey, rice and chestnuts. Sour fans should check out the famous Jura brewery BFM, Brasserie des Franches Montagnes.

Ovomaltine: it's a mix-in-milk powder made from malt, egg and milk, and flavoured with cocoa. Initially made to mprove the diet of Swiss children, it is now enjoyed worldwide, according to its website, in more than 100 countries.

(And no, English speakers, that's not a spelling mistake—the original name of the product was misspelled on its British trademark registration, leading to its English name of Ovaltine.)

RIVELLA

Of course the national soda pop of Switzerland is made with milk. First produced in 1952, Rivella is one of Switzerland's most iconic drinks. It's made from milk serum (also known as whey), herb and fruit tea extract, water, sugar and fizz. The whey is what makes the drink particularly Swiss. For centuries, dairy farmers enjoyed drinking this by-product of cheese production, which was later adopted as a health product by early Swiss nutritionists.

ORDERING COFFEE

- Espresso: small shot of strong coffee
- Café créme: cup of coffee with cream served on the side
- *Milchkaffee/Schale/Renversé:* cup of coffee with warm milk
- Cappuccino: shot of coffee with milk foam
- Latte Macchiato: shot of coffee with warm milk and milk foam

MEET YOUR EXPERT

Angelica Cipullo has spent the last eight years helping to grow Girlfriend Guide, Zurich, a digital lifestyle platform designed to help women fall in love with exploring Switzerland.

Angelica's professional highlights include working with sports sponsorships in the USA, then at an arts centre in the UK. She has spoken at TedxYouth Zurich.

Angelica loves splashing in Swiss lakes with her three children, hiking forest trails with her dog and undertaking bucket list adventures with her husband and best friend, David.

LEISURE

On any given Sunday in Switzerland, if you spend a few hours at a train station, we guarantee you're likely to see a lot of hustle and bustle. But not the weekday kind with laptops and suits. The fun kind. The kind that gives you goose bumps. The kind that makes you feel inspired. The kind where you stare in awe as people head by in every direction with skis, snowboards, rollerblades, bicycles, theatre tickets and so much more.

This is a place where you'll feel motivated…excited…and adventurous. Can you envision it? Sledding three kilometers down into a valley? Cycling around picture-postcard lakes surrounded by snowcapped mountains? Dancing in a sea of hundreds of thousands of techno fans?

Or is your vision more low key? Do bubbling thermal baths bring you bliss? Is your ideal late night the kind that involves museum hopping? Or are you eager to listen, up close, to the world's most talented jazz musicians?

Whatever makes you tick, our advice is to ignite your passion and go make Switzerland your leisure playground!

THE LOWDOWN
- Savvy tips on ways to keep costs low and adventures high
- How to embrace the outdoors at festivals, open-air cinemas, lake fronts and on the ski slopes
- The secrets to enjoying Switzerland's natural resources, with everything from thermal baths to downhill cycling

MUSEUMS

Including galleries, gardens and zoos, Switzerland has over 1,000 museums showcasing 71.3 million objects. In fact, according to Switzerland Tourism there is no other country on earth with as many museums per capita as Switzerland. Every year Swiss museums have more than 12 million visitors and provide almost 100,000 individual tours. The overall accessibility and ease of visiting helps make the Swiss museum scene so attractive.

- Most museums have coin operated lockers for jackets, bags, etc.
- Displays are usually in several languages, and if not, you can expect printed pamphlets or audio-guides.
- Most museums have lovely cafes with full-service kitchens, plus designated picnic areas where you can bring your own lunch and drinks.

The museums.ch app and website are our favourite tools for getting an overview of which museums are in which city and what's currently happening. You can easily search by location and interest to find what's best for you. Even if museums are not on your weekly check-list, there are a few annual highlights you don't want to miss-especially International Museum Day, Long Night of Museums, and Art Basel.

FOR KIDS

Museums have fantastic activities for kids but they are often not on the English page of the website. But don't be discouraged! Most museums host drop-off activities, in-museum scavenger hunts and other activities aimed at making children's experiences engaging. You just might have to do a bit of digging!

SAVE AT MUSEUMS

Tip	Why we love it
Basel Kunstmuseum	Free admission on the first Sunday of the month and after 5pm Tuesdays–Fridays
Bern Museum Card	Unrestricted entry to all Bern museums with 24-hour card (28Fr) or 48-hour card (35Fr)
Coop Hello Family Members	Free membership with various discounts including at the FIFA World Football Museum, Glasi Hergiswil and Papiliorama
Geneva Open Door Day	Free entry to all museums on the first Sunday of each month
Geneva Museum Pass	A 40Fr annual pass offering unlimited access to and reductions at Geneva's 16 museums
Museums-PASS-Musées	Annual card valid at 320 museums throughout Germany, Switzerland and France
Raiffeisen MemberPlus-program	Free access to 500 museums for cardholder and up to 3 children
Swiss Museum Pass	166Fr gets you entry to over 500 museums. Discounted rates for SBB GA and Half Fare cardholders. A 30Fr discount on the initial annual pass is possible when redeeming a Migros Cumulus-Bon.
SBB RailAway Kombi	65+ Art, Culture and Museum combination offers and rail discounts with savings up to 50%
Zurich Kunsthaus	Free admission to the General Collection on Wednesdays
Zurich Card	Unlimited public transportation and museum access for Zurich with the purchase of a 24-hour card (27Fr) or 72-hour card (53Fr)

BUCKET LIST

- Aliens: HR Giger in St-Germain Castle (Gruyères)
- Butterflies: Papiliorama (Kerzers) (pictured)
- Dogs: Barryland – the St. Bernard Museum (Martigny)
- Family Outing: Technorama Swiss Science Centre (Winterthur)
- Film Buffs: Chaplin's World (Vevey)
- Hands-On: Swiss Knife Valley Visitors Centre (Ingenbohl)
- Perfect Precision: Swiss Museum of Transport (Lucerne)
- Sports Fanatics: FIFA World Football Museum (Zurich)
- Summer Only: Swiss Open-Air Museum Ballenberg (Brienz)
- Up Close: Swissminiatur (Melide)

LIVE PERFORMANCES

Swiss life definitely involves music! And we're not talking about dim concert halls and crowded rooms. We're talking about music played at 3,000 metres above sea level. We're talking about pitching a tent in summer for six days of concerts. We're talking about long-standing traditions. And if all this doesn't have you rushing to download the event calendars, what really might grab you are the accessibility and uniqueness of Switzerland's performances. Many events offer free open-air performances set against drop-dead gorgeous backgrounds.

MY FAVOURITES

Best for…	
Classical Music	**Engadin Festival** For just under 80 years, this mountain region has hosted high-calibre orchestras at elegant locations, including the prestigious town of St. Moritz
DIY	**Curtain Call** Get involved locally with one of Switzerland's English speaking performing groups: Geneva English Drama Society, Bern's Upstage, The Village Players of Lausanne, The Semi-Circle in Basel, Zurich Comedy Club, The English Theater Group of Zug, and Simply Theatre Academy for Kids in Zurich/Zug and Geneva/Vaud.
Families	**The Street Performers Festival** 100 shows throughout Locarno featuring pantomimes, stage plays, dance performances, jugglers, tightrope walking, fire eaters, musicians, clowns and more. Don't forget to tip to give thanks for the 4 days of free shows!
Jazz	**Bird's Eye Jazz Club** A hidden gem in Basel you'll love for letting you get up close to amazing artists.
Musical Theatre	**Thunersee Spiele** An annual open-air production in Swiss German along the waterfront of Lake Thun with the Eiger, Mönch and Jungfrau as the backdrop.
Open-Air	**Paléo Festival** Often sold out before it starts, 9,000 daily campers rock to 280 concerts above the town of Nyon thanks to an organisation of 5,000 volunteers
Opera & Ballet	**Geneva and Zurich Opera Houses** These cities might battle it out for best, both boasting beautiful opera houses with world-renowned performers. Annually, they each host a free Open Day with rehearsal viewings, workshops, family programs and more.
Out of the Box	**Rüttelhütte IN AIR Festival** Launched thanks to a crowdfunding campaign, this festival is now known for running the world's first indoor camping area and first Swiss black light mini golf course
Postcard Pictures	**Zermatt Unplugged** The chic village explodes with concerts, but the ultimate experience is mountaintop music enjoyed at 3000m
Prestige	**Montreux Jazz Festival** One of the most prestigious festivals. Top events sell out quickly but a limited number of same-day tickets are released last-minute.
Summer	**Open Air St Gallen** Since 1977 concert-goers have been thronging to St. Gallen to pitch a tent, dip in the river and enjoy international headliners as well as young talent spanning the pop, rock, indie and electronic music genres
Techno	**Street Parade** Thirty lovemobiles, hundreds of DJs and seven stages in a massive party around Zurich. You've never imagined Switzerland like this. You must see it to believe it!
Venue	**KKL Luzern** The concert hall (pictured) is regarded as one of the best in the world. Music enthusiasts rave about the unique acoustics.

SPORTS

If you agree that mountains are for climbing and lakes are for swimming, Switzerland is the place for you. However, on the professional sports front, apart from World Cup years, you won't find the pubs crowded with cheering fans. If you're a fan of local sports, however, most cities have their own team in the Swiss Super League (football), Swiss Ice Hockey, the Swiss Rugby Federation and Swiss Basketball League.

FUN FACTS

- In 2003 Switzerland's Alinghi sailing team became the first European team to win the America's Cup.
- Switzerland has hosted two Olympic Games, eleven Ice Hockey World Championships, and one World Cup, and co-hosted one UEFA European Football Championship.
- Swiss star Roger Federer is undoubtedly one of the greatest tennis players of all time. He has won 20 Grand Slam titles and over 100 career ATP Titles.
- Since the modern Olympic Games began, Swiss athletes have won a total of 192 Summer Olympic medals and 138 Winter Olympic medals.

TWO WHEELS

Cycling is an amazing way to see the sights of Switzerland and schweizmobil.ch is an excellent planning tool. (See 'Travel' chapter for info about taking bikes on trains.) And don't miss the 20 different Slow Up car-free days scheduled on routes in cities all over Switzerland on summer weekends – attracting 500,000 annual participants.

GET SPORTY!

Sport	Two-Second Scoop	Highlight
Adventure Sports	These days, paragliding and rock climbing are practised on every suitable hill and canyoning is the ultimate water experience.	Interlaken is an epic centre of adrenaline!
Downhill Cycling	Many Swiss ski areas' answer to the summer season. Ride the lifts up and tear down on specially-built trails. Gnarly bikes often available for rent.	Excellent parks at Klosters, Laax and Lenzerheide. For really advanced adventures go to Verbier, or cross the French border to Morzine.
Golf	Ninety-six courses country-wide with Migros Golf Parks offering seven under the theme "Golf for Everyone"	Golf4Fun is an active expat golfing community of 30+ nationalities.
Rope Adventure Parks	Thirty experiences in forests, mountains and more with thrilling fun like speedy 250-metre zip lines and obstacle-courses 25 meters above the ground	Many cater to families and have special courses starting at four years of age. Brave adults are encouraged to try the newly opened Verbier course with a 3.5 meter free fall.
Running	Lake and forest running paths are everywhere, but if you want to take it up a notch, check out *Run the Alps* by Doug Mayer.	The classic Jungfrau Marathon has an altitude gain of 1829m.
Vitaparcourse	Over 500 forest courses throughout Switzerland are a fun way to stay in shape with up to 43 exercises at 15 workout stations.	Try a stunning location like Zermatt, Crans Montana or St Moritz, taking you past bridges, rivers and woods.

WINTER ACTIVITIES

Switzerland's mountains are the quintessential winter wonderland, and when it's grim and foggy in the cities it's often sunny and clear in the Alps. While downhill skiing is for sure all the rage from November to late March, there are actually a ton of other ways to have fun including sledding, snowboarding, winter hiking, ice skating, cross-country skiing and social games like curling.

Ice skating: rinks are scattered all over the country – both indoors and outdoors – and almost all hire out skates, helmets and supports to help younger kids.
- Oeschinensee (Kandersteg): the natural rink on a frozen lake under snow-capped mountains is quite memorable. In some years the entire lake is skatable.
- Not exactly a rink, but a trail! Skate along the three kilometre snowy forest path from Bad Alvaneu to Surava.
- Annually, Ice Magic opens in the centre of Interlaken featuring five connecting ice rinks alongside the Christmas markets.

Sledding: helmets and bravery required.
- Under-the-stars sledding is a great twist on a standard date night. Try the illuminated 3.5 kilometre Eiger Run and warm up afterwards with fondue at the Brandegg alpine chalet.
- For babies and toddlers, most equipment rental locations have safety seats to help keep littles ones secure.
- Fideris hosts one of Switzerland's longest tobogganing runs with a length of 12 kilometres.

Winter swimming: if you desperately want to get away from the snow, Switzerland has many indoor swimming pools and water parks including Europe's largest indoor water park, Alpamare in Freienbach. Aquabasilea in Pratteln and Splash & Spa Tamaro in Rivera also offer awesome days out with no wool sweaters required!

CROSS COUNTRY SKIING

Switzerland has great Nordic skiing trails (and you may even get passed by four-time Olympic gold medallist Dario Cologna). Most are free, but some have ticket fees of 10–15Fr. Ski hire is readily available.

- If seeing the sights is your priority, follow the young Rhone through forests and open trails from Oberwald to Niederwald.
- Join 13,000 other athletes and participate in the largest cross-country skiing event at the Engadin Skimarathon, crossing the Silser, Silvaplana and Champfer lakes.
- In Verbier, a gondola ride takes you to the La Chaux Trail at 2200m, a 6km trail with gorgeous views.

DOWNHILL SKIING

The cost of lift tickets varies wildly, with the most expensive at Laax for 85Fr while at Robella a day pass is only 20Fr.

To rent or buy: always a big question. All ski resorts have on-site rental shops as do most Migros Sports shops – the shopkeepers usually speak multiple languages and are quite thorough in finding the right fit. Season rentals offer competitive rates in comparison to purchasing.

Ski school: the Swiss Ski School has 170 locations throughout Switzerland and offers a Learn to Ski in 3 Days programme for ages 9 to 99, with a free repeat course if the promise isn't fulfilled – that you can ski down a blue slope easily after three days.

SAVVY SKI TICKETS

Tip	Why we love it
Birthday Pass	Some resorts, such as Vals and Pizol, offer a free day pass on your birthday.
Family Discounts	Check resort websites for deals as there are loads of offers for kids including Free Ski for 6 and under, Saturday Specials, Free Helmet Rentals and more.
Magic Pass	Unlimited access to over 1,000km of slopes (many of which are in the French-speaking region) 459Fr (in advance) or 899Fr during the season
Pre-Season Sales	If you know where you want to ski, buying in the summer or early autumn can save you up to 50% on season passes.
SBB Snow & Rail	Combination train and lift passes at 36+ mountain resorts with reductions of at least 10% as well as complimentary luggage travel vouchers and 15% rental discounts
Swiss-Ski	Save up to 20% with a 50Fr annual membership.

FUN IN THE SUN

With 1,600 lakes, it's no surprise that Switzerland's summer scene focuses on lakes, rivers and pools. Poles are swapped for paddles, and fondue pots for barbecues.

Designated public swimming areas open up along lakefronts and on some rivers, and many indoor pools open outdoor sections. Facilities vary, but we love the ones with a bit of action like floating trampolines, over-water zip lines, stand-up paddling rentals and diving boards. Most locations will have locker rooms, umbrellas and restaurants. As usual in Switzerland, the swimming experience is pretty civilised and stress free, but don't expect lifeguards; parents are responsible for their kids at all times. You can often pay less than 10Fr for public swimming, and season passes will save you even more money if you're a frequent visitor.

FISH OUT OF WATER

Summer isn't only about action. Some of our favourite low-key summer activities include:

- **The Big Screen**: sit under the stars and catch a film at one of the many open-air cinemas, and be sure to mark your calendar for the Allianz Tag des Kinos. Annually, on the first Sunday in September, over 500 cinemas host 5Fr movies.
- **Lake Cruise on Lake Lucerne**: the historic paddle-steamers offer views of Titlis and Pilatus and stops at the picturesque villages of Vitznau and Weggis, as well as themed nights like New Orleans Jazz Music. Many other lakes offer similar cruises.
- **Circus Knie**: one of Switzerland's best-known productions for the past 100 years, they perform 320 times at 33 venues throughout Switzerland during the warmer months.

SUMMER HOT SPOTS

Best for...	
Family Time	**Connyland** An amusement park with theme rides, water attractions and live shows in northeastern Switzerland
Fun Day Out	**Aare Rafting** Float down the river from Thun to Bern
Girls Night Out	**Rimini Bar Zurich** A nightclub with concerts and DJs in the evenings
Kayak Enthusiasts	**Lake Lucerne** Gorgeous panoramic mountain scenery with views of castles, Mt Pilatus and the Rigi
See & Be Seen	**Geneva Bains de Paquis** For a 2Fr entry, if you can find a spot, this is the place to be.
Thrill Seekers	**Viamala Gorge** Canyoning with Swiss River Adventures in Graubünden is a unique experience for those who crave action and adventure.
Weekend Getaway	**Monte Tamaro** An outdoor park with bobsled, zip line, 15-meter high jump and adventure trails
Wild Swimming	**Verzasca Valley** Stunning canyon scenery in Ticino

MIND
AND BODY

The Swiss place great emphasis on physical and mental health, which is often termed "wellness". Utilising the country's natural resources, visits to thermal baths, hammams, saunas, medical spas and beauty salons are part of the culture. Not to mention the plethora of yoga, pilates, acupuncture, massage and meditation opportunities available.

Wellness experiences: bathing and sauna experiences are quite popular in Switzerland for both recreation and the belief that they can help everything from muscle aches to poor blood circulation to skin allergies. Switzerland boasts numerous natural springs – both hot and cold – and you'll find everything from free fountains to high-end resorts across the country. While saunas remain the go-to for après-ski relaxation, hammams have recently taken centre stage, luring city slickers to intense detox experiences.

Most of these facilities are open 365 days a year, and prices start from 15Fr but vary considerably depending on the venue. Many offer daily entrance passes, three-hour passes and multi-pass subscriptions, usually with different prices for hotel vs. non-hotel guests and add-ons like massage treatments and towels.

Les Bains de Lavey and Walliser Alpentherme & Spa Leukerbad are quite popular thermal bath experiences, but we highly recommend trying Hammam & Spa Oktogon in Bern to experience a unique cleansing ritual.

WELLNESS

Best for...	Not to Miss!	Two-Second Scoop
Architectural Delight	The Art of Alpine Luxury 7132	5-star Vals hotel featuring a thermal bath made from 60,000 quartzite slabs by award-winning architect Peter Zumthor
Au Natural	Lenkerhof Gourmet Spa Resort	The 5-star resort offers amazing treatments utilizing their local mountain crystals, stones and river sand.
Family Fun	Bains de Saillon	Three thermal pools, one semi-Olympic pool, a Thermal River and children's zone with a giant toboggan, water slide and paddling pool
Hot Hammams	Le Mirador	Located in Mont-Pelerin above Montreux, this spa has awesome views of Lake Geneva, the Alps and the Lavaux vineyards
Lifestyle Makeover	Ayurveda by Giardino	Multi-day programmes focused on nutrition, activity and mindful relaxation at 5-star resorts
Mind & Body	Sparkling Yoga and Top Hill Retreats	Both host high-end mountaintop fitness, yoga and meditation retreats in English

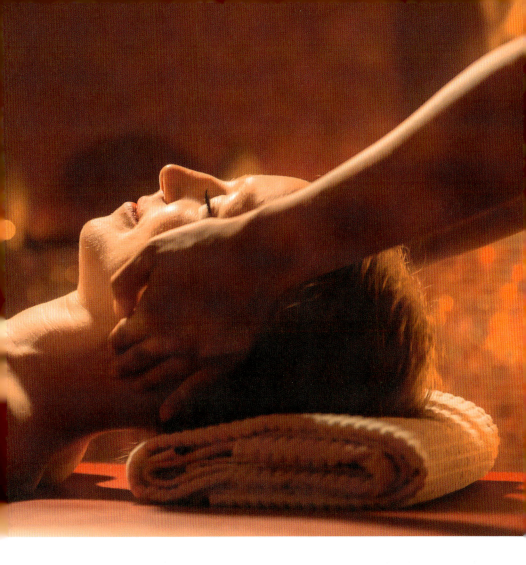

SPA ETIQUETTE

- Showers are required before entering any type of public bathing area.
- Many spa facilities are mixed, even the nude ones, which don't allow any clothing (though you can wrap yourself in towels). If this concerns you, check for women-only times.
- Tipping is appreciated but not required. Many locations will have little piggy banks at reception where you can leave a 5–10% cash tip. If tipping by credit card, you usually have to inform the cashier before they begin the process.
- Many places have a 'family day' during which children may join the sauna, etc.
- As a hotel guest, it's quite common to wear your bathrobe and slippers when travelling between your room and wellness areas.

MEET YOUR EXPERT

Christian Langenegger grew up in Canada in a Swiss household. He studied and worked in Germany and Austria before returning to Switzerland in 2009. For five years, he ran a language school that taught German to adults. During that time and while working in his craft beer bar, he heard about the trials and tribulations that newcomers have adapting to life in Switzerland. He has also witnessed many people successfully integrate into life in Switzerland. Christian has been a contributing writer to Newly Swissed Online Magazine since 2011.

SOCIAL LIFE

Swiss cities feature high on all of those quality-of-life surveys out there, from *Monocle* magazine to Mercer, a human resources consulting firm. However, look at expat surveys – like those from HSBC and InterNations, which put more emphasis on social life – and Switzerland doesn't always top the charts. Why does Switzerland rate as one of the best countries to live in when it comes to general surveys, but fall short when foreign residents are asked about their social life? Cold, closed, and unsociable – these are just a few of the words used to describe the Swiss. But there is hope. Those with Swiss friends will tell you once you have one, you have one for life.

Put on your hiking shoes, get out your grammar books and we'll help you find the best way to build a social life in Switzerland. You'll learn that the Swiss are active people, keen to get out into the mountains that cover 60% of the nation. With four languages, an urban-rural divide and nearly 25% non-Swiss nationals living in Switzerland, you're sure to find a group with whom you identify. From building a circle of international friends to joining a club and finally sitting at your local bar, this chapter will teach you to break the Swiss 'coconut shell' and create a social life for yourself in the alpine nation.

THE LOWDOWN
- The importance of learning a local language
- How and where to socialise with the Swiss
- How to find friends or even a partner in Switzerland

LEARN
A LANGUAGE

To socialise with the Swiss, you need to speak their language. Those coming to Switzerland can pick from four national languages, though you're most likely to choose one of the three major ones: German, French or Italian. English, while widely understood and spoken to varying degrees by many Swiss, is a signal for "I'm not from here."

As you can read in the chapter 'Becoming Swiss', there are language requirements for obtaining Swiss citizenship. But don't wait to learn a local language until you need it for administrative purposes – start socialising with locals as soon as you arrive. You might never speak perfect *Züritüütsch*, *français neuchâtelois* or *Italiano ticinese*, but any attempt to speak a local language will make breaking the ice with locals easier. Even a few words make a big difference, and your enjoyment of Switzerland depends on it.

Swiss-German, Swiss-French and Swiss-Italian all have their differences from those languages spoken in Germany, France or Italy. These are called 'Helvetisms', and many dictionaries like the *Duden* (German) and *Petit Larousse* (French) will mark them.

There are many reasons why Switzerland has so many dialects. Geography is one reason, as the country consists of many valleys and areas were isolated from each other for long periods. The other is that municipalities hold the most political power, so there was never a push to have everyone speak the same way. Lastly, the three major languages influence each other a great deal; words borrowed from other languages run rampant amongst the dialects

BEFORE & AFTER

Before you come to Switzerland:
- take an intensive crash course. Try to find a Goethe Institute (German), an Alliance Française (French) or a Società Dante Alighieri (Italian). Even a Berlitz course will give you a foundation.
- use audio courses to get used to hearing the language and practise simple phrases. The biggest name here is Pimsleur. You need to listen and repeat if you want a headstart.
- if your employer is bringing you to Switzerland, negotiate for language classes and time to learn.

Upon arrival:

- find a local language school and start with group instruction to save money and meet other people who are adapting to life in Switzerland.
- Migros schools, Bénédict, Berlitz, and Inlingua offer language classes in most towns and can get you started for about 20Fr/lesson bought in blocks of 40+. Smaller classes will run you about 45Fr per hour. Expect to pay around 120Fr an hour for a private tutor.
- many municipalities offer basic language training and may even offer child supervision during courses.
- taking courses via Skype with teachers in other countries is also a way to make things cheaper (around 30–40Fr an hour for private lessons with a legitimate teacher), but it requires discipline and a stable internet connection.
- schedule your lessons in the morning or during the day, and don't underestimate how hard it is to hit the books after a day of work.
- watch television, listen to the radio and try your hand at reading by picking up the free newspapers like *20 Minuten/20 minutes*.
- insist upon speaking the local language with Swiss acquaintances, even if it feels awkward at first.
- sign up for tests and set goals.

LANGUAGE SKILLS

The Common European Framework of Reference for Languages is used for academic and official purposes. It rates your language skills on a scale from A1 to C2.

Level Group	Level	Hours needed*
A: basic user	A1: breakthrough or beginner	80–200
	A2: waystage or elementary	200–350
B: independent user	B1: threshold or intermediate	350–650
	B2: vantage or upper intermediate	600–800
C: proficient user	C1: effective operational proficiency or advanced	800–1000
	C2: mastery or proficiency	1000+

*Expected number of classroom hours to reach stated level

FIND YOUR GROUP

The easiest way to build a social network is to find people you share something with besides work. This is true in Switzerland even more than in other countries. Your hobbies and passions are a great place to start.

My girlfriend Elizabeth comes from the USA. She's an old-time fiddle player and because she had lived and worked abroad before, she knew how important it would be to find her niche. When she arrived in Switzerland, she looked online for an old-time music group and didn't find one, so she set up a group on meetup.com for old-time jams. Today there are more than 100 members of the group and jams take place twice a month. Elizabeth isn't the only person who has connected to people via music. One of my former students from Australia joined a brass band that played at carnival, and a Scottish student joined a Highland band. Music connects, but so do other interests.

Use tools like meetup.com, InterNations, English Forum and other platforms to connect with people. Whether it's cooking, hiking or stand-up comedy, there are all sorts of groups out there. The good thing about these groups is that they attract Swiss and non-Swiss alike.

JOIN THE CLUB

A quarter of all Swiss are in a sports club and there are over 18,500 of them, ranging from archery to skiing. If it's a sport, there is probably a club for it. Like the meet-up groups above, sports clubs are great places to meet people, especially locals, as most Swiss are very physically active.

The Swiss take their clubs seriously; you can't just show up and have fun. Clubs generally have yearly dues and offer the possibility of taking on leadership roles. But if you're really looking to get in deep with the Swiss, joining a club is the best way to do it. Like bowling? Maybe you'll join the Bowling Club Uzwil or one of the sixteen other bowling clubs in the country. Like running, drinking and having fun? Try the Swiss chapter of the Hash House Harriers. There aren't only sports clubs, though: there are more than 57,000 associations in the country to choose from. Is photography more your thing? There are 72 different photography clubs. If you don't find what you're looking for, you can start it. Even the Swiss will tell you that the best way to socialise with the Swiss is to join a sports club or association.

Find a club near you here: vereinsverzeichnis.ch.

TOP TIP

Check out the video "How to Make Friends with a Swiss Person", available on YouTube, by the Swiss comedy duo Deville (pictured).

If a brilliant podcast is more your thing, Jo Fahy (UK) and Simon Zryd (CH) host Swiss & Chips about life in Switzerland. They answer questions and provide useful insights as well as organise events in the Bern area.

YOU'RE NOT ALONE

If you're looking to meet people from your home country or who have a connection to it, or to find people who speak your native tongue, here are some tips:

Socialising:
- American Women's Clubs
- International Women's Clubs
- National Clubs ("Nationality" + Club + Switzerland in Google will turn up suggestions)
- InterNations

Networking:
- chambers of commerce (the British-Swiss Chamber is particularly active, but several others exist)
- professional groups
- alumni groups
- Toastmasters (public speaking)

Be careful of any brand-new organisations that charge membership fees. New groups are sprouting up all the time, and only the rare new group has any added value. In that regard, the chambers of commerce, alumni groups and national clubs are a safer bet.

FINDING
YOUR FEET

The Swiss press enjoys reporting on resident foreigners who fail to fit in. Many Swiss claim foreigners are not as interested in Switzerland's customs and traditions as they are themselves. But the truth is, many newcomers are fascinated by their new home, and the best place to start your process of integration is right in your own neighbourhood. If you take the time to learn some local history, shop locally, attend neighbourhood festivities, and inform yourself about the basics – from the post office to recycling bins – you will be rewarded. Your interest plus demonstrable knowledge of Switzerland (the more local, the better) is the best reply to the main argument many have against foreigners, namely disinterest. If you can show that you are aware of your surroundings and the people and culture, you'll be more quickly accepted.

BE LIKE TONY

Tony is originally from Liverpool but he's made Switzerland his home. Despite living in the trendy Seefeld neighbourhood of Zurich, there is not a part of the city that he does not know or visit frequently. He knows people all over the city and where to find the best deals. Moreover, despite not speaking a high level of German, he chats to people every chance he gets. If you want to integrate into Swiss society, be curious and talk to people, like Tony. Here's how:

When you first arrive:

- many cities and municipalities will send you an information packet. Many municipalities (including all the big cities) invite people who have recently moved to the city to a free welcoming event (Swiss and non-Swiss alike). It's a good place to meet others in a similar situation and learn basic information like where to find recycling bins and how to prepare your rubbish for pick-up.

Read:

- free local and national newspapers, particularly the culture sections
- blogs like: Newly Swissed, New in Zurich, Girlfriend Guide, Harry's Ding, Ron Orp, etc.
- your calendar marked with Swiss holidays and local events. They vary from canton to canton and are a chance to catch the Swiss at their best.
- posters for cultural events – on trams and trains and in bars, or on poster pillars in parks or on the pavement at junctions

Visit (or follow on social media):

- community centres
- local museums
- free lectures at local universities in English or the local language
- lidos and public swimming pools that are popular in summer
- local markets (typically on Saturdays)
- independent cafés, restaurants, shops and businesses. Building a relationship with staff will help you feel like a local.

Volunteer:

- many municipalities have listings for volunteer opportunities.
- language exchanges. Many people are looking for tandem partners to practice their language skills. You can improve your newly acquired language and help a local learn your native language.
- join the parent-teacher association at your child's school. This gives you an ability to converse with other parents and applies to both local and international schools. Volunteering in schools, earlier unknown in Switzerland, is quickly becoming more common. Speak with your child's teacher.
- Switzerland has a strong work placement and internship culture. If you're not working, consider looking for an organisation or business where you can help out. These positions are generally paid (1,000–2,000Fr per month for full time workers) and last a minimum of six months.

BREAKING THROUGH

The first rule to life in Switzerland is: introduce yourself. Unlike in other parts of the world, where new neighbours and colleagues will show up at your door or desk to greet you and introduce themselves, in Switzerland the introduction needs to come from the newly-arrived person. Likewise, you may know your neighbours' names and when they do their washing, but that does not mean they are your friends and they might not jump at an invitation for dinner.

An easy way to make the first move is to invite your neighbours to what the Swiss call an *Apéro*, which is quite like an open house. Be sure to plan at least a month in advance. Your neighbours will most likely bring some gifts. This sometimes-awkward ritual is the best way to show everyone you're friendly and interested in meeting them.

AT WORK

Many foreigners are used to the idea that they make their best friends at work. The Swiss have a clear work-life separation. Private matters are not discussed at work and work is left at the office (with the exception of discussing your association or club, which can garner you respect). But there are some ways to get around this rule:

- go for lunch with your colleagues. The predetermined time is less intimidating for them and they will most likely offer you a tasty nugget of personal information from which you can start a deeper relationship. Don't talk about work.
- find people in your office who are also newcomers to the city. Someone from Basel working in Zurich may feel almost as foreign in their new surroundings as you do, and a native French or Italian-speaking Swiss in the German-speaking part might feel more in common with you than their fellow Swiss.
- be the life of the party. After-work *Apéros* might last a mere hour, but your organising them shows initiative.

SLOW PROGRESS

The four stages of knowing people in Switzerland:
- first a stranger
- then an acquaintance
- then a colleague
- and finally (maybe) a friend.

FOREIGN OR LOCAL

You are most likely to make different types of friends in Switzerland: expats, foreigners who intend to stay, and Swiss.

- Expats are the easiest to befriend, because these people are usually open, outgoing and like to network. The downside is that they are transient and will most likely move away after a few years. Expat friends will often be your first contacts here and introduce you to other people.
- Foreign locals are people like you, who are not from Switzerland and with whom you can connect more easily because they are also trying to integrate, and you share in the experience. Furthermore, they plan on staying here for some time or indefinitely. The best place to meet these people is as fellow parents at your child's school and through the chamber of commerce.
- International Swiss: these are Swiss who have spent time abroad. They've grown up in another country, or studied or worked away from Switzerland. These Swiss tend to be open to non-Swiss friends and like to connect with people from the countries where they have spent time. If you work for a multinational, you'll probably have some of these in your office. You'll also find that they frequent Irish and English pubs in Switzerland.
- Swiss: the Swiss split into two groups: local and non-local. It's easier to befriend non-locals, as they are also trying to integrate into the area of Switzerland that they are now living in, and they share this experience with you. The locals are the hardest because they have a circle of friends and family and are not necessarily looking for new friends.

In all cases, those willing to put in the effort will eventually make friends. Try to balance your friends to have people around you who will not move away quickly. Furthermore, you're likely to start becoming Swiss in your thinking about friendship and not call every acquaintance a friend so fast in the future.

SWISS ROMANCE

According to the Federal Statistics Office, over a third of marriages in Switzerland in 2018 were between Swiss and non-Swiss and over 15% were between two non-Swiss. That means your chance of snagging a partner in Switzerland is pretty good (if you don't already have one). Younger generations might find it easier, as millennial Swiss have travelled more and have grown up with social media. Just like all things in Switzerland, though, these things take time and vary from canton to canton.

Swiss women were late to gain the right to vote (1971, federally). As a result, even younger women still carry the weight of growing up in a patriarchal society. This fact divides them into three camps: while some of women actively defend domesticity – staying home and caring for children – others activity fight against it, and the third group, spanning a broad spectrum, balance traditional Swiss family values and their personal, professional lives. If you're looking to find a Swiss woman as a partner, you will want to gently probe where on the spectrum she stands.

Swiss men tend to be proper and well mannered. German-speaking Swiss men, unlike their Italian and French-Swiss cousins, tend to be more reserved and shyer. Traditional Swiss men are typically looking for a partner to meet domestic expectations; this is especially true in the countryside. If you like home life and potentially want to be a stay-at-home parent or work part-time, a Swiss man might be the man of your dreams. If that is not your idea of the ideal relationship, look for Swiss men who have studied or worked outside of Switzerland or are open to non-traditional relationship models.

DATING

A quick search around the internet about dating in Switzerland will tell you that foreigners find it difficult, especially foreign women. Lesley Lawson Botez, a Geneva-based psychologist and author, believes it is more difficult for foreign women who are in Switzerland with a job, because they are on their A-game, work long hours and are looking for a partner who is as driven as they are, which limits the field. Trea Tijmens from the Zurich- and Geneva-based *Success Match* believes that all foreigners looking for a partner in Switzerland need to stay positive and open to finding someone who does not check all their boxes. Of course, all of the standard dating platforms like Parship, Bumble, Tinder, Grindr etc. also work in Switzerland.

IN A RELATIONSHIP

Like all relationships, romance with a Swiss partner comes with its ups and downs. You'll have an instant connection to your partner's friends and family. Most likely your Swiss partner is well-educated and enjoys a high standard of living. Moreover, if you get married, and you want to become Swiss – at least on paper – you'll be eligible for the facilitated naturalisation process.

However, a dual-culture relationship has its own particular set of complications, and you should openly discuss these with your partner. When you fight with your partner, it's easy to blame the cultural difference. Because nationality and language are such omnipresent issues, many tend to blame them as the root cause of tension. Often, however, the real problems are more profound and need to be discussed. In addition, the Swiss partner will often be the person to take care of administrative, legal, financial and other formal matters that require linguistic competency and a solid knowledge of procedures, rules and norms, so it is wise to talk about how much you value your autonomy – and what you can do to get it back.

MEET YOUR EXPERT

Greg Zwygart is the editor-in-chief of *Mannschaft Magazin*, a monthly publication (in German) for gay and bisexual men in Germany and Switzerland. At age 18 he decided to leave Switzerland behind for the hustle and bustle of New York. He felt that the small alpine country had nothing to offer a young gay man. But fear not: gay and lesbian life in Switzerland is not half as bad as that teenager made it out to be. Greg moved back in 2010 and has been convinced ever since that there is no place he'd rather live.

16 GAY AND LESBIAN

As you might have guessed, Switzerland is not considered top of the list when it comes to the ultimate destination for gays and lesbians. Whereas European hubs such as Barcelona, Berlin and London offer packed calendars for the rainbow community, events in Switzerland are few and far between. This doesn't mean that Switzerland isn't attractive to LGBT visitors. Zurich is home to the biggest gay and lesbian community in the country, with weekly nightlife options such as the Cranberry Bar and Heaven Nightclub. But the community is also out and about in other cities. Drag queens regularly host gay bingo in Basel, the gay and lesbian sports club in Bern wins multiple medals at international competitions, and Geneva and Lucerne – among other cities – are home to annual queer film festivals. Head up to the Alps in January for Gay Skiweek in Arosa, which attracts guests from all over the world. Add a high rate of acceptance among the population to the list and you can look forward to a comfortable and safe day-to-day life in Switzerland as a gay man or lesbian.

THE LOWDOWN
- Get to know the community and where they hang out
- Discover every aspect of LGBT life in Switzerland
- Catch up on the legal situation in daily life and in the work place. Find out how accepting the Swiss really are and what they think about public displays of affection

ZURICH

As the biggest city in Switzerland, Zurich is also a popular hotspot among gays and lesbians. It's the heart of the Swiss community with a large selection of nightlife, sports and cultural activities. Heaven is the only explicitly queer club and especially popular with the younger club crowd. Depending on the evening, local and international DJs play different styles of music, with regular drag shows taking centre stage. For after-work drinks head over to the Cranberry bar and try their signature cocktails, such as *Schlampe* (literally, slut) or *Chlorpfütze* (puddle of bleach). Zurich's reputation as a mecca for same-sex love dates back to the 1940s. An underground organisation for gay men called *Der Kreis* (or The Circle) published an eponymous magazine that quickly attracted a growing readership in Switzerland but also in Germany, Britain and the USA. While neighbouring countries were rebuilding their cities and slowly recovering from World War II, a buzzing subculture for gay men flourished in Zurich with Barfüsser Bar as the central meeting point; it still exists today as a sushi restaurant. Lavish costume balls attracted men from all corners of the country and abroad. The authorities, however, weren't happy with this colourful scene going on in their city and, as in many other Swiss towns, the police kept a 'homo register', in which they recorded the names of all known homosexual men and the people they associated with. The 2014 film The Circle takes a look back at those turbulent times and tells the love story of Röbi Rapp and Ernst Ostertag, two lifelong LGBT-activists. This film by director Stefan Haupt received several awards and was the Swiss entry at the Oscars for Best Foreign Language Film.

THINGS TO DO IN ZURICH

- Cranberry Bar (cranberry.ch) and Heaven Club (heavenclub.ch) are located within walking distance of the heart of downtown Zurich and are both popular hangouts. Cranberry is open daily, Heaven on Fridays, Saturdays and nights before public holidays.
- Different parties take place at regular intervals and cater to a variety of music tastes: Heldenbar (Wednesdays, alternative), Angels (circuit), Kiki (electronic), Offstream (alternative), Boyahkasha (R&B, drag) and Ladies Temptation (lesbian). The websites gay.ch and her2her.com provide information about upcoming dates.
- For twenty years the queer cultural month, Warm May (warmermai.ch), has been held every May.
- Pink Apple is an annual film festival in May that screens queer movies from all over the world.
- Gaysport Zürich (gaysport.ch) offers a variety of sports, including badminton, boot camps, tennis and yoga.

ZURICH PRIDE

With over 50,000 visitors, Zurich Pride Festival (zurichpridefestival.ch) is Switzerland's biggest LGBT event. Organisations, clubs, political parties and companies such as Google, Swiss Post, SBB as well as Credit Suisse and UBS take part in the pride march which, unlike in many other European cities, is not an exclusive event. The public is not only allowed but also encouraged to take part in the colourful parade! The subsequent open-air festival is free and often features LGBT favorites, such as Conchita Wurst, Betty and Vengaboys. There is also a political stage and various information booths staffed by LGBT organisations for those seeking a quieter, more political pride experience. During Pride, several official and unofficial pride parties pop up all over Zurich.

RAINBOW SWITZERLAND

You're not going to Zurich but to another corner of Switzerland? Have no fear – as long as you're not sentenced to milking cows on a lonely alp, you will find accessible community life in other parts of the country too. Although Basel, Bern, Geneva, Lausanne and Lucerne have much smaller LGBT populations than Zurich, these cities also have their fair share of queer happenings.

- Check out these annual LGBT film festivals: Luststreifen in Basel, Queersicht in Bern, Pink Panorama in Lucerne and Everybody's Perfect in Geneva.
- From gay bingo to drag shows and queer carnival festivities, gaybasel.org keeps you in the loop on local events in Basel.
- Tolerdance is one of the oldest gay parties in Switzerland, going strong for over 25 years! The party takes place every fourth Saturday of the month with alternating DJs playing pop and electronica. See bern.lgbt for the lowdown on all events in Bern.
- Frigay Night and Queerbad are the places to be in Lucerne.
- The website 360.ch informs you about news and events in French-speaking Switzerland. In German-speaking Switzerland, gay.ch gives you an overview of parties and events. Head over to her2her.com for the scoop on parties and get-togethers for lesbian and bisexual women.

Many of these events take place only sporadically or once a month. The fact is that many bars and parties for gays and lesbians have closed in recent years, including in Zurich. On the one hand the internet with its social media and dating platforms has diminished the demand for the classic gay bar; on the other hand cheap flights have had a considerable effect on community life as well. Party animals jet to Berlin or Barcelona for the weekend – major cities with festivals and events that are unrivalled in Switzerland.

PRIDE ROMANDE

Pride Romande is the second-largest pride event in Switzerland, albeit less commercial and more political than the one in Zurich. The festivities are usually organized by LGBT organisations and take place in a different city every year, mostly in French-speaking Switzerland. In addition to cities such as Delémont, Fribourg, Geneva and Lausanne, Pride Romande has also been to Bern and Lugano. The pride parade usually runs through the city centre and is, like in Zurich, open to everyone. Visit the Pride Village for food stands, political speeches and entertainment, followed by an official party at a local club. Check the internet or contact local LGBT organisations to find out which city will host the upcoming Pride Romande.

TRANS PEOPLE

The legal and social situation for trans people in Switzerland leaves much to be desired. For example, the current law on the protection of gays, lesbians and bisexuals against discrimination does not address gender identity. A change of name and gender on legal documents involves a lengthy bureaucratic process and a judge's decision. Depending on the judge and the canton, surgery might even be required – a decision that has been successfully challenged in the past. Unlike Germany and Canada, Switzerland does not recognise a third gender. In Swiss daily life, trans people do not enjoy the same level of acceptance as gay, lesbian and bisexual persons so. Transgender Network Switzerland estimates that currently every fourth trans person loses their job after coming out. By launching the new campaign TransWelcome (transwelcome.ch), the organisation hopes to raise more awareness among companies for the concerns of trans people.

WHERE IS EVERYONE?

Moving from a big city to Switzerland often involves feeling lonely for any newcomer. The fastest way to get involved in the local scene is, of course, through dating apps. Especially popular with gay men are Grindr, PlanetRomeo and Tinder; lesbian women turn to Her2Her and Tinder. While my lesbian sister tells me that it's easy to strike up a conversation with women, I know from experience that it can be a lot more difficult for men to establish long-term contacts – especially when sex is not the main focus. The Swiss tend to be reserved when it comes to getting to know one another so it's not surprising that on platforms like Grindr or PlanetRomeo you'll find many faceless profiles and photos of naked torsos. My recommendation: show your face, write something about yourself and let people know that you are looking to build meaningful friendships.

Don't be afraid to meet new people the old-fashioned way, by venturing out of the comfort of your home and joining an association. After all, this typically Swiss institution is also popular with gays and lesbians! Check out one of the outdoor providers or LGBT sports groups mentioned in this chapter.

If you are more the cultural and political type, reach out to the local LGBT film festival or LGBT organisation as volunteer work is always appreciated. In Bern and Zurich there are choirs for gay and bisexual men called schwubs (schwubs.ch) and schmaz (schmaz.ch). The choir Rosa (chor-rosa.ch) in Zurich is open to all genders.

GET SPORTY

The Swiss are outdoorsy people, so it's no surprise that there are sporting activities aplenty for gays and lesbians. So why not get yourself moving? You'll not only do your health a favour but also get a chance to meet new and likeminded people. Pink Alpine (pinkalpine.ch) and Outdoor Sports for Gays (gaypeak.wordpress.com) offer hiking, mountain bike tours and winter sports for newbies and the more advanced. For those looking to combine skiing or snowboarding with some *Glühwein* and après-ski, check out Arosa Gay Skiweek (arosa-gayskiweek.com). The LGBT sports groups in the cities of Basel (lgsportbasel.ch), Bern (glsbe.ch) and Zurich (gaysport.ch) feature different sports with training opportunities. 360.ch provides information on sports in French-speaking Switzerland.

GET STEAMY

Unlike bars and clubs, saunas for gay men have more or less survived the internet revolution as meeting places, either for sexual adventures or making new contacts – or both. In addition to dry saunas and steam baths, most venues have a bar where beer and cocktails make it easy to strike up a conversation. Popular saunas are Pink Beach in Lausanne, Sundeck and Aqualis in Bern, Mann-o-Mann in St Gallen, Sunnyday in Basel and Bains de l'est in Geneva. On selected weekends, Moustache in Zurich brings in a DJ to create a club atmosphere.

INFORMATION

Pink Cross (pinkcross.ch), the Swiss federation of gay and bisexual men, the Swiss Lesbian Organisation LOS (los.ch) and Transgender Network Switzerland (tgns.ch) represent the political interests of LGBT people in Switzerland and organise various get-togethers for their members. *Mannschaft Magazin* (mannschaft.com) and gay.ch are media outlets for LGBT news worldwide, 360.ch and swissgay.ch for French-speaking Switzerland.

STAY HEALTHY

Checkpoint Zurich is a sexual health centre for gay men and provides testing for common sexually-transmitted diseases. The team of physicians and other specialists focuses on HIV, PrEP and questions about coming out, and offers psychological consultations. Checkpoints are also located in Basel, Bern, Geneva and Lausanne. Though some centres have walk-in days, you will generally need an appointment. Depending on your health insurance policy, medical services provided by the doctors can be billed directly to your insurer, but not the costs of tests (mycheckpoint.ch).

GAY AND LESBIAN STARS

As Switzerland's main fashion, finance and entertainment hub, Zurich is home to many gay and lesbian celebrities. Popular faces on Swiss radio and television include Sven Epiney, Mario Grossniklaus and business journalist Reto Lipp. Other personalities include comedian Jonny Fischer, pop singer Michael von der Heide and singer Tiziana Gulino. The most famous lovebirds in Switzerland are without doubt model Tamy Glauser and the former Miss Switzerland, Dominique Rinderknecht – dubbed #Tamynique by the media. Not forgetting Corine Mauch, the mayor of Zurich since 2009.

GET NETWORKING

Like other corporations, Swiss Post and SBB have internal networks for LGBT employees for activities that go beyond the normal working day. Professional and private networking is also possible through members' organisations: Network (network.ch) is the association for gay executives and entrepreneurs, with several regional groups all over Switzerland; Wybernet (wybernet.ch) is dedicated to lesbian professionals.

YOUR RIGHTS

Switzerland has some catching up to do when it comes to the legal situation for gays and lesbians. The usual human rights' poster-child lands midfield when compared to other European countries (rainbow-europe.org). Reasons for this include the lack of protection against hate speech and discrimination as well as the absence of marriage equality. Another example are restrictive blood donor rules applied to gay and bisexual men. There is change on the horizion, but at a leisurely pace – as anyone living in Switzerland might expect. In February 2020, Swiss voters approved a law on protecting sexual orientation from discrimination. By 2021, the legal commission of the National Council must submit a draft law for marriage equality – almost eight years after the parliamentary initiative was taken up!

Still, Switzerland took on a pioneering role with civil unions. In 2005, it was the first country to legalise same-sex partnerships through a popular vote. Registered couples have similar rights to married couples, excluding adoption and simplified naturalisation of a foreign partner. Lesbian couples are at a disadvantage compared to heterosexual women in that they receive a lower pension after their partner's death. With the legalisation of same-sex marriage, civil unions would be discontinued and all existing partnerships converted to marriage.

Although homosexuality was decriminalised as early as 1942, gays and lesbians in Switzerland still struggled with stigmatisation for a long time, culminating in the AIDS crisis of the 1980s and early 1990s. Today, gays and lesbians are widely accepted, especially in urban and suburban areas. According to a survey conducted by the research institute gfs, 74% of the Swiss population is in favour of marriage equality.

BE SAFE

According to a recent OECD study, only one third of all gays and lesbians in German-speaking countries are out on the job, although the workplace in Switzerland is usually very accepting. Even the Swiss army trains its officers in aspects of diversity and inclusion. At job interviews, you are free not to answer questions about your marital status, your sexual orientation or whether you plan on having children. When it comes to public displays of affection, play it like the Swiss and use discretion. If you plan on holding hands with your partner, be prepared for some curious looks and/or one or two comments from strangers, even in larger cities.

Unfortunately there have also been reports of violence against gay couples in the street, mostly at night. If that happens, it is advisable to inform the police and the LGBT helpline (lgbt-helpline.ch).

ADOPTION

In Switzerland, same-sex couples in a registered partnership are not allowed to adopt children, but gay or lesbian individuals are – a paradox that will come to an end if marriage equality and adoption rights are legalised. Step-child adoption was introduced in 2018. This means that a person in a civil union can adopt the children of their partner from a previous relationship and act as legal guardian. At present, lesbian couples are barred from accessing reproductive medicine, including sperm donation. Surrogacy is prohibited in Switzerland, even for heterosexual couples. More information is available from Regenbogen-familien, the association of rainbow families (regenbogenfamilien.ch).

CIVIL UNIONS

Are you looking to fall in love in Switzerland? Your chances are good! According to the Swiss Federal Statistical Office, more than half of all civil unions in 2017 between two men were between a Swiss and a foreign citizen. With the exception of adoption rights and simplified naturalisation, registered partnerships are equal to marriage and afford partners legal security when it comes to inheritance and medical matters. Your income, however, is subject to joint taxation and your pensions will no longer be calculated separately, meaning that they will be smaller than the sum of two individual pensions. Civil unions are also open to foreign nationals. Same-sex couples who have married abroad will have their marriage 'downgraded' to a registered partnership in Switzerland.

MEET YOUR EXPERT

Margaret Oertig originates from Scotland and has lived in Switzerland since 1987. She has worked for many years as an intercultural communication trainer for companies in Switzerland and abroad. She is also the author of *The New Beyond Chocolate – Understanding Swiss Culture* and *Going Local – Your Guide to Swiss Schooling*, both published by Bergli Books. Margaret is a lecturer at the FHNW (University of Applied Sciences and Arts, Northwestern Switzerland). Her husband is Swiss and they have two adult daughters.

17
ETIQUETTE

There is more to etiquette than meets the eye in Switzerland. This chapter provides tips and explanations to help things go smoothly in your interactions with the locals around the country. Even if you don't get it quite right first time, people will appreciate your efforts as a sign of respect for their local language and customs.

You may notice that your client adviser at the bank addresses you formally by your surname, as does the letting agent for your rental accommodation. The correct use of greetings and names is a form of ritual behaviour that Swiss people find very important. They are used to differentiating between first name and surname relationships and the nature of the relationship also affects whether they shake hands when they meet or kiss or hug, even at work.

Other topics in this chapter include what you should wear to a social event, when you should arrive and what are good topics of conversation. Some key rules related to food and drink and public transport are also provided.

THE LOWDOWN

- Navigate Switzerland's complex code of greetings
- Master everything you need for social events, from the ubiquitous apéro to a formal dinner
- Get on with your neighbours and learn the Do's and Don'ts of small talk

GREETING

All around Switzerland, people greet each other with a ritual expression such as *Grüezi*, *Bonjour* or *Buon giorno*. See the greetings table below for more examples. Keep the following in mind:

- say the ritual greeting expression to neighbours, shop assistants and work colleagues.
- make firm eye contact as you greet people.
- use the person's name with the greeting if you know it in German-speaking Switzerland.

Relationship categories: the Swiss divide their social environment into people with whom they use first names and those with whom they use surnames. They use:

- surnames with strangers and clients.
- first names with family and friends.
- first names by mutual agreement with work colleagues and neighbours.
- first names, if they're young adults talking to other young adults, even if they are strangers.

Please see opposite for more on this topic.

Kiss, hug or shake hands: people shake hands, kiss or hug when they meet, depending on their age, relationship and location. This is how it works.

- Shaking hands is the most formal custom.
- Air or cheek kissing is the custom with friends and family: male to female or female to female.
- Men rarely kiss other men; they shake hands even with their male family and friends.
- Some people kiss three times; young people might only kiss once.
- Hugging and/or kissing is most common among young adults, but is growing more common among people of all ages.
- At work, shaking hands is the safest approach, unless the other person initiates kissing or hugging.

FORMAL greetings

	German-speaking	French-speaking	Italian-speaking
Hello	*Grüezi* (High German: *Guten Tag*)	*Bonjour*	*Buon giorno*
Goodbye	*Adieu, Adé, Uf Wiederluege* (High German: *Auf Wiedersehen*)	*Au revoir*	*Arrivederci*
Use of name with greeting	*Herr/Frau Müller*	*Not required, or Monsieur/ Madame*	*Not required, or Signor/Signora*
Way to say "you"	*Sie*	*Vous*	*Lei*

INFORMAL greetings

	German-speaking	French-speaking	Italian-speaking
Hello	Hoi/Hallo/Sali	Salut	Ciao
Goodbye	Tschüss/Ciao	Au revoir	Ciao
Use of name with greeting	First name	First name (optional)	First name (optional)
Way to say "you"	Du	Tu	Tu

PEACHES & COCONUTS

The peaches and coconuts model provides an easy way to understand the complicated subject of using first names (or not) with people. The outer layer of the peach or coconut represents a person's public space and the inner layer their private space. Put simply, people who take a peachy approach to relating to others will talk in a relaxed, friendly manner to new people they meet, as if they were already friends. They are comfortable using first names with (almost) everyone as a way of breaking down barriers. This approach tends to be used by Americans and people from other English-speaking cultures who are fairly mobile.

Those who take a coconut approach tend to make a clearer distinction between their friends and family on the inside of the coconut and others on the outside of the coconut. Swiss people tend to make this distinction. They will use first names with their friends and some work colleagues to express a degree of familiarity and surnames with others to express a respectful distance. They do not feel the need to break down barriers with everyone.

ENTERTAINING

Typical occasions to which you might be invited are brunch, coffee, an apéro, dinner or a party. Brunch, coffee and dinner will probably have a fixed starting time, while an apéro or party might be more flexible. Check the wording on the invitation. An apéro could consist of drinks and snacks. An *apéro riche* is more like dinner, but it is not served as a sit-down meal. If no finishing time is given, and there is plenty of food around, people could stay for hours. A birthday party in the evening is likely to be a sit-down dinner rather than a stand-up party where you mill around, glass in hand. People sometimes invite others to birthday dinners in restaurants rather than at home. Then the host pays for everything, including all alcohol (usually bubbly, beer and wine). When arriving at an event, keep in mind:

- if there is a fixed starting time, arrive within five minutes of it in German-speaking Switzerland, and within 15 to 30 minutes of it in Ticino and Romandie.
- if you are going to be late, text your host to apologise and say when you'll be arriving.
- when you arrive at a small gathering, introduce yourself to everyone already there, shaking hands and saying your name.
- in German-speaking Switzerland, greet each person by name, if you know it. If you've forgotten someone's name, you should apologise and ask them to remind you of it. (The older you get, the more forgiveable this is.) Asking shows you think their name is important and want to get it right.
- avoid crossing arms with others while shaking hands as it is meant to bring bad luck. This can happen if there are four or more people trying to shake hands with each other at the same time.

SAYING CHEERS

- Wait until the host initiates saying cheers before you start to drink. Join in saying cheers, looking round at everyone at the table. This is _Prost_ or _Zum Wohl_ in German, _Santé_ in French and _Salute_ or _Cin cin_ in Italian. There are other local variations too.
- Clink glasses with everyone sitting near you, and say cheers again. Everyone then takes their first sip at the same time.
- In theory, with a large group, people do not clink glasses, but in practice they will often get up from their seats and reach over to do so with people further along their table.
- Thank your host for the invitation when saying cheers.
- Wait until the host indicates that you should start to eat.

SOCIALISING

Swiss people generally don't strike up a conversation with strangers when out and about, e.g. in shops, restaurants or on public transport. They tend not to see the point in sharing their opinions or experiences with people they will possibly never see again. The exception may be if you have (unwittingly) done something wrong, like parking in the wrong place.

At social gatherings, people will be happy to share their opinions and experiences on certain topics, but will not talk very personally with people they do not know well. Popular, fairly neutral topics of conversation include:
• holidays, day trips or shopping
• hobbies, gardens or sport
• books, concerts, festivals, films or Netflix series
• local news and events, such as building a new car park
• their children's school level, free time activities, etc

If you want to chat a bit more personally, you could talk about:
• where you come from
• whether they have visited the country/town you come from
• how often you go back there
• where they grew up (possibly not where they live now)
• the regional dialect they speak (for German-speaking Swiss)

WATCH OUT!

Small talk topics considered less appropriate include:

- local news and politics which could be seen to be controversial, such as closing down the local refugee centre
- illness, politics, sex, religion or money
- details about your job or workplace politics
- your problems or your family's problems
- funny stories about your family that could sound critical of someone

PRESENTS

Swiss people may give generous gifts as thanks for practical help, such as taking in the mail or watering a neighbour's plants when they are away. Some will bring a present from their holiday location, while others give a bottle of wine.

The Swiss tend to be good at remembering to wish people a happy birthday, but are cautious about giving birthday gifts to others they do not know well. They are aware of the possibility of starting something that will become an expectation for years to come. The obvious exception to this is when they are invited to a birthday party and take a generous birthday gift.

Hosts are quite pragmatic about asking for money as a birthday or wedding gift. They may even specify on the invitation that they would like money towards a holiday or honeymoon, rather than lots of smaller presents. If they don't specify this, you can ask them if there is anything they would like. They will then tell you if they are saving for something.

Guests give generous gifts when invited to someone's home. Typical gifts when invited to dinner are wine, flowers, chocolate and even a well-chosen book. They will also take a small gift when invited for a coffee. Guests will usually not offer to bring food, eg a salad or dessert, unless they move in international circles and are used to doing this. They may also not be familiar with the idea of pot luck meals, where everyone brings a dish to share. Guests tend not to write thank you texts or cards. The gift is the thank you.

DRESS CODES

In general, the Swiss do not adhere to strict <u>dress codes</u> and you may search in vain for clear guidelines on what to wear to an event in your free time. Cultural values of autonomy, authenticity and pragmatism result in people deciding for themselves what they feel comfortable wearing. They will turn up to the opera, theatre, concerts, etc in anything from suits and cocktail dresses to jeans and t-shirts. Schoolteachers and their pupils tend to dress casually, often in jeans and t-shirts, and this sets a relaxed standard for later life.

As an exception to the above, very posh hotels may stipulate a dress code for dinner, eg a jacket and tie for men. Another exception is the sauna, where you are expected to wear nothing at all and may be thrown out if you turn up in swimwear. There are also designated nudist bathing zones (known as *FKK*, or *Freie Körperkult* in German) by some rivers, lakes and even swimming pools. The etiquette there would be not to scream if you see a naked person walking towards you.

Swiss people tend to dress casually for parties and some also dress fairly casually for weddings. You can ask your host what others will be wearing, and follow suit. Clothes are neat (usually well ironed) and understated and people like to spend their money on brand names rather than extravagant design. You are unlikely to see a lot of gaudy dresses, frills or sparkly bits.

TOP TIP

If a formal invitation states the dress code as 'Smoking', that doesn't mean only smokers can attend. A 'smoking' is worn for a black-tie event, as it is a dinner jacket or tuxedo.

WORK ATTIRE

Things are a bit more complicated when it comes to clothes for work. It depends largely on the company culture or even the department culture. Four categories are listed below, with simple examples of what people typically wear.

Business formal: for interviews, important meetings, or in the financial sector and consulting (client-facing)
- men: grey, blue or black suit with blue or white shirt and tie, black shoes
- women: grey, blue or black suit or dress with trousers or skirt, black shoes, not open-toed
- TIP: if you have a job interview and want to see what the locals buy, look up suits on Swiss clothing store websites such as Globus and PKZ (*Anzug* in German and *costume* in French).

Business casual: working in office (not client-facing)
- men: trousers and long-sleeved business shirt, no tie, sports jacket, black or brown shoes
- women: dress or trousers/skirt with blouse or smart t-shirt, blazer, range of shoe colours

Smart casual
- men: trousers, dark blue or black jeans and shirt or polo shirt, jacket
- women: skirt or trousers, blue or black jeans and blouse or t-shirt, jacket or cardigan

Casual
- jeans and t-shirts or shorts and flipflops

You may find a real mix of styles in some international companies, with marketing managers dressed in a business casual style and data managers in shorts and flipflops. Presumably the data managers have earned the right to dress as they please.

ENCOUNTERS

There are a few things to keep in mind when you encounter others on the street, in shops and when using public transport.

Staring: people have a tendency to look strangers in the eye when out and about. They may not even be aware they are doing this. They might seem to be staring at you as they wonder whether to cook rice or pasta for dinner. On the other hand, they may be deliberately giving you a meaningful look, for example if they think you are talking loudly on your phone on the tram.

Keeping to the right: another tendency is for people to veer to the right as they pass each other on the pavement as if they were cars. If they don't do this, they are probably foreign or are out walking their dog. The dog gets to decide where to walk, usually close to a hedgerow with its interesting smells.

Queuing: there is not a highly developed queuing culture in Switzerland. If there are many customers at a meat counter, for example, the assistants may ask the customers, "Who's next?". You may need to be alert to who comes after you and speak up for yourself or move forward when it's your turn.

Some places, such as large post offices and busy train stations, have introduced ticketed queuing to get over this problem; be sure to take a ticket.

People may not form an orderly queue to get off and on trains and trams. At the ski lift, you need to defend your place in the queue and spread out your ski sticks to block people who are trying to overtake you (this is where snowboarders without sticks have a disadvantage).

Finding a seat: when travelling on public transport, people sometimes take up adjacent seats with their bags while the bus, tram or train is half-empty. They may then not get round to moving them as the seats fill up.

    If you are looking for a seat, it is up to you to take the initiative and ask if the seat is free (*Ist der Platz noch frei?* in German, *Est-ce que cette place est libre?* in French and *È libero questo posto?* in Italian). Standing beside a blocked seat and looking meaningfully at it does not usually work. Looking old does not always help either.

Noise levels: Swiss people are conscious of noise levels and tend to talk quietly in public places, unless they get carried away in a large group out on a day trip. Some people talk loudly on their phones, and others look annoyed about this. Everyone is silent in the first class silent compartment on trains. People working on their laptops may remind others of this rule if they start chatting to each other.

Eating and drinking: there may be a no eating or drinking rule on buses and trams in your town. In theory you could be fined if you contravene this rule. There are many unwritten rules and expectations around eating on trains. Commuters apparently hate it when their fellow passengers eat smelly food on the train, or scrape out their yogurt pots too loudly, but you will not be fined if you do this.

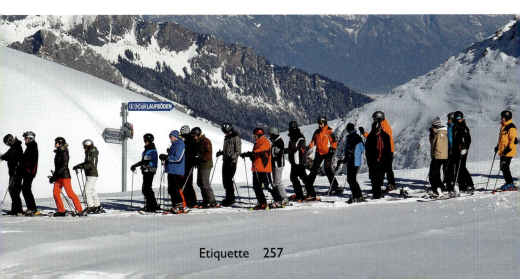

MEET YOUR EXPERT

Diccon Bewes is a British travel writer and author of five books on Switzerland, including the number one bestseller, *Swiss Watching*. He arrived back in 2005 and fell in love with Switzerland and its people (and chocolate) so started writing about his life here. In doing so, he became an accidental expat expert and regularly speaks about the joys and trials of living in Switzerland. Recently he took the momentous decision to become Swiss. You can follow him via his website dicconbewes.com, on Twitter (@dicconb) or on Facebook (facebook.com/ SwissWatching).

18

BECOMING SWISS

Once you know how to recycle your paper, understand what direct democracy is and realise that not all the cheese has holes, then you're ready for the final step. You're ready to become Swiss, something roughly 42,000 other resident foreigners do every year. Of course, this being Switzerland, that isn't a simple process, or a cheap one. And, as with most things Swiss, the precise rules for acquiring citizenship depend on where you live. There are basic federal regulations, which cantons and municipalities can add to, so that it might take longer, cost more and involve more steps – or the exact opposite, depending on the local rules. That's because to become Swiss, you actually have to apply at the local level, and be accepted as a citizen of your municipality first.

In this chapter we'll explain how the naturalisation process works from application form to passport. We'll outline the documents you'll need, the tests you'll face, the costs you'll incur and the time it will take – remembering, as always, that every canton and municipality has its own quirky rules.

THE LOWDOWN
- Naturalisation rules for foreigners explained
- A guide to the essential paperwork
- Language levels needed to become Swiss

THE RULES

For many people the route to citizenship is through <u>ordinary naturalisation</u>, based on residency. This falls under the competence of each canton, so your application to become Swiss starts at a local level. Federal law details the basic criteria for ordinary naturalisations, with these the most important for applicants living in Switzerland. You must:

- possess a C <u>permit</u>.
- have lived in Switzerland for at least ten years, three of them within the five years prior to application.
- respect the values of the <u>Federal Constitution</u>.
- not pose a risk to Switzerland's internal or external security.
- show that you are successfully integrated in Switzerland.
- speak and write a national language to a certified minimum level.
- respect public security and order (that means, no criminal record, no current debts and no outstanding taxes).
- participate in economic life (and not be in receipt of any social security benefits), or be in education or training.

You also have to show that you are familiar with the Swiss way of life, eg knowing about Swiss geography, history and politics, participating in the social and cultural life of Switzerland, and having regular contact with Swiss citizens.

These are national criteria but implementation is up to the cantons and municipalities so, for example, cantonal residency rules vary within the obligatory ten-year minimum. It's only two years in Geneva and Zurich whereas many cantons require five, while some municipalities also apply minimum residency requirements. Move house to another canton, or even another <u>municipality</u>, and you may have to start counting again, so always check.

Children born here are not automatically Swiss if neither parent is Swiss, and so face similar rules. The two big differences are: the years lived here between ages 8 and 18 count double towards the ten-year minimum, as long as residency is at least six years; and a language test isn't needed if the child's mother tongue is a national language or he or she has completed five years of obligatory school in Switzerland in a national language.

<u>Dual nationality</u> is allowed as long as the other country permits it as well.

DOCUMENTS

To start the long process of ordinary naturalisation, you'll need these documents in particular to prove that you qualify to become Swiss.

- **C permit**
- **Residency certificate:** this proves that you've lived in your municipality for the minimum required period.
- **Passport:** your nationality isn't important as all citizens are treated the same.
- **Birth certificate:** this must not be more than six months old (the certificate, not the birth) so order a copy from your home country.
- **Proof of marital status:** if you're married, divorced or widowed, you'll need proof. If you're single, you'll be asked to show that you've never been married.

THE SIMPLE ROUTE

For the lucky few, there is a faster and cheaper way to become Swiss: simplified naturalisation. This applies to foreign children who have one Swiss parent or to anyone married to a Swiss citizen. These applications are decided by the State Secretariat for Migration, in consultation with the canton concerned.

For foreigners living in Switzerland and married to a Swiss national, the standard rules still apply, for example minimum language proficiency and knowledge of Switzerland. The big benefit is that minimum residency is reduced to five years, which must include the one leading up to the application, and you must have been married for at least the past three years.

Same-sex couples in a registered partnership cannot benefit from this simpler process. The foreign partner is subject to all the ordinary naturalisation rules, except that he or she can apply after only five years' residency and once the partnership is at least three years old.

The rules do vary for foreigners who live abroad and apply for citizenship via marriage or ancestry. Best to check with the nearest Swiss embassy or consulate.

THE APPLICATION

Becoming Swiss is voluntary, so about a third of resident foreigners have lived here more than the minimum ten years but are not naturalised. Citizenship is not a right, but must be earned. You have to apply and seek approval, and the process depends on the local rules as federal laws are quite broad in this respect. Most applications roughly follow the same procedure: eligibility checks, application form, language tests, Swissness tests, official paperwork, interview and eventually approval (or not). The costs and timings are as variable as everything else in Switzerland.

Application form: it's usually long and detailed so be prepared to fill in your education since kindergarten, your employment history over the past ten years, personal details of your parents and spouse/partner, and maybe even why you want to be Swiss. You must also name three character witnesses, who should be Swiss and live in your municipality or canton.

Language tests and official paperwork: see boxes

Swissness test: some cantons (eg, Bern and Aargau) test your knowledge of Switzerland with a formal written exam, but in others your Swissness is tested during the naturalisation interview. There are few textbooks or practice questions to help you prepare but typical subjects covered are geography, history, politics, the economy, education and the tax/benefit system – all at national, cantonal or local level.

FILM TIP

For a bit of light relief, watch the delightful film, *Die Schweizermacher*. It's from 1978 but much of it is still true, and still funny, today.

Interview: you're required to pass a naturalisation interview at municipal level. Get ready to be grilled by one (or more) local officials on why you're applying, how integrated you are, what leisure activities you enjoy and what you know about your community.

Home visits: these are less common now, though many places still allow them.

Costs: the fixed federal fee is 100Fr per adult, or 150Fr for spouses making a joint application. Then come the cantonal and municipal fees, which usually total around 3,000Fr. Simplified naturalisation is normally much cheaper, at about 900Fr.

Timings and approval: see overleaf

Schweizer Pass
Passeport suisse
Passaporto svizzero
Passaport svizzer
Swiss passport

Applicants have to reach certain levels of proficiency in a language test. The federal minimum is A2 for written and B1 for oral (based on the Common European Framework) but cantons can make it harder for ordinary naturalisations, eg in Thurgau the levels are B1 and B2 respectively. For all ordinary naturalisations, the language tested is that of the municipality where you live, so a native German-speaker living in Nyon has to pass the tests in French. In bilingual municipalities, eg Biel-Bienne, you can choose either official language.

PAPERWORK

These official certificates are normally needed during your application, and generally they should be current, eg not more than three months old. Each can be ordered from the relevant authority, usually at a cost of 20 to 60 francs.

- **Tax:** to show that you owe no taxes.
- **Social security:** to show that you have not received any benefits in the past three years (in some cases up to ten years), or that you have repaid them in full.
- **National insurance:** to show that you are up to date with your contributions to the state pension scheme.
- **Debt collection register:** to show that you pay your bills on time and have no outstanding debts.
- **Criminal record:** to show that you have no previous convictions in Switzerland.

Homeowners, students, pensioners and the self-employed will have to produce further documents to prove their particular circumstances.

THE TIMELINE

In most cantons it takes around two years for an ordinary naturalisation to be completed but, unusually for Switzerland, it isn't an exact science. The law does have set time-limits for the process but exact timings depend on where you live and how many other applications are being processed at the same time. Simplified naturalisations are very often completed more quickly.

You can roughly reckon on about a year from first contact to the crucial interview, during which time you have to pass all the relevant tests and provide all your documentation. The interview is the climax of your direct involvement, and also the pivotal point of the process. You have to pass it to go any further.

GOOD TO KNOW

If your application for ordinary naturalisation is rejected, you can normally apply again but will have to start from scratch — and you're unlikely to get a refund. You might also be able to appeal to the cantonal authorities if you think your rejection by the municipality was unfair. For simplified naturalisations, you can appeal to the Federal Administrative Court.

Then your application has to be approved by the municipality, which in some smaller places is still done by a popular vote in person. In other words, your friends, neighbours and strangers get to decide if you can be Swiss. In larger municipalities such a vote is impractical, so many have a system a bit like planning permission: applicants' names are published and Swiss citizens have 30 days in which to object. Other places leave approval up to the local parliament or immigration commission.

Finally, your naturalisation must be approved by the federal authorities, which is mostly a formality as the critical decisions are taken at municipal and cantonal level. With that done, you can become a citizen of your municipality, often via a public ceremony. That's it: you're Swiss! And then you can start the application for a passport, but that's a whole other story.

THE PROCESS

An abridged version of the whole process for an ordinary naturalisation.

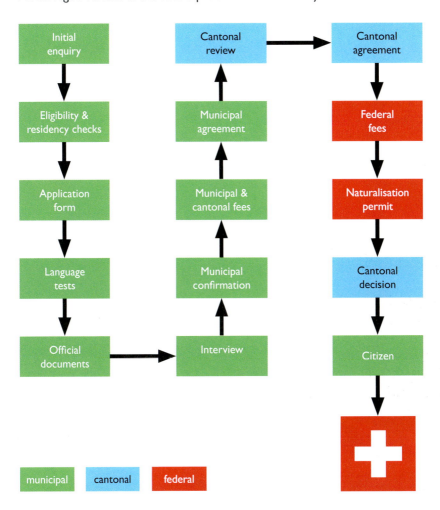

IF THEY SAY NO

Perfectly ordinary foreigners sometimes make the news in Switzerland simply because they didn't become Swiss. For example, the Dutch-born vegan woman who was rejected (twice) by voters in her Aargau municipality. The reason? She was too annoying because she campaigned against cow bells; her appeal to the canton was successful. Or the trilingual Brit in Canton Schwyz who failed his interview for not knowing the population of his community or which canton was home to raclette. Sometimes it's less tangible, such as the Muslim couple in Lausanne rejected for not being well integrated: they refused to shake hands with members of the opposite sex. They won't be travelling with a Swiss passport even if they made the headlines abroad.

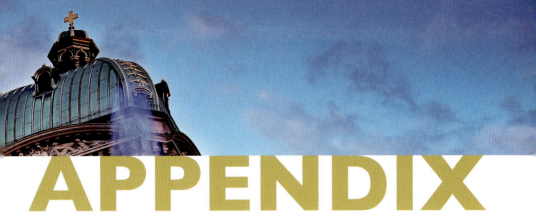

APPENDIX

Essential information about Switzerland:

Area: 41,285km² (134th in the world)
Population: 8,544,527 (100th in the world)
Population density per km²: 205.5 (48th in the world)

Boundaries: 1,899km
- Italy: 744km
- France: 572km
- Germany: 362km
- Austria: 180km
- Liechtenstein: 41km

Place furthest from the national border: Uttigen (BE), 69km

Highest point: Dufourspitze, 4634m
Lowest point: Lago Maggiore, 193m
Average altitude: 1307m

Distance north to south: 224km
Northernmost point (SH): 47° 48' 30" N, 8° 34' 5" E
Southernmost point (TI): 45° 49' 4" N, 9° 1' 0.8" E
Middle point of Switzerland: Älggialp (OW) 46° 48' 4" N, 8° 13' 36" E
Distance west to east: 352km
Westernmost point (GE): 46° 7' 56" N, 5° 57' 21" E
Easternmost point (GR): 46° 36' 55" N, 10° 29' 32" E

DID YOU KNOW?

If Switzerland were ironed out so that it was all flat, its surface area would increase by 5,200km² or 12.5% – equivalent to adding a canton the size of Valais.

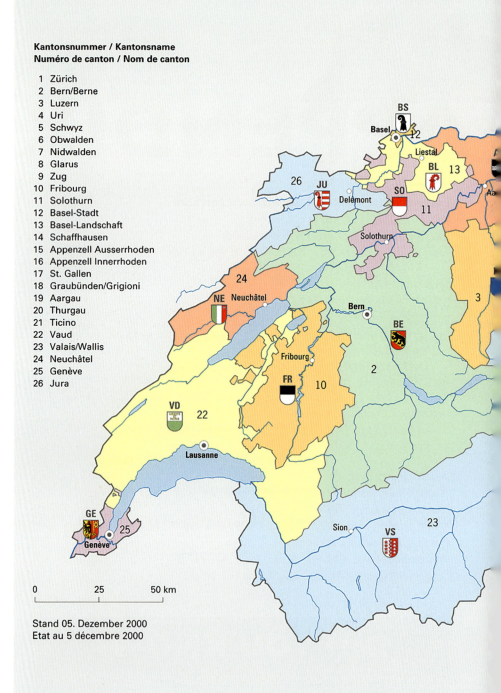

Kantonsnummer / Kantonsname
Numéro de canton / Nom de canton

1 Zürich
2 Bern/Berne
3 Luzern
4 Uri
5 Schwyz
6 Obwalden
7 Nidwalden
8 Glarus
9 Zug
10 Fribourg
11 Solothurn
12 Basel-Stadt
13 Basel-Landschaft
14 Schaffhausen
15 Appenzell Ausserrhoden
16 Appenzell Innerrhoden
17 St. Gallen
18 Graubünden/Grigioni
19 Aargau
20 Thurgau
21 Ticino
22 Vaud
23 Valais/Wallis
24 Neuchâtel
25 Genève
26 Jura

0   25   50 km

Stand 05. Dezember 2000
Etat au 5 décembre 2000

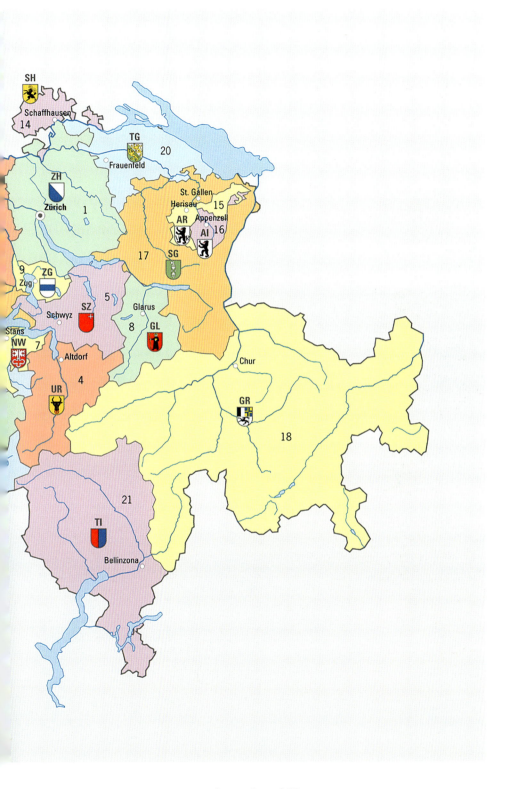

SH
Schaffhausen
14

TG
Frauenfeld
20

ZH
Zürich
1

St. Gallen
Herisau   15
AR   Appenzell
AI   16
SG
17

9   ZG
Zug

5   SZ
Schwyz   Glarus
8   GL

Stans
NW   7
Altdorf
UR
4

Chur

GR
18

21

TI
Bellinzona

THE 26 CANTONS

Each canton has an official two-letter abbreviation.

AG (Aargau)

Capital: Aarau
Area: 1404 km²
Population: 670,988

AI (Appenzell Innerrhoden)

Capital: Appenzell
Area: 172 km²
Population: 16,105

AR (Appenzell Ausserrhoden)

Capital: Herisau
Area: 243 km²
Population: 55,178

BE (Bern)

Capital: Bern
Area: 5959 km²
Population: 1,031,126

BL (Basel-Landschaft)

Capital: Liestal
Area: 517 km²
Population: 287,023

BS (Basel-Stadt)

Capital: Basel
Area: 37 km²
Population: 193,908

FR (Fribourg)

Capital: Fribourg
Area: 1671 km²
Population: 315,074

GE (Geneva)

Capital: Geneva
Area: 282 km²
Population: 495,249

GL (Glarus)

Capital: Glarus
Area: 685 km²
Population: 40,349

GR (Graubünden)

Capital: Chur
Area: 7105 km²
Population: 197,888

JU (Jura)

Capital: Delémont
Area: 838 km²
Population: 73,290

LU (Lucerne)

Capital: Lucerne
Area: 1493 km²
Population: 406,506

NE (Neuchâtel)

Capital: Neuchâtel
Area: 803 km²
Population: 177,964

NW (Nidwalden)

Capital: Stans
Area: 276 km²
Population: 42,969

OW (Obwalden)

Capital: Sarnen
Area: 490 km²
Population: 37,575

SG (St Gallen)

Capital: St Gallen
Area: 2026 km²
Population: 504,686

SH (Schaffhausen)

Capital: Schaffhausen
Area: 298 km²
Population: 81,351

SO (Solothurn)

Capital: Solothurn
Area: 791 km²
Population: 271,432

SZ (Schwyz)

Capital: Schwyz
Area: 908 km²
Population: 157,301

TG (Thurgau)

Capital: Frauenfeld
Area: 991 km²
Population: 270,709

TI (Ticino)

Capital: Bellinzona
Area: 2812 km²
Population: 353,709

UR (Uri)

Capital: Altdorf
Area: 1077 km²
Population: 36,299

VD (Vaud)

Capital: Lausanne
Area: 3212 km²
Population: 793,129

VS (Valais)

Capital: Sion
Area: 5224 km²
Population: 341,463

ZG (Zug)

Capital: Zug
Area: 239 km²
Population: 125,421

ZH (Zurich)

Capital: Zurich
Area: 1729 km²
Population: 1,504,346

Population data from Federal Statistical Office

THE LAKES

The total area of all lakes in Switzerland is 1422.4 km², or a little larger than Canton Aargau. Within Switzerland Lake Brienz is the deepest at 261m, and these are the five largest:

- Lake Neuchâtel: 215.2km²
- Lake Lucerne: 113.7km²
- Lake Zurich: 88.2km²
- Lake Thun: 47.7km²
- Lake Biel: 39.5km²

Four lakes are shared with neighbouring countries:

- Lake Geneva (with France)
  Total area: 580km²,
  Swiss part: 345.3km²
- Lake Constance
  (with Austria & Germany)
  Total area: 536km²,
  Swiss part: 172.9km²
- Lago Maggiore (with Italy)
  Total area: 210.2km²,
  Swiss part: 40.5km²
- Lago di Lugano (with Italy)
  Total area: 48.7km²,
  Swiss part: 30.0km²

THE RIVERS

The total length of all flowing water in Switzerland is 61,000km, equivalent to one and a half times round the equator.

- Rhine: 375km*
  Direction: North
  Outflow: North Sea
- Aare: 295km
  Direction: North
  Outflow: River Rhine
- Rhône: 264km*
  Direction: South
  Outflow: Mediterranean Sea
- Reuss: 158km
  Direction: North
  Outflow: River Aare
- Linth-Limmat: 140km
  Direction: North
  Outflow: River Aare

* Swiss section of the river

THE MOUNTAINS

About 23% of Switzerland sits at over 2000m, and around 2% is over 4000m, with 48 named peaks. Some of the best-known mountains don't break that 4000m barrier, for example, Eiger (3970m), Titlis (3238m), Säntis (2502m) and Pilatus (2132m). Possibly the most famous Swiss mountain, the Matterhorn, comes in at 4478m, but that's not enough to make the top ten highest peaks:

- Dufourspitze*   4634m
- Dunantspitze*   4632m
- Grenzgipfel*   4618m
- Nordend*   4609m
- Zumsteinspitze*   4563m
- Signalkuppe*   4554m
- Dom   4545m
- Liskamm Ost   4527m
- Weisshorn   4506m
- Täschhorn   4491m

* All peaks in the Monte Rosa massif

THE FEDERAL DEPARTMENTS

Each of the seven federal departments is represented by a Federal Councillor.

- DDPS   Federal Department of Defence, Civil Protection and Sport
- DETEC   Federal Department of the Environment, Transport, Energy and Communications
- EAER   Federal Department of Economic Affairs
- FDF   Federal Department of Finance
- FDFA   Federal Department of Foreign ffairs, Education and Research
- FDHA   Federal Department of Home Affairs
- FDJP   Federal Department of Justice and Police

THE MAIN POLITICAL PARTIES

There are six political parties with five or more seats in Federal Parliament. The party names and abbreviations are different in French and Italian. From right to left, politically speaking, the main parties are:

SVP – Schweizerische Volkspartei (Swiss People's Party)
Right-wing collection of nationalists, farmers and millionaires

FDP – Freisinnig-Demokratische Partei* (Free Democratic Party)
Both liberal and centre-right, which is a hard balance to sustain

CVP – Christlichdemokratische Volkspartei (Christian Democratic Party)
Somewhere in the centre, trying to be all things to everyone

GLP – Grünliberale Partei (Green Liberal Party)
They're green and they're liberal. Rather like Shrek with a conscience, only cuter

SP – Sozialdemokratische Partei (Social Democratic Party)
Eternal idealists who think Switzerland could be a better place with more taxes

Die Grünen – (Green Party)
Worthy ecologists saving the world one vote at a time; it could take a while

*Officially known as FDP.Die Liberalen after merging with the Liberal Party in 2009

THE MUNICIPALITIES

Switzerland is divided into 2,202 municipalities. Only 25 of them have a population of more than 30,000, and over half of the Swiss population lives in a municipality with fewer than 10,000 inhabitants.

Ten largest by population

Zurich	409,241
Geneva	200,548
Basel	171,513
Lausanne	138,905
Bern	133,798
Winterthur	110,912
Lucerne	81,401
St Gallen	75,522
Lugano	63,494
Biel/Bienne	54,640

Ten smallest by population

Corippo (TI)	12
Kammersrohr (SO)	29
Bister (VS)	32
Schelten (BE)	34
Rebévelier (BE)	42
Lohn (GR)	42
Berken (BE)	43
Clavaleyres (BE)	46
Linescio (TI)	48
Cerentino (TI)	49

Source: Federal Statistical Office

EMERGENCY NUMBERS

General emergency
112
Ambulance
144
Fire
118
Police
117
Rega
1414

Rega is the Swiss Air Rescue service (rega.ch), a non-profit foundation financed by members' subscriptions. It costs 30Fr a year, but does not replace health insurance.

GLOSSARY

ENGLISH	FRANÇAIS	DEUTSCH
annual working time	**temps de travail annuel**	**Jahresarbeitszeit**
accident cover	couverture accident	Unfalldeckung
alpine descent of the cows	désalpe	Alpabfahrt/Alpabzug
alternative medicine	médecines alternatives	Alternativmedizin
annual contract	contrat annuel	Jahresabo (Jahresvertrag)
apprenticeship	apprentissage	Lehre
asparagus season	saison des asperges	Spargelsaison
assisted suicide	suicide assisté	Sterbehilfe
association	association / club	Verein
baccalaureate school	**gymnase / collège / lycée**	**Gymnasium**
basic insurance	assurance de base	Grundversicherung
benefits	prestations complémentaires	Zusatzleistungen
bill, please	l'addition, s'il vous plaît	zahlen, bitte
birthday party	fête d'anniversaire	Kindergeburtstagsparty
car dealer	**concessionnaire automobile**	**Autohändler**
car hire	location de voitures	Autovermietung
carnival	carnaval	Fasnacht
chestnuts	marrons	Marroni
child benefit/family allowance	allocations familiales	Familienzulagen
child-minder	assistante maternelle / puéricultrice	Tagesmutter
children's doctor/paediatrician	pédiatre	Kinderarzt
co-ownership stake	part de copropriété	Mieteigentumsanteil
collision car insurance	assurance casco intégrale	Vollkasko
community centres	salle communale / maison de quartier	Gemeinschaftszentren
comprehensive car insurance	assurance casco partielle	Teilkasko
Council of States	Conseil des États	Ständerat
crèche/day care	crèche	Krippe/KiTa
criminal record	casier judiciaire	Strafregister
cross country skiing	ski de fond	Langlaufen

ENGLISH	FRANÇAIS	DEUTSCH
curling	curling	Eisstockschiessen
debt collection register	**Registre des poursuites**	**Betreibungsregister**
deductible/excess	franchise	Franchise (Selbstbehalt)
deposit slip	bulletin de versement	Einzahlungsschein
direct democracy	démocratie directe	Direkte Demokratie
disability insurance	assurance-invalidité (AI)	Invalidenversicherung (IV)
double majority	double majorité	doppelte Mehrheit
dress code	code vestimentaire	Dresscode
driving licence	permis de conduire	Fahrausweis (Führerschein)
drop-in health consultation services	consultations en santé sans rendez-vous	Mütter- und Väterberatung
dual nationality	double nationalité	Doppelte Staatsbürgerschaft
duty free	duty free / boutique hors taxe	zollfrei
emergency	**urgence**	**Notfall**
employment contract	contrat de travail	Arbeitsvertrag
enjoy your meal	bon appétit	Bon appetit
escrow account	compte bloqué / compte en séquestre	Treuhandkonto
European Economic Area (EEA)	Espace Économique Européen (EEE)	Europäischer Wirtschaftsraum (EWR)
extract from the debt collection register	extrait du Registre des poursuites	Betreibungsregisterauszug
Federal Central Authority	**Autorité centrale fédérale**	**Zentralen Behörde des Bundes**
Federal Constitution	Constitution fédérale	Bundesverfassung
Federal Council	Conseil fédéral	Bundesrat
flea market	marché aux puces	Flohmarkt
free movement of persons	libre circulation des personnes	Personenfreizügigkeit
further education	formation continue	Weiterbildungen
GA travelcard	**abonnement général (AG)**	**Generalabonnement (GA)**
gay	gay	schwule
general ward	division commune	allgemeine Abteilung
Half Fare travelcard	**carte demi-tarif**	**Halbtax**
health insurance	assurance maladie	Krankenversicherung
health insurer	caisse maladie	Krankenkasse
hiking path	sentier de randonnée	Wanderweg
historically listed	patrimoine culturel	Heimatschutz / Denkmalschutz

ENGLISH	FRANÇAIS	DEUTSCH
hunting season	saison de la chasse	Jagdsaison
ice skating	**patinage sur glace**	**Eislaufen**
imputed rental value	valeur locative imputée	Eigenmietwert
interaction zone	zone de rencontre	Begegnungszone
land registry	**Office du registre foncier**	**Grundbuchamt**
laundry room	buanderie	Waschküche
leasehold	droit de superficie	Erbbaurecht
legal insurance	assurance protection juridique	Rechtsschutzversicherung
lesbian	lesbienne	lesbisch
limited partnership	partenariat limité / société en commandite	Kommanditgesellschaft
loyalty card	carte de fidélité	Kundenkarte
lunch club	repas de midi / cantine	Mittagstisch
magic formula	**formule magique**	**Zauberformel**
mandatory referendum	référendum obligatoire	obligatorisches Referendum
marriage preparation	préparation du mariage	Vorbereitung der Eheschliessung
maternity leave	congé maternité	Mutterschaftsurlaub
milk buns	petits pains au lait	Milchbrötchen
municipality	commune / municipalité	Gemeinde
nanny	**nounou / maman de jour**	**Kindermädchen**
National Council	Conseil national	Nationalrat
naturalisation	naturalisation	Einbürgerung
number plate	plaque d'immatriculation	Nummernschild
OASI	**AVS**	**AHV**
occupational private retirement funds	prévoyance professionnelle	berufliche private Altersvorsorge
optional referendum	référendum facultatif	freiwilliges Referendum
ordinary naturalisation	naturalisation ordinaire	ordentliche Einbürgerung
organic	bio / biologique	bio/biologisch
out-of-school club	garderie	Hort
outdoor pool	piscine en plein-air	Badi
outpatient	ambulatoire	ambulant
paddle-steamer	**bateau à vapeur / bateau à aubes**	**Dampfschiff**
part-time work	travail à temps partiel	Teilzeitarbeit
paternity leave	congé paternité	Vaterschaftsurlaub

ENGLISH	FRANÇAIS	DEUTSCH
payment summons	commandement de payer	Zahlungsbefehl
permanent life insurance	assurance vie / assurance épargne	Lebensversicherung / Sparversicherung
permit	permis	Bewilligung
permit	permis	Genehmigung
personal liability insurance	assurance responsabilité civile	Privathaftpflichtversicherung
personal property insurance	assurance ménage	Hausratversicherung
plate of game	menu de chasse	Wildgericht
playgroup	groupe de jeu	Spielgruppe
popular initiative	initiative populaire	Volksinitiative
postal code	code postal	Postleitzahl (PLZ)
premium	prime	Prämie
premium reduction	réduction de primes	Prämienverbilligung
prescription	ordonnance	Rezept
property transfer tax	impôt sur la mutation immobilière	Grunderwerbsteuer / Liegenschaftssteuer
recycling centre	**déchèterie**	**Recyclinghof**
references	références	Referenzen
registered partnership	partenaire enregistré	Eigetragene Partnerschaft
road traffic department	Office cantonal des véhicules / Office cantonal de la circulation / Service des automobiles	Strassenverkehrsamt
roadside assistance	assistance dépannage	Pannenhilfe
Romansh	romanche	Rätoromanisch
second-hand shop	**magasin de seconde main**	**Brocki/Brockenhaus**
simple partnership	partenariat simple	Einfache Gesellschaft
simplified naturalisation	naturalisation simplifiée	erleichterte Einbürgerung
sledding	traîneau	Schlitteln
special alliance	Sonderbund / Sondrebond	Sonderbund
spousal maintenance	contribution à l'entretien du conjoint	Unterhalt des Ehegatten
stone throwing	lancer de la pierre	Steinstossen
supplemental insurance	assurance complémentaire	Zusatzversicherung
Swiss Confederation	Confédération suisse	Schweizerische Eidgenossenschaft
Swiss Estate Association (SVIT)	Association suisse de l'économie immobilière (SVIT)	Schweizerischer Verband der Immobilienwirtschaft (SVIT)
Swiss Homeowner's Association	Société suisse des propriétaires fonciers (APF)	Hauseigentümerverband (HEV)

ENGLISH	FRANÇAIS	DEUTSCH
Swiss National Day	Fête nationale suisse	Schweizer Nationalfeiertag/ Bundesfeiertag
Swiss wrestling	lutte suisse	Schwingen
temporary accommodation	**logement provisoire**	**provisorische Unterbringung**
tenants' association	Association cantonale des locataires	Mieterverband
term life insurance	couverture en cas de décès / assurance décès	Todesfallversicherung
third-party liability car insurance	assurance automobile conducteur tiers	Motorfahrzeughaftpflicht- versicherungen
Three Kings' cake	gâteau des rois / galette des rois	Dreikönigskuchen
tip	pourboire	Trinkgeld
toy library	ludothèque	Ludothek
trans people	personnes trans	trans Menschen
TV licence	Serafe	Serafe (Empfangsgebühr)
union	**syndicat**	**Gewerkschaft**
vaccination	**vaccination**	**Impfung**
VAT	TVA	Mehrwertsteuer (MwSt.)
visa	visa	Visum
voluntary private retirement savings	prévoyance privée	freiwillige private Altersvorsorge
wild garlic	**ail des ours**	**Bärlauch**
will	testament	Testament
withholding tax	impôt à la source	Quellensteuer
work placement	stage / placement en entreprise	Berufspraktikum / Praktikum

PHOTOS

Page	(Subject) and ©copyright
cover photos	*Front cover (top to bottom):* Alpine descent of the cows, Lenzerheide ©gdefilip/Shutterstock; Oeschinensee ©Eva Bocek/Shutterstock; Zurich market ©Zurich Tourism; Zurich tram ©Zurich Tourism; Swiss francs, ©pixabay; Lucerne ©Eva Bocek/Shutterstock *Back cover (top to bottom):* Geneva market ©Geneva Tourism; Zermatt ©ansharphoto/Shutterstock; Mountain biking near Chur ©Graubünden Ferien *Back flap (top to bottom):* Sauriermuseum Aathal ©Zurich Tourism; Brunch ©Rawpixel.com/Shutterstock
7–8	(Interlaken) ©Diccon Bewes
8–9	©RVillalon/Shutterstock
10–11	©Staatssekretariat für Migration
13	©Alexandros Michailidis/Shutterstock
16	(Zurich Airport) ©Staatssekretariat für Migration
18–19	©brunocoelho/Shutterstock
20–21	©Graubünden Ferien
23	©alexandre zveiger/Shutterstock
24–25	©MIND AND I/Shutterstock
26–27	©alexandre zveiger/Shutterstock
28–29	(Geneva Christmas market) ©Geneva Tourism
30	(Ticino house) ©Pixabay
32–33	©Everett Collection/Shutterstock
35	©Bern Tourism
36	©rblfmr/Shutterstock
39	©stockfour/Shutterstock
40–41	©Photographee.eu/Shutterstock
42–43	©Geneva Tourism
44–45	©Bern Tourism
46–47	©FJZEA/shutterstock
48–49	©Dmitry Rukhlenko/Shutterstock
50–51	(Parliament Building, Bern) ©Bern Tourism
52–53	(Waldseemüller map) Zentralbibliothek Zürich, Map Department
54–55	(WWII escape map) ©Zentralbibliothek Zürich, Map Department
56–57	(Languages in Switzerland) ©The Federal Statistical Office
58–59	pixabay
60	(Landsgemeinde, Appenzell) ©Diccon Bewes
62–63	©fstockfoto/shutterstock
65	(Charlie Chaplin statue, Vevey) ©Diccon Bewes
66–67	(Watchmaking tools) ©Geneva Tourism
68–69	©Zurich Tourism
70–71	(Corippo) ©Diccon Bewes
72–73	©Zurich Tourism

Page	(Subject) and ©copyright
75	(Recycling in Geneva) ©Charles Lewis/Shutterstock
76–77	©Michal Stipek/Shutterstock
78	pixabay
80–81	(Maloja Pass) ©Andrei Bortnikau/Shutterstock
82–83	©Maryna Patzen/Shutterstock
84–85	(Lucerne market) ©Pani Garmyder/Shutterstock
86–87	(Shopping in Migros) ©Sorbis/Shutterstock
88–89	(Bern market) ©Bern Tourism
90–91	©Grzegorz Czapski/Shutterstock
92–93	©Zurich Tourism
94–95	(Lecture at the ETH) ©ETH Zurich / Alessandro Della Bella
96	(Swiss education system) ©EDK CDIP CDEP CDPE
99	(Sauriermuseum Aathal) ©Zurich Tourism
101	Anna Nahabed©Shutterstock
103	(Basel Holbein fountain) ©Basel Tourism
104	©FamVeld/Shutterstock
106	©Zurich Tourism
108–109	(Lake Lucerne) ©Diccon Bewes
110–111	(Landwasser Viaduct) ©Diccon Bewes
112–113	(Mount Pilatus aerial cableway) xbrchx/Shutterstock
114–115	(Lake Lungern) ©kavalenkau/Shutterstock
116–117	©Byjeng/Shutterstock
119	(Freddie Mercury statue, Montreux) ©Diccon Bewes
120–121	(Fairmont Le Montreux Palace) Roman Babakin/Shutterstock
123	©Swiss Travel System AG/Tobias Ryser
124–125	(Ticino hiking sign) ©Diccon Bewes
126–127	(Gotthard Pass) ©Stefano Ember/Shutterstock
128–129	(Furka Pass) ©Michal Ludwiczak/Shutterstock
131	(Rhine Falls) ©Zurich Tourism
132–133	©A_stockphoto/Shutterstock
134–135	©Niyazz/Shutterstock
136	©Denis Linine/Shutterstock
138–139	©pixabay
140	©Sedrun Disentis Tourismus
142–143	©i viewfinder/Shutterstock
147	©Zurich Tourism
148–149	©pixabay
150–151	©Tom Wang/Shutterstock
152–153	©Everett Collection/Shutterstock
154–155	©Constantin Culic/Shutterstock
156-157	(Ice storm in Geneva) ©Mahathir Mohd Yasin/Shutterstock
158–159	©pixabay
160–161	©Blackforest-Photography/Shutterstock
162–163	©Pixeljoy/Shutterstock

Page	(Subject) and ©copyright
164–165	©Bumble Dee/Shutterstock
166–167	©Bern Tourism
168–169	©VGstockstudio/Shutterstock
170–171	(Naked hiking in Grindelwald) Jaro68/Shutterstock
172–173	©Lysenko Andrii/Shutterstock
175	©HiddenCatch/Shutterstock
176–177	©pixabay
178–179	©pixabay
180–181	(Lötschental Tschäggättä) ©Lötschental Tourism
183	(William Tell statue, Altdorf) ©Oleg Znamenskiy/Shutterstock
184	(Jass cards) ©Diccon Bewes
185	(Swiss wrestling) ©Alistair Scott/Shutterstock
186–187	(Lenzerheide) ©gdefilip/Shutterstock
187	(Silversterchlausen, Urnäsch) ©pixabay
187	(Chienbäse, Liestal) ©Diccon Bewes
187	(Carnival, Basel) ©Swiss-Ives/Shutterstock
187	(Chalandamarz, Graubünden) ©peterdonatsch/Graubünden Ferien
188–189	(Fireworks above the Rhine Falls) ©Pixeljoy/Shutterstock
188	(Le Pleureuses, Romont) ©Frédéric Rochat
188	(Sechseläuten, Zurich) ©Zurich Tourism
189	(Cow fighting, Hérens) ©mountainpix/Shutterstock
189	(Alphorn Festival Nendaz) ©Etienne Bornet
190–191	(Candy onions, Zibelemärit, Bern) ©Diccon Bewes
190	(Chästeilet) ©Interlaken Tourism
190	(Alpabfahrt) ©Diccon Bewes
190	(Chestnuts) ©pixabay
191	(Zibelemärit, Bern) ©Bern Tourism
191	(Fête de l'Escalade, Geneva) ©GenevaTourism
191	(Klausjagen, Küssnacht am Rigi) ©www.dietz.ch/SNGK
192–193	(Muesli) ©Andie Pilot
194	(Birnbrot) ©Graubünden Ferien
194	(Basler Läckerli) ©sidefin/Shutterstock
194	(Zopf) ©pixabay
195	(Zürcher Geschnetzeltes) ©Zurich Tourism
195	(Zuger Kirschtorte) ©Andie Pilot
195	(Glarner Kalberwurst) ©Samuel Trümpy
195	(Capuns) ©Andie Pilot
196–197	(Raclette) ©beats1/Shutterstock
196	(Cardons) ©denio109/Shutterstock
196	(Saucisson Vaudois) ©Andie Pilot
196	(Meringues) ©Nathalie Dulex/Shutterstock
197	(Plums) ©Andie Pilot
197	(Abricotine) Public domain
197	(Chestnuts) ©tabak lejla/Shutterstock

Page	(Subject) and ©copyright
199	(Three Kings' Cake) ©Natalia Ruedisueli
200	©Oscity/Shutterstock
201	(Swiss Army grilled cheese) ©Andie Pilot
202–203	(Fondue) ©beats1/Shutterstock
204–205	©Geneva Tourism
206–207	©mavo/Shutterstock
208–209	(Cine Transat) ©Geneva Tourism
210–211	(Hatching butterflies at the Papiliorama) ©Susanne Keller
212–213	(KKL Lucerne) ©KKL Luzern
214–215	(Mountain biking near Chur) ©Graubünden Ferien
216–217	©Graubünden Ferien
218–219	(Jumping into the Aare) ©Bern Tourism
220–221	(Massage at Bain Bleu) ©Geneva Tourism
222–223	(Rhine swimming in Basel) ©Basel Tourism
224–225	©Maxx-Studio/Shutterstock
226–227	(Comedy duo Deville) ©SRF
228–229	(Rheingasse, Basel) ©Basel Tourism
230–231	©pixabay
232–233	©Geneva Tourism
234–235	©Zurich Tourism
237	©Zurich Tourism
238–239	(Pride parade, Lugano) ©Stefano Ember/Shutterstock
240–241	(Schwubs choir) ©Daniel Geiser
242–243	©Zurich Tourism
245	©Lital Israeli/Shutterstock
246–247	©Zurich Tourism
249	©michaeljung/Shutterstock
250–251	©Rawpixel.com/Shutterstock
252–253	(Parc des Eaux Vives, Geneva) ©Geneva Tourism
254–255	©Zurich Tourism
256–257	©Alexander Chaikin/Shutterstock
258–259	©Marc Studer/Shutterstock
260–261	©Shutterstock
262–263	©Marlon Trottmann/Shutterstock
266	(Parliament Building, Bern) ©Bern Tourism
268–269	(Cantonal Map) © Federal Statistical Office

INDEX